REGULATING SOCIETY

REGULATING SOCIETY
Marginality and Social Control
in Historical Perspective

Ephraim H. Mizruchi

THE FREE PRESS
A Division of Macmillan Publishing Co., Inc.
NEW YORK

Collier Macmillan Publishers
LONDON

THE FREE PRESS
A Division of Macmillan Publishing Co., Inc.
866 Third Avenue, New York, N.Y. 10022

Collier Macmillan Canada, Inc.

Printed in the United States of America

printing number

1 2 3 4 5 6 7 8 9 10

Library of Congress Cataloging in Publication Data

Mizruchi, Ephraim Harold.
  Regulating society.

  Bibliography: p.
  Includes indexes.
  1. Social structure.   2. Marginality, Social.
3. Social control.   4. Social conflict.   5. Social change.   I. Title.
HM131.M56   1983   303   82-48161
ISBN 0-02-921660-5

To Ruth

"Revolutionary millennnarianism drew its strength from a population living on the margin of society."—Norman Cohn, *The Pursuit of the Millennium*

"The extra-ordinary expansion of enrolments in Oxford and Cambridge meant the creation of a small army of unemployed or under-employed gentry. . . . Neither the central bureaucracy, nor the army, nor colonial expansion . . . nor even the law could absorb them all. The result was frustration and resentment among large numbers of nobles, squires and gentry."—Lawrence Stone, *The Causes of the English Revolution, 1529–1642*

"It was not human biology but human society which created the surplus labour in the countryside."—E. J. Hobsbawm and George Rude, *Captain Swing*

"This pool of unemployed is the 'surplus population' of England. When they are out of work these people eke out a miserable existence by begging and stealing . . . by turning their hands to anything that will bring in a copper or two. . . . Those who—goaded by their distress—summon up enough courage to revolt openly against society become thieves and murderers."—Friedrich Engels,*The Condition of the Working Class in England*

"The three military-religious orders (Knights Templars, Hospitallers, and the Teutonic Knights) were surely means of imposing discipline upon unruly warriors and of directing their energies to socially acceptable outlets."—David Herlihy, personal communication

"You don't find a home in the Army."—GI Joe World War II

" 'Well, returned Verena, it's all very comfortable for you to say that you wish to leave us alone. But you can't leave us alone. We are here, and we have got to be disposed of. You have got to put us somewhere. It's a remarkable social system that has no place for *us*,' the girl went on. . . ."—Henry James, *The Bostonians*

"Economic policies are not to be explained in terms of economics alone."—R. H. Tawney, *The Agrarian Problem in the Sixteenth Century*

Contents

Preface

The basic idea that organizations may be created to absorb and control the potentially dissident in our society has been with me for three decades. An "off the cuff" comment made by one of my undergraduate professors during a lecture in social anthropology was the source of this idea. St. Clair Drake's comment that "Roosevelt and Hopkins organized the WPA arts projects to get the rabble rousers off the street corners" has intrigued me for many years.

An interest in bohemianism, growing out of a field research project, also under Professor Drake, has been another source of the perspective I have developed here. Begun as a participant observation study with Howard Kamin, a fellow student, I carried on alone with the research struggling with the problem of conceptualizing and organizing the data in a theoretically meaningful manner. My later reading and reflection led me to the historical data which were used to write the chapter on bohemianism in this book.

It was when I came to know something of the medieval Beguines that I realized how important and useful the historical data could be to understanding the group absorption process. My exposure to Professor David Herlihy, in a year long symposium on alienation in which we were both participants, made me aware of the similar functions of the bohemian and beguine patterns. I had already used the term "abeyance" in an earlier paper and had made reference to Professor Drake's remark, described above, in my earlier book on anomie. Herlihy's perspective suggested that the historical data might be used to expand and deepen my understanding of the relationship between unintegrated persons and organizational patterns.

I do not recall how I came to be interested in monasticism. Monasticism is such an old organizational form that it must be that it would be difficult for a sociologist to be unfamiliar with it. Whatever the case the historical research on which this book is based has deepened my interest in the subject.

Finally, with respect to this brief introduction, I had originally planned to write chapters on two case studies which were never completed. A study of war and military organizations as well as a study of mental hospitals were to be included in this book. I decided, several years ago, that I had already undertaken an extremely complex intellectual task and that adding two more case studies might be—given the theoretical goals of this project—superfluous. I have, instead, made references from time to time, to those contexts as they help elucidate the theory.

A great many colleagues and friends have had varying degrees of input into my research and thinking. Some have aided by being good listeners, others have read and criticized what I had written in earlier papers and versions of the book. Still others have read versions of the completed manuscript prior to revision and publication. I cannot remember all of them and for that reason I hope those who are not mentioned here will be generous in their understanding.

Among those who have made the most direct contributions are: Lewis Coser, William Form, Robert K. Merton, James Powell and Michael Schwartz. Others include: Mark Abrahamson, Georgianna Appignani, Michael Barkun, Joseph Bensman, Isabella Bick, Guthrie Birkhead, Norman Birnbaum, Brenda Bolton, Susan Borker, Richard Braungart, Leonard Cain, Donald T. Campbell, D. Glynn Cochrane, Rose L. Coser, Natalie Z. Davis, Ron Ehrenreich, Suzanne Fleming, Israel Gerver, Barry Glassner, Gerald Grant, Harvey Greisman, Anne-Marie Guillemard, Walter Hirsch, Jerry Jacobs, Morris Janowitz, Judith Long, Helena Z. Lopata, Julia Loughlin, Theodore J. Lowi, Stanford Lyman, Victor Marshall, M. Marian Mayer, Allan Mazur, William McCord, Paul Meadows, Omar K. Moore, Ed Muir, Lena W. Myers, Thomas Pastorello, Robert Perrucci, Robert Pickett, Ned Polsky, Elwin H. Powell, Joanna Prins, Gunter Remmling, D. B. Robertson, Bernard Rosenberg, Deena Rosenberg, Barry Schwartz, Richard D. Schwartz, Manfred Stanley, Arthur Stinchcombe, Nicholas Tatsis, Gladys Topkis, Arthur Vidich, Isidore Walliman, Mary Jane Whitestockings, Charles Willie and Eviatar Zerubavel. Pat Zohler, Dorothy Smith, and Joann McDonald typed the largest share of the manuscript. Gloria Katz, Ruthe Kassel, and Virginia Moran helped expedite completion of this project.

In addition to the special thanks which I owe to Professors Drake and Herlihy I would like to acknowledge my debt to the late Louis Schneider, my teacher and friend. Before Lou's untimely death he read the chapters based on medieval history and provided much support when I had doubts about the value of this project. The reader familiar with Schneider's work will recognize how profound is my intellectual debt to him.

Still another former teacher to whom I owe a debt of gratitude is the late Rose Hum Lee. It was she who insisted I go on to graduate study.

Several others have played a special role in relation to this project. George Zito, in addition to being a constant sounding board and severe critic has helped in countless ways, including a careful reading and critique of the completed first draft of the manuscript. Jerome Mazzarro, my longtime friend and colleague, critically read and made valuable suggestions for the final draft of this book. Gary Spencer responded to the abeyance idea with understanding and enthusiasm. He has been a constant source of moral support. Mark Mizruchi took valuable time from the manuscript of his first book to read, criticize and make suggestions for revisions. Susan Mizruchi, whose field is literature, has been my most enthusiastic supporter. She quickly grasped what I was attempting to do and constantly showered me with suggestions and relevant quotations from Shakespeare, Henry James and others. David Mizruchi was also a sounding board who provided a bridge between my abstractions and his own observations while a staff member in an organization that is unequivocally geared to the abeyance process, a school for the emotionally and intellectually handicapped. The dedication of this book to Ruth is, of course, in recognition of far more than her contribution in this particular sphere.

I want to thank especially, Charles Smith of the Free Press, my longtime friend and editor; Joyce Seltzer, who edited this book; and both Michael Sander and Toni Ann Scaramuzzo, who saw this book through production.

Although it is conventional to hold that I alone am responsible for any of this book's shortcomings it is nevertheless true. It was I alone who decided whether to use or ignore, for whatever reasons, the many excellent suggestions made by those named above.

EPHRAIM H. MIZRUCHI

Syracuse, New York
September, 1981

REGULATING SOCIETY

Prologue

Societies for the most part tend toward an orderly flow of people both from one place to the next and from one social organization to another. In order for this flow to occur without incident, certain social processes occur that control the intensity of the impact of people on places. One important continuous and dynamic pattern, which also contributes to the maintenance of the status quo and to social change, is what I have chosen to call *abeyance*.

Abeyance is a holding process that occurs within and between social organizations of various types, some institutionalized and others not. All organizations may be thought of as possessing certain degrees of elasticity, i.e., capacities to expand and contract the number of positions to which people can be assigned. It is this variable capacity of organizations in society that makes it possible for abeyance to work. When there are too many people in society at a given point in time, i.e., surplus populations, certain organizations may expand or new organizations emerge to absorb these people. When people are needed in another organizational context, participants may be expelled or may choose to leave.

The source of the surplus or shortage of population in relation to positions in organizations may be biological, i.e., a result of increased birthrates or lowered death rates, or both; or the origins of what may be termed an imbalance may be attributed to organizational phenomena. My perspective here is structural, and the conceptualized units with which I deal are organized social patterns. Thus I do not deny the importance of surpluses or shortages of population resulting from biological processes. These processes are, after all, very much influenced by social structural phenomena. What I seek is a theory that is sociological in the strictest sense, setting aside, for example, biological, psychological, and economic perspectives. All theories are abstractions and as such they deal with only portions of reality. My focus, then, in the book that follows these brief remarks is on certain *social* processes that are central to all societies and all times. Abeyance occurs within and between organizations.

Closely associated with abeyance, in ways that I describe in the forthcoming pages, are social control and marginality. My assumption is that when people are only marginally integrated into society—i.e., only

1

weakly tied into important social structures, including family and work organizations—they are more vulnerable to their own impulses and the appeals of others to deviate from a society's expectations and norms. Thus marginal people are more likely to participate in diverse behaviors judged by their contemporaries as deviant, including moral and political protest.[1] Surplus populations are marginal populations, and thus are more prone to dissident behavior. Organizations contributing to the abeyance process simultaneously control, intentionally or unintentionally, their charges. This is, in part at least, their raison d'être. Absorption and social control go hand in hand.

My assumption that the abeyance and social control process occurs both intentionally and unintentionally brings me to the heart of the matter, so to speak. This process, like most others impacting on society, is typically unplanned and unrecognized, i.e., latent.[2] It is well to keep in mind that people do not always anticipate or assess or understand how and why they perform or will perform in a social context. Nor are a given person's interests congruent with the interests of his kin, his peers, or society at large. There is no necessary connection between a person's motives, manifest or latent to him, and a society's presumed need at a given moment in time. What is judged as "good" at the societal level may be an outcome of what is "evil" at the level of personal motivation. "Evil" may also result from good intentions.[3]

In the context of abeyance and social control I am assuming that these processes typically, although not always, occur *without* the awareness of those who participate in them or those who derive losses or benefits from them. If, for example, we go to the army when called, it is patriotism or coercion that moves us, not a nation's need to provide places for unemployed youth and others. Societal processes are organized; otherwise life would be even more chaotic than experience tells us it can be. But how this organization works cannot be explained by metaphors like "the invisible hand" or such simple sociological assumptions as those which stress the continuity between child-rearing practices, the norms that regulate them, and presumed societal needs. Careful, thoughtful research on how these factors are connected to other central processes will surely help us unravel these issues. My effort here is toward that kind of understanding. To develop my theory I study aspects of five phenomena, using historical data, that illustrate the abeyance and social control processes as both manifest and latent. Western monasteries, medieval Beguinages, bohemian communes, compulsory apprenticeship settings and schools, and the WPA writers' and artists' projects of the 1930s are the organized patterns I have selected to illustrate my theory.

The history of Western monasticism, from its origins in the fourth century to the present, is a story of expansion and contraction. Originat-

ing as an absorber of the surplus populations who fled the urban settings of the Roman Empire in the East, the monastic system has been
both the permanent and temporary resting place of diverse masses of
Christians. Organized, in the beginning, under the Rule of St. Benedict—which called for obedience to "the precepts of spiritual counsel
extracted from the Gospels," obedience to the Rule itself, and obedience
to the abbot, who was to be "obeyed as the voice of God himself"—
monasticism was the central organ of the Church from the time of its
origins until the rise of orders and the expansion of urban-commercial
activities during the thirteenth century.[4] Because of the emphasis upon
obedience and the capacity of the abbot to impose sanctions on both his
monks and his lay followers, monasticism also functioned as a social
control system. In its capacity to absorb lay its strength as a control
mechanism. As personnel were expelled, other organizational forms
absorbed and controlled them. Monasticism was and is capable of expanding and absorbing personnel as societal conditions require.

The thirteenth-century decline of monastic influence occurred about
the same time as the growth of new religious orders, including the
Franciscans and Dominicans. But other organizations that were less
than orders emerged at this time as well. Among these were groups of
women called Beguines. Originating in the Low Countries and spreading to the Rhineland, these organized forms absorbed and placed under
control women who, as migrants from rural to urban areas, were a
surplus population. Attaching themselves temporarily, or, in some
cases, permanently to groups of religious adherents, these women performed some of the jobs ordinarily done by nuns. Since they did not
take vows they were free to leave their urban communes, or Beguinages,
as alternative opportunities, including marriage, emerged. Like the
monk, nun, or layperson temporarily attached to religious houses, the
Beguine was also under serveillance and control.

Somewhat later, historically, the life-style that is called "bohemian"
arrived. Influenced by aspects of the life of the minstrel, the troubadour,
and the medieval and Elizabethan actor, and given a name associated
with the religious protestors of the late Middle Ages, bohemianism became associated with a voluntary form of communal living. At times
urban and at other times rural, these forms have provided the moder-
ately deviant members of Western societies opportunities for integration
into accepting groups. These groups, too, expand and contract under
the pressure of surplus population, absorbing and controlling those who
voluntarily join them. Participation in these organizations is also temporary, an alternative to integration into more traditional social structures.

Overlapping with bohemianism historically is compulsory education. Beginning during the early nineteenth century and growing out of
legally mandated apprenticeship, the latter beginning in the thirteenth

century, it also arose under the pressure of surplus population. Schools have expanded and contracted with increases and decreases of unintegrated youth. Unlike the other forms just described, going to school is mandated by law, and thus it represents the use of statutes and direct state intervention into the absorption and control of potentially unintegrated and dissident populations.

The most conspicuous modern effort to create structures for this purpose was the establishment of the various federal job programs of the 1930s in the United States. The WPA, including the various arts projects, was a device for providing not only funds for the unemployed but work, under surveillance and control, for millions of Americans. The outright intervention of government in the process of absorbing and controlling those who might engage in revolution and other forms of deviant behavior represents the opposite pole from the religious, often long-term, commitment of persons associated with the monastic system.

My goal in this study is to formulate a theory which will help illuminate hitherto neglected societal processes that contribute to fluctuations in the rates of change, maintenance of the status quo, and the control of group dissidence. The processes themselves exist and have always occurred in society. I raise them to the level of the reader's awareness and articulate a conceptual scheme that is applicable to a wide variety of societal and historical contexts. Thus I am interested in explaining general phenomena associated with all societies independent of time and place. By so doing I do not reject the significance of situational and historical variation. I intentionally abstract from the particular only that which I understand to be generalizable. In so doing I risk an inadequate explanation of a specific occurrence for the sake of understanding a limited aspect of all occurrences. Abstract theories do not explain all of the variations associated with concrete happenings.

Because this is a work using the data gathered, for the most part, by historians, some will attempt to judge my effort from the perspective of historical scholarship. It is not my intention to pretend to be a historian or to explain all of the historical circumstances that led to the emergence of the patterns with which I deal. I am interested in organizational forms and interorganizational processes that emerge under most, if not all, historical conditions. I will ignore, at the risk of horrifying the historian, some of the unique causal aspects of the contexts with which I deal.

The method that has been used is akin to what Stinchcombe has recently called historical analogy.[5] I have studied a number of diverse historical cases which, upon initial inspection, seemed to be characterized by similar sociological patterns. After extensive reading of a wide variety of historical literature I formulated a relatively simple theoretical perspective. I then focused on selected aspects of the contexts and patterns which were to constitute my historical case studies. As my reading and reflection became more focused I began to see the pattern with greater precision and understanding. At that point I conceptualized six variables that I felt were central to the processes I was attempting to describe and explain. I then returned to the specific cases and assessed the data from the standpoint of these variables. Thus I have worked up and back from data to conceptualization and from the emerging analytical framework back to the data.

Hence, to repeat, the historical data that describe the processes in which I am interested represent only a special slice of the pie of reality. By abstracting a particular aspect of what has occurred in a given social-historical context I risk losing the ability to understand a phenomenon in its totality. This risk must be taken if sociologists are to formulate concepts and theories that are generalizable to broad classes of societal phenomena. Because my goal is different from the historian's, the reader is cautioned to bear in mind that my concepts may not be identical in meaning with those used in history. For example, I treat monasticism as a form of social organization which, although undergoing changes over the past two thousand years, continues nevertheless to have certain special characteristics. Whether the system that emerged in the fourth and fifth centuries is divergent in some respects from that which began at Cluny some five hundred years later may or may not be of interest in assessing the theory I am proposing here. Sociologists will agree that structures and functions may vary over time. Some organizations may change but their contribution to a community or society may remain the same, and, conversely, the organization may remain somewhat the same but its function may change. In this study it is what the organization does that is central, and how it does it that I am attempting to explain.

This study examines social forms and the processes that influence their response to societal conditions as well as their contribution to societal change. My goal is to conceptualize and theorize in the interest of a general theory of societal process. The theory, I assume, is applicable to a wide variety of societal contexts occurring in an equally diverse number of historical settings.

The theory is articulated in terms of six variables, which I discuss in each historical context: (1) temporality; (2) commitment; (3) inclusiveness; (4) division of labor; (5) institutionalization; and (6) stratification. These variables describe the relative capacity of an organization, at a point in time and under specified conditions, to absorb or expel people as external societal conditions change. This is a theory of absorption and expulsion processes. The unit of analysis is the organization.

This theory is not only applicable to the past. It has implications for social policy in contemporary societies. There are hypotheses which are derivable from this framework, and these suggest that focusing on the abeyance process does lend itself to formulation of clear statements of anticipated relationships as well as contexts for observations to test these hypotheses.

Each variable of the six on which I have focused suggests a hypothesis about the relationship between an organization's readiness and response to a societal condition and the condition itself. And each hypothesis, assessed under relatively controlled conditions, can be tested. Any number of examples is derivable from my analysis, but one will suffice to illustrate my point.

Using the state college as an example of an organization responding to the abeyance process, the greater the surplus of college-age youth in the population the lower will be the standards for admission and the greater will be the inflation of academic grades. This hypothesis, under the assumption that all other conditions are held constant, is derived from my inclusiveness variable, which implies that the greater the societal pressure for an organization to absorb and hold personnel the more open will admission requirements be. The pressure for abeyance is a result of the emergence of a surplus population, either because of biological factors or, more relevant to my theory, because of the contraction of status vacancies in another organizational context or failure to absorb in an organization that traditionally absorbs youth. For example, the labor market has declined in its usefulness as an alternative as a result of the pushing out of youth through child-labor legislation.

To do a test of this hypothesis it is important to consider other factors that might be influencing entrance requirements and standards and the confounding effects of these factors on the interplay between the variables on which we are making observations. Careful research using experimental models makes such a test possible. For example, once the educational system has expanded the number of status vacancies—as was the situation during the 1960s in the United States—organizational functionaries may attempt to maintain their fiefdoms by pressing for continued high inclusiveness, thus maintaining organizational size; i.e., they may lower standards in order to attract students even though their former contribution to societal abeyance processes is no longer useful. Thus the colleges may compete with organizations that have status vacancies which need to be filled. The result may be problematic for society.*

---

*Other hypotheses that readily come to mind are: the more inclusive the membership the faster the rate of absorption, e.g., educational organizations; the less the degree of specialization the faster the rate of absorption, e.g., the WPA writers' and artists' projects; the less the degree of hierarchical organization the greater the rate of expulsion, e.g., bohemian communes; the greater the commitment to an organization the lower the rate of expulsion, e.g., monasteries; the more institutionalized the pattern the greater the motivation to participate in structures that hold people in abeyance, e.g., schools.

Focusing on abeyance, as I held throughout this study, not only increases insight into societal processes and articulates ongoing but hitherto latent processes; it also contributes to the development of propositions and hypotheses that can be tested, interpreted, and incorporated into general theories of society. The connections between my perspective and some of the other theories are examined in Chapter 7.

But these processes with which I deal, when understood, can have an impact on social policy as well. Because of such phenomena in Western societies as increasing longevity of human life and increasing technological capacities, including assembly-line work carried out by robots and some clerical work carried out by computers, we will need to find meaningful places and activities for a great many more people than in the past. Understanding that the surplus populations of the contemporary world are not simply a result of biological factors will have some bearing on societal decision-making. Reflecting on how some societies in the past have responded to these phenomena can have practical consequences.

To articulate this theoretical perspective I introduce the theory, briefly, in Chapter 1. In Chapters 2 through 6 I explicate, illustrate, and expand the theory in the context of diverse social and historical occurrences. Chapter 7 returns to the theoretical issues that emerge out of the analysis of the case studies and digs into the assumptions that must be examined to understand the processes at work. Some readers may want to read the final chapter first, returning to it after completing Chapters 1 through 6. This approach may have special appeal for the theoretical social scientist. Finally, I have attempted to avoid excessive technical terminology, choosing instead to define terms in a relatively simple way. I hope the reader will find this book both enjoyable and educational.

CHAPTER 1

Too Many People, Too Few Places

"A society composed of an infinite number of unorganized individuals, that a hypertrophied state is forced to oppress and contain, constitutes a veritable sociological monstrosity."
—Émile Durkheim

Heretics, vagrants, bohemians, and other types of marginally integrated people have always been objects of anxiety and scorn. These responses are concomitant with society's capacities to label, conceptualize, and stigmatize. Whether it was the medieval period in Europe, the Elizabethan in England, post-Revolutionary France, or the United States during the 1930s and the 1960s, sentiments directed toward doing something about marginal groups helped create organized forms to contain them. Throughout the medieval period monasteries appeared and waned, Beguinages came into existence, and vagabonds and vagrants were pressed into apprenticeships. In Elizabethan England the poor laws and the Bridewell system were created; in post-Revolutionary France bohemians became organized into urban clusters; in early-nineteenth-century England schools were created to contain surplus youth; and during the 1930s the WPA projects were initiated, in part, to absorb and control unemployed (and thus marginally integrated) Americans. How these forms have evolved and how they work to control the impact of the seemingly unattached on society is the subject of this study.

The challenge to society of a short-term or long-term imbalance between people and places has received relatively little attention from modern social scientists. Demographers and policymakers have, to be sure, indicated concern over the practical impact of too few jobs to absorb available manpower, or, conversely, shortages of labor to fill vacant positions. Articulation at the level of theory of the societal dynamics that create these imbalances, and the way imbalances impact on and are responded to by diverse segments of society, has been neglected. A systematic effort to build concepts and theories that will aid us in understanding not only those processes which are most salient but those which are latent is long overdue. The growth of concepts and theories to help meet these challenges will simultaneously raise practical issues about how society may rationally respond to them.

This particular effort adheres to the basic assumptions associated with formal scientific method. The most important assumption orienting this study is that the more diverse in time and place are the contexts to which a theory applies the more convincing is the theory. According to this criterion, the theory I am assessing in this study, to the extent that it is supported by observation of social events, is important.

The question of what kind of sociology is being practiced here is difficult to answer. Some will choose to call this historical sociology. Others will choose to describe it as sociological history. My inclination is to think of it as theoretical sociology. The fact that I use historical data and, particularly, select case studies from medieval, Renaissance, and pre-modern Europe and England as well as the United States during the 1930s and 1960s does not itself make this historical sociology or sociological history. What historical data allow me to do is identify a universal pattern.

Short-term or long-term imbalances between people and places—and the consequences, real and imagined, of these imbalances—require some response from society. Whether the response is intentional and recognized or unintentional and latent is of importance to understanding these processes. One of the most important of the contributions that sociologists make to the understanding of societal processes is the transformation of what is latent into what we call "manifest."[1] Raising awareness, or consciousness, regarding society's essential processes makes it possible to anticipate, recognize, and control their direction.

Modern sociological theory has benefited, in this regard, from the work of two major figures, Karl Marx and Émile Durkheim, both of whom recognized that society itself creates marginal populations. Marx and his close associate Friedrich Engels were particularly concerned with surplus populations, those large masses of unemployed who are generated both by themselves and by economic and political elites acting in accord with the systems of production associated with capitalism. Creating and maintaining a greater number of workers than jobs keeps the cost of labor down. Since capitalism is a system directed to profit, and having more workers than jobs enhances profits, a surplus population may be perceived as necessary. The existence of such a surplus may be viewed by some segments of society as tolerable and by others as intolerable. The widespread exchanges in the press and from the

podium between Thomas Malthus, apologist for the status quo, and
both Marx and Engels, critics of the system, attest to the view that what
appears necessary for a social system to survive is often a matter of
judgment rather than sociological fact.

Marginality, particularly in the form of relatively weak integration
into organized groups, was a major concern of Durkheim's. According
to Durkheim, people in Western societies without ties to and regulation
by organized groups are particularly prone to self-destruction and other
forms of deviant behavior. The degree of vulnerability is a result of the
nature of the bonds between people and the effectiveness of the regula-
tive system, i.e., norms, in exerting control over the goal-oriented behavior of society's members.

The existence of large numbers of relatively unattached and unintegrated people in modern society was attributed, by Marx and Engels on
the one hand, and Durkheim on the other, to the impact of the Industrial Revolution on Western societies. These observers were in agreement that marginality is an undesirable and unacceptable condition in
society. More recent observers have selected the theme of marginality as
well. Implicitly recognizing that an imbalance between people and
positons in society is the source of marginal population, regardless of
the origins of the imbalance, Roger H. Tawney, Norman Cohn, and
Frances Piven and Richard Cloward have examined the roots and impact, in diverse societal contexts, of marginality and its relationship to
social protest.[2]

Marginality, Deviance, and Social Control

The sociological questions surrounding surplus populations and marginality in relation to given organizations in society involve issues larger
than social protest. The study of social movements, largely directed to
describing and explaining how protest movements emerge, become organized, and impact on society, does deal with marginality and surplus
populations. Organized, effective movements to change societies clearly
require soldiers, as it were, with whom these instruments are built. But
the substantial, cumulative body of literature in that area, particularly
the research of the "resource mobilization" school, is directed to questions that are different from mine.* It is furthermore, not the populations as such in whom I am interested but the organizational processes
that create, manipulate, and control substantial portions of the potentially dissident in society. Organizations contributing to the abeyance

---

*I have read extensively in this literature, particularly the works of Tilly, Gamson, Michael
Schwartz, and others; of particular interest has been the work of Natalie Z. Davis, a social
historian (see Bibliography). In this context see my review of Michael Schwartz's *Radical
Protest and Social Structure* in *Contemporary Sociology*, 10, no. 3 (May 1981):428–429.

process may be a source of social control and maintenance of the status quo, on the one hand, and a source of protest and change, on the other. It is also possible for two or more of these functions to occur simultaneously. Since relatively little attention has been directed to how social structures attenuate protest and change, this study emphasizes the social control dimension. If there is a question of direct relevance to the study of social protests, it is: Why do we not have more? The question of how they come about will be illuminated by my effort here but it is not central. What, then, is my interest in this study?

This study focuses on the interplay between *status vacancies* (i.e., positions in organizations), *abeyance* (a holding or slowing process of integration), and *social control* in a variety of trans-historical and trans-societal contexts. The expansion and contraction of occupational, kinship, and other positions is hypothesized as a factor conducive to the creation, emergence, and control of deviant behavior. *Control of the consequences of too many people and too few places is viewed as a problem that is not only economic but moral as well, since dissident behavior may be perceived as a threat to the normative system of a society.* The precise point at which sanctioning agents respond remains problematic. Certain structures emerge, either by design or by spontaneous social processes, to contain the temporary surplus of people. Established institutional patterns also exist that can expand and contract in order to absorb or release personnel. The process of holding personnel is called abeyance.

The various factors enhancing and inhibiting the abeyance process, the nature of this process, the structures that emerge, and their institutionalization or decline is my primary interest in this study. My goal is to conceptualize, to articulate, and to extend what is implicit in the sociological and historical literature.

The intellectual framework within which these questions are asked bridges social-scientific and humanistic disciplines. Among the important questions are: What is the range of tolerable deviance in society? What are the boundaries within which the balance between human freedom and societal constraints can simultaneously allow and encourage conformity, creativity, and change? At a more abstract and implicit level, how can societies attain a balance between change and both moral and rational-functional integration? Exploration of the specific processes to which my attention is directed here should help illuminate these basic sociological quesions and contribute, as well, to an increased capacity to interpret and communicate humanistic knowledge.

Heretics and Vagrants

Cohn, Tawney, and Piven and Cloward have grasped a similar theme. They hold that marginal populations become a source of concern in

society and that this concern is a stimulant to reaction by authoritie
Their work suggests that marginality is a phenomenon that may be
problem in any society, in any time. As such marginality is a universa
condition, at least in its potentialities, and understanding how and what
happens when marginality occurs is important for understanding the
universal attributes of societal phenomena.

In the interest of a generalizing theory it is useful to review, briefly,
these three studies as illustrative of the ubiquity of these phenomena.

Cohn's thesis is that revolutionary messianism requires a particular
set of social conditions that provide personnel to activate the ideology.

Cohn holds that the pattern of "voluntary poverty" was a crucial
factor in understanding the movements of the late medieval period in
Europe. A number of other authors have said the same thing, although
they described the same pattern as the *via apostolica*, the simulation of
the life-style associated with the stories of the original apostles of Jesus.
Unlike most of the historians who have described this pattern, however,
Cohn sought an explanation in terms of social structural conditions.

The pattern of voluntary poverty was not significant in and of itself.
It reflected the situation of marginality in which a large number of people, especially women, found themselves during the later Middle Ages
in northern and central Europe. Both those who were well-off and those
who were poor became marginal. Cohn reasoned that as the economic
circumstances of the relatively affluent populations improved beyond
their most extravagant expectations, as men entered monasteries, and as
women's expectations and liberation from male dominance increased, to
name but a few of the contributing factors, people were dislodged from
old attachments and became mentally free as well. This mental freedom
(my terminology) included elements of guilt over extravagant living on
the part of the populace and criticism of the churchmen for their lack of
adherence to spiritual norms. The movements of voluntary poverty,
including the Brethren of the Free Spirit as one major example, provided
structures for the integration of the marginal populations of the cities of
the late Middle Ages. Those without means also contributed members to
the movement. In Cohn's words, "Revolutionary chiliasm drew its
strength from the *surplus population* living on the *margin* of society—
peasants without land or with too little land even for subsistence; jour-
neymen and unskilled workers living under the continuous threat of
unemployment; beggars and vagabonds—in fact from that amorphous
mass of people who were not simply poor but who could find no assured and recognized place in society at all."[3]

My second example of the ubiquity of social structure as a source of
marginality is R. H. Tawney's classic study of sixteenth century England, in which he noted how the emergence of surplus populations
created a rootless, unintegrated mass not unlike those who were in
evidence on the Continent somewhat earlier and for somewhat other

reasons. The "tramp" is the sixteenth-century counterpart to Cohn's marginal messianist.

Although the people to whom Tawney was referring were seemingly different from those whom Cohn describes, they are sociologically similar. The tramps and vagrants (Tawney uses both characterizations) were clearly marginal once they were thrust out of the structures in which they had been integrated. Their marginality was in relation to the towns and cities toward which they migrated once their positions as agricultural laborers were no longer available to them. They remained marginal, and thus surplus, until other positions expanded to provide integrating structures for them. As in the case of the central and northern European groups who became messianists, the rootless, mobile mass in sixteenth-century England was feared. The response to this "terror," as Tawney describes it, was an effort to slow down the rate of increase of surplus populations through legislation and to find means of social control over those who were already in a marginal situation. The response was both economic in the form of alms and stipends and social in the form of mandatory engagement in institutionalized activities, one of which was apprenticeship for the younger vagrants.

Tawney's thesis was that for a long time before and especially during the sixteenth century, rural England had been undergoing an increasingly revolutionary change in agriculture and rural social structure. This change led to the eviction of a great many peasants from their homes, and thus from their place in the social structure.

From a situation which was anything but static, but which involved a relative balance between personnel and available positions in the occupational structure, there arose a surplus population. That this population was more a creation of institutional processes than the result of demographic factors is extremely important to keep in mind. For the present, in reviewing Tawney, it is essential to consider the response to this outpouring of human mass on the part of both local and national authorities.

That the existence of this large surplus was viewed with alarm is evident in the many documents which Tawney assembled. The problem of the vagrant taxed the imagination and effort of townspeople on the one hand and the organs of the national state on the other.

> He is denounced by moralists, analysed into species by the curious or scientific, scourged and buffeted by all men. The destitution of the aged and impotent, of fatherless children, is familiar enough. It has been with the world from time immemorial. It has been for centuries the object of voluntary charitable effort; and when the dissolution of the monasteries dries up one great channel of provision, the Government intervenes with special arrangements to take their place a whole generation before it can be brought to admit that there is any problem of the unemployed, other than the problem of the sturdy rogue.[4]

The government intervened under an act of Henry VIII which directed "city and country authorities to relieve impotent beggars 'by way of voluntary and charitable alms.' They were also for the first time given power to apprentice vagrant children."[5]

From a humanitarian perspective it is relatively easy to laud the sensitivity and foresight of the English elites in response to their brethren. A great many documents, unearthed by Tawney, indicate that there was also great moral outcry against the ravages of Enclosure and its consequences. One of these reflects the drama that must have characterized the debates surrounding Enclosure. *The Crying Sin of England in not caring for the Poor, wherein Enclosure such as doth unpeople Towns and Common Fields is Arraigned, Convicted, and Condemned by the Word of God,* by John Moore, Minister of Knaptoft, in Leicestershire, 1633, provides an example of humanitarian outrage. But the response of elites was not primarily motivated by humanitarian concern. It was, Tawney holds, a police measure. Every effort seemed to be made to hold the masses in their place, which was the village; and if these failed to work, sanctions, including whipping, could be imposed. "If the poor being thrust out of their houses go to dwell with others, straight we catch them with the Statute of Inmates; if they wander abroad, they are in danger of the Statute of the Poor to be whipped."[6]

In sum, efforts to relieve the destitute were not a result of the enforcement of moral obligations attributable to medieval ideas, "but an attempt on the part of the powerful Tudor State to prevent the social disorder caused by economic changes, which, in spite of its efforts, it had not been strong enough to control."[7]

This inability of the State to prevent and control social disorder was reflected in the many peasant uprisings between 1500 and 1650. Varying in numbers involved and intensity of outrage on the part of the rebels, these protest movements were the last great upheavals that resonated from the protest movements of medieval Europe. Although they were different in some respects, there were common elements as well. The English rebels who struck out against the effects of Enclosure were not the poor and destitute. These were people who owned land and were fighting to keep what they had. The messianists described by Cohn were also better off for the most part than a substantial portion of the populations of medieval central and northern Europe. It will be recalled that their life of poverty was "voluntary." Thus, as analysts of revolutionary movements now realize, it is typically not the destitute who initiate and participate in these uprisings but those who are, at least, better off than the economically and socially poor.[8]

Although both types of movements were organized, rather than the result of spontaneous, idiosyncratic outbursts, they differed in a major respect. Revolutionary messianism attempted to change the nature of the relationships between men and their religious organizations. Not only did the protesters seek to attain an alteration in the moral ideas of their age, they wanted to displace the established Church as a mediator between man and God. That they threatened the Establishment was clear. The sixteenth-century English rebel, however, was concerned with one relatively simple matter: to reestablish a set of economic relationships that he had enjoyed prior to the wholesale, rampant proliferation of Enclosure. He was primarily conservative, largely satisfied with other aspects of his life situation. Effective government intervention was all that would be necessary to mollify him. The total rejection of a life situation, which characterized the quest of the revolutionary messianist, was foreign to him.[9]

If it was the relatively well endowed rather than the destitute who were in the vanguard of the English riots associated with Enclosure, why so much concern over the vagrant? "It was that agrarian discontent created a permanent supply of inflammable material, which a spark might turn into a conflagration."[10] Thus began the pattern, associated with both England and the United States, of anticipating and reacting through state intervention to intentionally forestall dramatic change and revolution. Two hundred years later, the Speenhamland Law demonstrated a similar perception of the effect of the Industrial Revolution on the large mass of the poor.[11] Although the result was judged by some to have been catastrophic, the law nevertheless represented a major effort to deal with the problem of surplus population and marginality in a systematic manner. That legislative intervention can both create and dislocate, in order to relocate surplus populations and integrate them into organized activities, will be taken up below. For the moment it is important to keep in mind that the emergence of surplus populations and its concomitant marginality, does not go unnoticed in society. Time and time again we observe the relatively stable, well-integrated people in society responding with fear and anxiety in anticipation of the actions of an uncontrolled mass, unleashed from the fetters of institutional engagement.

To be aware that surplus populations tended to evoke concern and response from both the general public and authorities is to describe only part of a complex, subtle process. Since the first response is often the police or social control reaction, it is essential to ask about the nature of state intervention beyond the mere provision of alms and poor relief. This is especially important because in many cases, as I have noted in my example of revolutionary messianism, the problem may be perceived as moral rather than economic. It is, furthermore, essential to look at the dynamic interplay between the structures that initially integrated the now-marginal populations and those that could absorb and reintegrate them, for the existence of a marginal population could not be tolerated for long.

Cohn suggested that the millenial movements of central and northern Europe provided positions for those who joined them. These positons, or statuses, were alternatives for those who had been thrust out of or could not find other positions as a result of limited opportunities. During the medieval period, for example, profound social changes associated with kinship patterns and expansion of opportunities for men as crusaders or monks contracted opportunities for women. As a surplus population, particularly in towns and cities, women far outnumbered men. The Beguines, to whom I will devote much attention below, and other religious movements provided status vacancies that women could fill. Thus, new integrating structures emerged to engage these marginal women and provided them with a recognized position.

With respect to the surplus created by Enclosure, as another example, it is useful to look at the original functions of land tenure. The intentional effort to intervene to slow down the impact of Enclosure was related to the awareness of authorities that the pattern of land tenure functioned, in part at least, to maintain a reservoir of military manpower. Thus the authorities viewed the organization of agricultural life in terms of both social control and abeyance, the holding function. Unlike the situation in medieval Europe, the processes surrounding surplus populations and response to it in sixteenth-century England were rational and intentional on the part of the authorities. Likewise, although the protest movements of the English agrarians were specific, controlled, and intentional in organization, those of the millenialists involved inadvertent control over participants. It was not only the authorities—in this case the Church—who accomplished the social control of protesters; there was also the fact of participating in organized group activities. The Brethren of the Free Spirit, for example, by developing patterns for shared activities, inadvertently put themselves under control. These patterns helped to buffer and slow the impact of protest and change.

These two sets of movements are instructive because they provide examples along a continuum of social controls ranging from the exercise of formal authority to those that are a latent product of group involvement. In either case we can observe that something happens in society when the challenge of surplus population and widespread marginality occurs.

The Disreputable Poor and Demographic Flow

A more recent study than either Cohn's or Tawney's deals explicitly with the regulation of potential dissidents. In a study of modern poor relief, particularly in the United States since the New Deal, Piven and Cloward directed their attention to the absorption and control aspects of poor relief. They held that the "chief function" of relief is to regulate labor: "when mass unemployment leads to outbreaks of turmoil, relief programs are ordinarily initiated or expanded to *absorb and control* enough of the unemployed to restore order; then, as turbulence subsides, the relief system contracts, expelling those who are needed to populate the labor market."[12]

Reviewing some of the sources selected by Tawney and taking a number of cues from Sidney and Beatrice Webb's classic, *English Poor Law History*,[13] and Karl Polanyi's *The Great Transformation*, Piven and Cloward attributed the nature of the reactions to, and patterns of, poor relief to market forces. Recognizing that under traditional conditions where work and status positon is ascribed—ie., assigned by birth, gender, or other characteristics—the problem of motivating workers and directing them to pursue tasks deemed desirable by higher authorities is relatively rare. In a free market economy, however, allocating labor is much more complicated and difficult. Since "manpower distribution is mainly the result of monetary incentives and disincentives,"[14] the need for labor in a given industry or place is subject to the changing conditions and, more dramatically, vicissitudes of the market. Since the need for labor fluctuates, it is necessary to have a mechanism that will help regulate the extremes surrounding temporary surpluses and scarcities of manpower.

Piven and Cloward have observed that surplus populations constitute, in the eyes of reacting publics and elites, a threat to the established order of the communities and society in which they occur. They note that social control is central to the regulation of surplus populations and that regulating labor is a special case of maintaining order. They focus on mechanisms, in this case the various types of poor relief, that play a major role in maintaining order. Finally, they recognize that the nature of maintaining order with respect to allocation of personnel to status positions varies by societal type. Thus it is possible to view, in these terms, the diverse range of reactions to surplus populations associated with medieval Europe, sixteenth-century England, and contemporary American society.

Although the emphasis on the economic system and work, in particular, might obscure the basic societal processes reflected in this analysis, it is nevertheless very closely related to my own assumptions. However, Piven and Cloward's focus on the relief system primarily in terms of its capacity to distribute resources, and in that manner regulate personnel, neglects a hitherto uncharted dimension, the organizational processes that absorb, control, and expel personnel as they are and are not needed to fill status positions in society. This is the abeyance process and function of organizations, to which I have alluded above, which is the major concern of this study.

REGULATING DEMOGRAPHIC FLOW.   Although Cohn in his study of medieval millenialism recognized the connection between superfluity of population, marginality, and participation in protest movements, he was less concerned with the control functions of the social contexts from which the marginals emerged or with the capacities of the movements themselves to regulate behavior. Tawney, by contrast, was much more sensitive to this aspect of collective phenomena.

Tawney, it will be recalled, noted that one of the important functions of the land tenure system in England was military. Landholders represented a "reservoir" of military manpower who could be expected to respond in time of war or similar emergencies. The landholding system kept reservists in place, as it were, until their services were needed by those in higher authority.

This idea of a reservoir of human potential is not unlike the Marxian usage of "warehousing," which plays a prominent role in Piven and Cloward's perspective. As the quotation from their study suggests, relief programs function to regulate the flow of labor in and out of the market, as needed. But the flow of labor is an aspect of a more fundamental process in society, and it is well to recognize that this is a special case of the more general problem of surplus population and societal regulation.

All societies must come to terms with the problem of too many people in relation to too few resources, whether food or positions. When food is critically scarce among some Eskimo tribes it is expected that the elderly will remain behind, effectively committing suicide, as younger tribe members move on to gather sustenance. Modern societies encourage conception under conditions of too few people and conception control and abortion when there are too many. Thomas Malthus's classic *Essay on the Principle of Population* (1798, revised 1803) reflects this long-standing concern with the asymmetry of population and resources.

But societies are equally concerned with the relationship between people and jobs, and, more generally, with the integration of people into collective activities. Tawney, for example, did explicitly recognize the social control dimension with respect to populations, and, more specifically, the police action dimension. Piven and Cloward's awareness was more implicit. How the relief system controls the labor surplus is not addressed in their study. The absorption-expulsion function is left to the reader's imagination.

The process of regulating demographic flow is the same process that controls the potential for dissident behavior. It is an organized process, sometimes leading to the formation of new social structures or the reorganization of existent ones, but more often impacting on already existing patterns associated with institutions. Thus, abeyance processes are patterned activities of diverse organizations in society. These functions are performed when circumstances require them. When not necessary they may be recognized as dormant, or, if efforts continue to hold personnel when they are needed in other social contexts, they may be viewed as dysfunctional, i.e., contributing to excessive strains* in society.

An example of an institutionalized process that at times performs the abeyance function is war. Malthus's recognition that war was a regulator of population, along with pestilence and disease, was based on a concern with elimination of population rather than temporary displacement. J. R. Hale describes how war provided an alternative for those who could not find work in Renaissance Europe.

> Next in volume was a multiplicity of men looking for work. The population of Europe was growing but slowly, *but faster than agriculture or the labour demands of towns could readily absorb.* This was especially true of Castile, the mountains of Central Europe and the less fertile islands and coasts of the Mediterranean. There was a steady flow of men from these areas seeking jobs, above all, as soldiers. Albanian mercenaries were found as far afield as Spain, though most sought service in Italy and were relied on particularly in Venice. Called stradiots because they were always on the road (Italian *strada*), they were joined by men from other sterile regions wandering in search of wars which others were too prosperous to risk fighting in themselves.[15]

Although the value of this example, taken alone, is limited because it describes population growth as a source of the surplus and intersocietal rather than intrasocietal patterns, and thus helps little in the development of a theory for societies as units of analysis, it is nevertheless instructive. Soldiering was recognized as one alternative to other positions in society when the latter were not sufficient for the integration of personnel. As more articulated societies emerged, with governments able to control mobility, state intervention enhanced social control. Renaissance Europe as described by Hale contrasted sharply with the sixteenth-century England that Tawney described. The latter was a nation in spite of internal strife and, ultimately, civil war. It was possible to intervene, more or less effectively, in the problems arising out of surplus populations. England did not simply depend on emigration, but made an effort to keep her population within and under control.

Perhaps it is no accident that those whom Hale describes had come from areas in Europe where the articulation of nation-states was at a particularly low level. Venice, the principal receiver of stradiots, was in contrast a well integrated city-state.

War is a possible alternative for absorbing surplus population not

---

*By "excessive" strains I imply that some strain is healthy and leads to desirable, creative change.

only because almost anyone can become a soldier but because there are always places where wars are ongoing. The existence of a surplus population can itself create a greater probability that a country will go to war. History is replete with examples. Thus a surplus population can be both a creator and creature, as it were, of war.

STATUS VACANCY AND DEMOGRAPHIC FLOW.   What I am proposing in this study is a sociological approach to analysing, interpreting and understanding a fundamental process in all societies. I have, for the purpose of increasing the salience of this process, coined the concept *abeyance*. Abeyance is a holding or slowing process that affects the relative stability or the rate of change in a society. It is conceptualized as an *interorganizational* process. What happens in one organizational sphere is explained, in this perspective, by what has happened or is happening in another organizational sphere. Thus it is important to know those things that are happening *within* a given organization which may have implications for the impact of one organization on another. In this study I want to know about the expansion and contraction of positions and the sources and consequences of this process. But concrete people are the actors in this process, and it is on them that, ultimately, abeyance impacts.

The sociological perspective includes the assumption that people are integrated or involved in collective phenomena both as persons and as occupants of positions in group settings. The person is placed conceptually in a group context in order to articulate that aspect of social relationships which mediates between the person and the larger, more impersonal society. The person relates to society not as such but as a group member and participant. Analytically and conceptually, each person is thought of as occupying a position, or *status,* and performing a *role* according to expectations associated with that position.[16] When sociologists describe action, i.e., dynamic aspects of collective phenomena, they use the role concept; in describing what is relatively static, the status concept is used.

In discussing the expansion and contraction of positions in a system, whether it be monasticism or employment in a modern commercial organization, it is often useful to conceive of a limited number of positions available to be filled by personnel. In contemporary terms this may mean that we will make predictions about the number of teachers and the number of students expected to assume positions in a given school system. At any point in time there may be too many or too few personnel in relation to the number of available positions. What happens when these discrepancies between personnel and structural opportunities occur is what this study is all about. For the capacity of a society to exert control over its personnel is directly related to the extent to which its members are integrated into organized social patterns. And they are integrated through the behaviors performed as occupants of statuses. Two types of discrepancy between personnel and positions in organizations may be conceptualized: status *vacancy* and status *superfluity*.*

The idea of status vacancy has received only limited attention in the sociological literature since it was introduced by Sorokin in 1927. Indeed, except for brief reference to "vacant statuses" by Lipset and Zetterberg and "vacancies in high places" by Sibley, little explicit attention has been paid to status vacancy at the conceptual level.[17]

That there are more or fewer positions to be filled in an occupational structure, that there are increased or decreased employment opportunities, and that there are greater or more limited opportunities for mobility into elite positions in given societies is clearly a matter of great interest to sociologists. As an important variable, status vacancy has not been altogether neglected, particularly by demographers. But its value as a sensitizing concept that might lead to an expansion of our perspective on broader processes and social structures has been too limited. My efforts here are directed in part to explication and application of status vacancy as a concept that is important to understanding the interplay among social processes associated with societal controls. Closely associated in a dynamic sense with status vacancy, the structural component, is a constantly ongoing process of demographic flow, at one time providing personnel to occupy vacant positions and at another time redirecting personnel to other pursuits. This expansion-contraction phenomenon, which must be viewed at both manifest and latent levels, plays an important role in the creation and reinforcement of certain social structures and movements as well as contributing to processes surrounding deviance and social control at a macrosocial level.

Status Vacancy: Vertical and Horizontal

Usage of the status vacancy concept has been too limited due to the tendency in the past to view this factor, primarily, with respect to vertical social mobility. Thus Sorokin, Sibley, Lipset and Zetterberg, and Perrucci, to name but a few, take into account the availability of higher-ranking positions in an occupational structure in order to assess the pattern and degree of upward mobility in a system. Indeed, the question of whether social mobility has actually occurred revolves about whether movement upward results from "the supply of vacant statuses" and the resulting "interchange of ranks," in Lipset and Zetterberg's framework, or from expansive mobility.

*Articulating status superfluity is beyond the scope of this study.

Expansive mobility refers to changes that occur in the structure of positions themselves. With the advent of factory-organized work and the increase of agricultural output per unit of manpower, for example, a number of previously existing occupational categories disappeared; also a number of other vacancies proliferated and new categories emerged. A large segment of the population was drawn into these positions en masse, not because they sought "higher" positions but because these were now readily available. Thus some vertical social mobility may only be apparent, rather than real, since it is the expansion and contraction of status vacancies rather than the mobility-oriented behavior of actors that is responsible for the altered occupational rank.

That no real increase in rank must occur in relation to movement toward vacancies is illustrated historically by the repeal of the Speenhamland Law and the enactment of the Poor Law Reform Act in England during the early part of the nineteenth century—two developments that forced peasants off the land into the factories and urban areas.[18]

But the occurrence of fluctuating employment on a massive scale is associated with a more subtle though general social process that requires some comment. The control of the supply of status vacancies in a society and the regulation of movement of personnel in and out of these vacancies is not a random, accidental process. Through a variety of techniques, some of which have already been suggested, both the demographic flow and the numbers and kinds of positions are directed by traditional normative means and by rational manipulation of social processes.

More important at this point, however, is to broaden our perspective on status vacancy beyond the realm of occupational structure and to move from vertical to horizontal perspectives. Every position in society is potentially vacant or occupied at some point in time independent of the process of ranking. Each formal role typically requires an actor to perform the expectations associated with it.

From the standpoint of structure, to name but one dimension, the organized social life of personnel may be focused not only on formal work contexts but on family, peer groups, and voluntary associations. Access to interaction in these contexts is also a matter of the status vacancy factor. The ratio of males to females is simultaneously a matter of entry into roles in marriage and a factor in access to family positions; and consequently, it is a factor in demographic flow, among other things. Peer and age-group involvement is an extremely important activity from the point of view of both personal development and societal maintenance and change, as S. N. Eisenstadt has shown.[19]

But access to the relationship associated with these contexts is similarly a matter of the availability of membership positions. Under some conditions—and this is most dramatically exemplified by the plight to-day of large numbers of aged Americans (it also occurs when we experi-ence rapid increase in the numbers of young people in society)—strains occur that create demands for societal response to disruption and change. It is partly in anticipation of these conditions, and also in re-sponse to them, that abeyance processes operate.

STATUS VACANCY AND SOCIETAL REGULATION.   Concern with an over-supply of population in relation to resources was a feature of societies long before Malthus wrote his *Essay*. Indeed, as Tawney has shown in *The Agrarian Problem in the Sixteenth Century*, concern with undersupply and oversupply of personnel in relation to work was a central feature of the controversy surrounding the passage of the Enclosure Acts. Earlier, in the fourteenth century, as a result of plague, depression, and famine, England was caught in an agrarian crisis while much of Europe suffered similar circumstances.[20] In terms of demographic flow, Renaissance Eu-rope was like an accordion, alternately expanding and contracting. Thus even before the age of social science and modern societies the need to respond to the imbalance between demographic flow and societal re-sources was manifest.

But to view the concern with regulating personnel for economic rea-sons alone would be to oversimply a very complex process. Indeed, oversupply of population as a factor in demographic flow is also too limited a perspective. That "Idle hands are the Devil's workshop" can be illustrated by many accounts of deviant behavior associated with periods of economic contraction.[21] That deviance also characterized pe-riods of economic expansion is illustrated by Durkheim. However, it is not the economic factor itself which is responsible for deviant behavior and society's efforts to exert control over the phenomena so charac-terized. Under conditions of rapid change and social dislocation so-cieties tend toward deregulation, or *anomie,* and this is reflected, accord-ing to Durkheim's classic study, in increased rates of suicide. That this deregulative process is an aspect of large-scale societal change was noted not only by Durkheim but by Karl Polanyi and others as well. Polanyi's analysis of the rise of the market economy at the cost of releas-ing the economic system from the traditional constraints of the larger society is remarkably similar to Durkheim's analysis of the sources of chronic anomie.[22]

Dimensions of Organizations

The abeyance process contributes to the regulation of the impact of surplus populations on society by holding potentially dissident marginal people in controlled situations. I have also said that the process is typically a normal activity associated with institutionalized patterns and that it may occur as a result of newly emergent patterns, intended or unintended. How does the process work and what is there about these organized patterns that makes it work?

These questions are best answered below in my description and analysis of a number of case studies taken from diverse historical and social contexts. As said earlier, by selecting seemingly unrelated phenomena I intentionally adhere to the principle that the more diverse are the contexts in which a particular social pattern can be discerned the more generalizable are the assumptions and hypotheses associated with the pattern, and hence the more scientifically significant is the theoretical perspective. In addition to the examples I have chosen to treat at length, there are, of course, a great many other contexts that may be analyzed, including military organizations, mental hospitals, and other total institutions, but my reference to them will be brief.

To understand the abeyance processes better, I have selected different aspects of organizations that may be thought of as variables. These are treated as continua with respect to the case studies. Thus each context exhibits more or less of a particular factor. These factors do not add up to an ideal type, in Weber's terms.[23] They are, instead, based upon induction and describe empirically observable phenomena. My goal, therefore, is not to create a typology, but, rather, to introduce a concept that has direct influence on observation of societal events. This does not preclude, however, a reader's desire to create an ideal typology from what I am presenting. The analysis will hopefully, lead to a variety of conceptual tools for the expansion and articulation of sociological theory, some of them not yet intended or recognized by me.

The relative weight of each variable in its importance to the abeyance process in general will, for the time being, remain implicit. Other variables may, in time, be added to the conceptual framework, and some that have been selected may also be deleted. My effort is consciously exploratory, although this does not justify weak analysis, irresponsible speculation, or unwarranted generalization. As stated earlier, the variables which are most relevant with respect to the abeyance process are *temporality; commitment; inclusiveness; division of labor; institutionalization;* and *internal stratification.* Effectiveness in regulating demographic flow in relation to the larger society, and in maintaining social control internally and externally, will vary according to these factors. The accompanying table illustrates the relative weighting of each factor in relation to the patterns to be described.

How these factors will be interrelated with each other, and under what social conditions, will vary. Clarity will emerge as I apply the

ORGANIZED PATTERN	Temporality	Commitment	Inclusiveness	Division of Labor	Institutionalization	Stratification
Monasticism	High	High	Moderate	Moderate	High	High
Beguines	Moderate	Moderate	High	Low	Low/Moderate	Low
Bohemianism	Low	Low	High	Low	Low	Low
Education	High	Low/High	High	Low	High	Moderate
Federal Projects	Low	Low	Moderate	Low	Low	Low

These variables have different values when they are absorbing and holding on the one hand and expelling personnel on the other. The reader will note that there are implicit hypotheses in this table.

framework to the case studies that follow. For the present it will suffice to explain what the variables are.

TEMPORALITY.   By temporality I refer to the relative length of time that the organizational pattern remains salient. The monastic system, for example, has persisted for more than fifteen hundred years in the West, whereas bohemianism is only several hundred years old. More critical than duration, however, is salience. Although the monastic system has been relatively important and conspicuous as a religious form, bohemianism remains outside of the network of institutions in society but emerges in different forms when abeyance is required. The specific organization that absorbs personnel may have great longevity, as in the monastery, or limited longevity, as in the "hippie" groups in the United States during the 1960s.

COMMITMENT.   Organizations vary in the degree of commitment required of members. As Coser has demonstrated in his study of "greedy institutions,"[24] the priesthood, for example, requires celibacy in order to remove any alternative potential for the priest's loyalty, thus tying him to the Church for life. In order for abeyance to work most effectively, members must be relatively *undercommitted* to the organization. Otherwise it is difficult to encourage people to leave the organization when the expulsion phase of the pendulum is required. Coser's perspective is thus expanded by adding the idea of undercommitment. What emerges is a continuum concept of commitment.

INCLUSIVENESS.   Organizations vary in their openness to members, some being more exclusive than others. In order to absorb surplus populations, organizations must be willing to accept almost anybody, regardless of the diverse social criteria used to select members in other contexts. Schools must be willing to accept almost anyone who fits some general age criterion. An army selects men and women on the basis of very undiscriminating factors, especially when its mandate is to increase its members.

DIVISION OF LABOR.   This variable is closely related to inclusiveness, although it is not the same. The abeyance process works most effectively when those to be absorbed are expected to perform only general tasks which require skills that can be learned by the lowest common denominator. Thus, again, the motivation to become a permanent member of the organization is less likely to emerge. The member who is being held in abeyance must not identify his or her future with that of the organization; it must be sought in other contexts.

STRATIFICATION.   Opportunities to succeed within the organization and to receive rewards from it are another inducement to tenacity of involvement. In order for the temporary member to see himself as a sojourner, he must be kept from entering the ranks of the permanent members.

INSTITUTIONALIZATION.   The abeyance process is enhanced when societal members believe that the "right thing to do" under certain circumstances is to participate in the activities of those organizations that are absorbing personnel. By making work, education, and patriotism, for example, ends in themselves society makes it easy to get people to go to work, school, or war. This is one of the most important variables influencing the capacity of societies to control masses of people without confrontation.

These are the variables that make the difference in abeyance and social control. Their usefulness as analytical tools will be clear as I review the case studies.

CHAPTER 2

Monasticism: The Total Way of Life

"Monasticism was the friend and the foe of true religion. It was the inspiration of virtue and the encouragement of vice. It was the patron of industry and the promoter of idleness. It was a pioneer in education and the teacher of superstition. It was the disburser of alms and a many-handed robber. It was the friend of human liberty and the abettor of tyranny. It was the champion of the common people and the defender of class privileges. It was, in short, everything that man was and is, so varied were its operations, so complex was its influence, so comprehensive was its life."

—A. W. Wishart

The monasteries of the West, from the time of their origin during the fourth and fifth centuries A.D. to the present, have performed a wide variety of activities significant to both Church and Western societies. Sometimes these monasteries have served as a source of stability; at other times they have contributed to changes; and often they have supported both. (The monastic system has been one of the institutions of the West that has enjoyed the greatest longevity.) As absorber of unintegrated Christians, socializer of children, surveillant of adults, conduit of charity, and, above all, keeper of the ideals of the Church, the monastic system has expanded and contracted with the ebb and flow of activities in other institutional spheres. Over its history the monastic system has made an important contribution to the abeyance process and its concomitant, social control. It is an excellent example of an organization whose form has remained somewhat the same over time but whose functions have changed as external conditions have required. It is this flexibility that has been the source of its persistence. It is this same capacity to adapt to the times that has been one of monasticism's important contributions to the survival of the Church over the past two thousand years.

Monasteries are like other social organizations that perform, at least in part, similar functions. Schools, prisons, hospitals, military organizations, and a host of other social structures have the capacity to expand and contract numbers of available positions, socialize, discipline, supervise, and control personnel. All of these other organized forms are, however, of more recent origin, and their tenacity has not yet met the test of longevity that characterizes monasticism. And none of them has, furthermore, performed as wide a variety of functions when compared to the monastic system.

Understanding how the monastic system came into being, how its organization has emerged and changed, how it has flourished and waned, particularly in the context of its contribution to the abeyance and social control processes, can help throw light on the nature of the processes themselves and the organizations that serve their implementation. It is to the origins of monasticism that I now turn.[1]

Origins

Western monasticism, the institutionalized pattern of religious activity carried out in organized seclusion from the secular world, emerged under acute societal conditions, the decline of the Roman Empire. No better description of what sociologists call *anomie*, the deregulation of normative constraints, can be provided than the one that Harnack presents in his classic essay on monasticism.

> No age, perhaps, was ever more deeply penetrated with the idea that the fashion of this world passeth away, that life is not worth living. In actual fact, a great epoch in human history was passing away. The Roman Empire, the old world, hastened to die, and fearful were its death-bed agonies. Sedition, bloodshed, poverty, pestilence within; without, the barbarous hordes on all sides. What was to be set against all this? No longer the power of a self-sufficient State, or the force of a uniform and tried ideal of civilization, but an Empire falling asunder, hardly held together by a decaying and disintegrated culture; and that culture itself hollow and untrue, in which scarcely a single man could keep a good conscience, or a free natural mind, or a clean hand. . . . It was then that monasticism, as a mighty movement . . . took its origin.[2]

Workman, following a similar theme, describes some of the specifics of this anomic phenomenon.

The Empire was slowly sinking into ruin, as much from weakness within, bad methods of finance, a poverty-stricken middle class, the concentration of all wealth in the hands of the few, a hopeless bureaucracy, the stereotyping of all society into hereditary castes, an army of hireling barbarians—more terrible to its masters than to its enemies—as by attacks from without. The despotism of the Empire as it grew old became at once feebler and more vexatious, exhausting a world which it would not even defend. It weighed upon all and protected none.[3]

Roman society had reached, by the fourth century, a state of extreme corruption, a situation ripe for a moral movement. Workman notes that "protest was bound to come . . . a similar revolt [occurred] in the early days that followed the break-up of Greek civic independence and the substitution of imperialism."[4]

Christianity, its message carried by the itinerant and seemingly ubiquitous preachers against the false gods of the secular, materialistic, and sensate life of the Roman elites, was a consciousness-raising phenomenon, and this ingredient is essential to a moral movement. Status protest, chaos, corruption, and romanticism led first to a movement to abandon the cities, where the impact of these phenomena was greatest, and then to the establishment of monastic communities—first in the desert, where hermits and groups of vagrants settled, and then in regulated settings, where work and secular renunciation were the normative emphases.

Manifestly, monasticism was a response to the secular world that was directed to renunciation of worldly pursuits. "Complete renunciation centered itself round three points: poverty, chastity and obedience; or the renunciation of the world, the renunciation of the flesh, and the renunciation of self-will." Groups of Christians could be brought together to pursue the physical labor that was necessary for self and group maintenance while at the same time adhering to a normatively rigorous spiritual life. However, if we are to accept Edward Gibbon's view, the monastic movement was not simply a religious phenomenon.

The monasteries were filled by a crew of obscure and abject plebeians, who gained in the cloister much more than they had sacrificed in the world. Peasants, slaves and mechanics might escape from poverty and contempt to a safe and honourable profession, whose apparent hardships are mitigated by custom, by popular applause, and by the secret relaxation of discipline. The subjects of Rome, whose persons and fortunes were made responsible for unequal and exorbitant tributes, retired from the oppression of the Imperial government; and the pusillanimous youth preferred the penance of a monastic, to the dangers of a military life. The affrighted provincials, of every rank, who fled before the Barbarians, found shelter and subsistence; whole legions were buried in these religious sanctuaries; and the same cause, which relieved the distress of individuals, impaired the strength and fortitude of the empire.[5]

Gibbon's view that monasticism appealed to a wide variety of motives is consistent with my own. That it functioned to integrate and simultaneously direct the activities of large numbers of diverse groups is more directly to the point. Monasticism was a means, at least in part, by which the unintegrated and poorly integrated were given places and brought under control by a latent societal process. As was the case for unintegrated young people with respect to war, education, bohemianism, and the Beguines, monasticism provided opportunities for integration and its corollary, social control.

This is not to suggest that the monastic system, in origin, was *intended* as a means for the absorption and control of surplus populations of men. But once organized, it gradually came to pass that the elites used the pattern to exert control over both the overzealous and those who were lax in their adherence to regulations passed down by Church authorities.

Although the ultimate origins of monasticism, like other origins, are obscure, it is clear that the Christians both in the East and in the West did not alone invent the form that finally emerged and proliferated throughout western Europe. The practice of retreat from the mundane life for religious purposes was known in the Orient and during the period preceding the rise of Christianity. It has been a tradition, however, judging by the consensus one finds among Church historians, to attribute the origins of Western monasticism to the hermits who withdrew from secular life in the Near East to the deserts and seashores of that region. It was when Christianity became transformed from "a religious movement to the legally instituted state church"[6] that the monastic system became organized in the West. Thus even the original organization of the monastic system exemplifies a pattern that emerged out of a setting in which surplus, marginal people seemingly voluntarily helped bring an end to a religious movement by joining with others in groups of relatively disciplined adherents. Even before the emergence of monasticism the basic concepts existed: "complete abstinence from all sexual intercourse, and . . . complete renunciation of the world."[7] From the former emerged the proscription on marriage for those who took vows, and notably members of the priesthood, and from the latter emerged the retreat from secular society that became organized into the monastic system. It was more than two hundred years after the founding of the Church that the hermits and monks appeared on the scene. And it was more than a century later before the mass exodus of Christians from Rome provided the recruits to transform monasticism from a

relatively limited mass of diverse groups and tendencies into an organized system capable of absorbing, disciplining, and socializing the un-
initiated refugees.[8]

To speak of monasticism is, however, more difficult than I have
heretofore suggested. A pattern that is almost two thousand years old
could not have survived if it had remained the same over so long a
period of time. While its function might have remained the same the
organization could have changed, and, conversely, while the functions
might have changed the organization could have remained similar.

Monasticism was and is a changing pattern, and this fluctuation is
true of the Church more generally. But for a long time, at least six
hundred years, it was within the monasteries that the Church resided.
During what may be called the early medieval period, from about the
fifth to the eleventh centuries, the monasteries were more than the
spiritual home of Christianity. They provided a haven for refugees from
war and other violence; alms for the poor; food for the starving; care of
the sick; and, above all, the training and education of youth and the
societal elites. During this period many of the most powerful members
of Western society's elites got their start as monks. The latter part of the
period was dominated by popes who had been monks and by a monk
who has been described as "the uncrowned pope,"[9] Bernard of
Clairvaux.

FUNCTIONS.   The diverse activities of the monasteries and the impact
that these activities had on the community and society within which
they occurred, i.e., their functions, may be conceptualized in two broad
categories. The spiritual relations between monastery and community
revolved about the penitential function, and the social relations involved
the recruitment for, training in, and provision of positions, i.e., status
vacancies, for all segments of society but particularly the nobility.

It is impossible to adequately understand medieval society without
taking into account the profound influence of religious belief on the day-
to-day activities of both the nobles and the mass of commoners. The
difference between the secular life and that which was held to be sacred
was, for the most part, negligible. Without organized states, in the modern sense, to confront the clergy, it was the Church that provided the
effort to unify all life, to bring all aspects of society, as E. Barker writes,
"under the control of Christian principle." Barker goes on to describe
the Church's scope of activities:

> Politically, it attempts to rebuke and correct kings for internal misgovern-
> ment, as when they falsify coinage, and for external misdoing, as when they
> break treaties; socially, it controls the life of the family by the law of marriage
> which it administers, and the life of the individual by its system of penance;
> economically, it seeks to regulate commerce and industry by enforcing just

prices and prohibiting interest, as it seeks to control the economic motive in general by its conception of property as a trust held for the general benefit and by its inculcation of charity; intellectually, it develops a single culture in the universities which are its organs, and in the last resort it enforces that culture by the persecution of heresy.[10]

This effort to impose a pattern of norms on the whole of Western societies was enhanced by the system of sanctions called penances, which could cost the deviant in both this world and in the afterlife. Sins, both serious and relatively trivial, could be the basis for the imposition of a penitential debt, which in turn might result in profit for the monastery. Whether the violator was required to undertake a fast in order to pay his debt or to recite prayers for a stipulated period of time, the monks were available to substitute for the sinner who could afford the price. And what the price was had often been indicated by the sanctioning agent, who was well aware that someone other than the sinner was likely to assume the privations of the penance.[11] If the sinner were to fail to fulfill his obligation before he died, he could, in keeping with the beliefs of the time, reasonably expect to suffer the unspecified but nevertheless consequential horrors imposed on a restless soul in the life beyond.

Although there were some lay people who could undertake, for a fee, the penitential debt, it was typically the monk, bound by vows, who performed the stand-in role. And since this required no special skill the monk enjoyed a sinecure for life.

Whether the pattern of penances and their fulfillment was based on fear of retribution in this world or the next, it was responsible for a vast network of social relationships between the secular society and the monasteries. Even more important, however, it created jobs, particularly the kind that required no special talents. As such the monastery could absorb a great many persons who might, for any number of reasons, not the least of which was limited alternatives elsewhere, be unable to find other employment. The spiritual function associated with penances thus spilled over into the sphere of the social functions as it provided status vacancies for a great many unemployables.

Socially the monastic system functioned to reinforce the system of ranks existing in the secular world. Although it was always possible for a person from a family of relatively low status to improve his rank by upward mobility within the monastery and then the Church, and finally, perhaps, by lateral movement from the religious elite to the secular, this was rare. It is sufficient to realize that because the monastic system was, for the most part, an aristocratic institution mere acceptance as a monk represented an increase in rank for those of lesser standing. Among the most important social functions performed by the monasteries in relation to the existing stratification system was the provision of status vacancies for the offspring of the nobility. R. W. Southern is to the point on the aristocracy's need for such niches:

> The economy of a great family required a monastic outlet for its members. At no time in the Middle Ages, and least of all in the early centuries, were the resources of society expanding fast enough to provide honourable positions in secular life for all the children of noble families. There were severe, and well-justified, restrictions on the practice of splitting up the family property, and it was a very serious problem to provide secure and acceptable positions for those members of the family for whom no sufficient endowment could be provided. The problem was especially serious for the girls of a family. They were not exposed to the hazards of an active military life, which created gaps and unexpected opportunities for the boys. There were not enough suitable marriages for all of them; and those who married were often widowed at an early age.[12]

The life-style and the relatively high prestige which the monks of that period enjoyed assured the aristocrats that neither downward mobility nor economic privation would ever be their lot in life. Indeed, as I suggest in the following chapter on medieval women, the rank systems of the external, secular society tended to carry over into the monastery in spite of the normatively prescribed ideals of the *via apostolica*, including the notion of voluntary poverty. However, for the extremely pious the monastery became a permanent home, a setting for a life committed to prayer, to work, and to isolation forever from kin and secular community. Monasticism, for those who adhered to the norms, was an alienating phenomenon in relation to some families.

Time and time again Montalembert, Lecky, and Duckett, to cite just a few, describe incidents which, in spite of exaggeration and romanticization, probably accurately portray a holy man or woman renouncing a spouse, mother, children, and other kin, never again to speak to them, see them, or touch them. This ideal of renunciation of the flesh in order to more fervently commit oneself to a religious calling was reinforced by the structure of relationships and isolation in the monastery. Although the monastery contributed in manifold ways to the larger social structures of which it was a part it remained, ideally, a religious organization. By the eleventh century the ideal form was well established.

INTERNAL ORGANIZATION.   As a religious organization the monastery was a community. Francis helps us understand its sociological form by contrasting two types of organization, Tonnies's *Gemeinschaft* and *Gesellschaft*. The primary difference between these two types of social organization is reflected in the normative distinction between what Francis called "life in religion" (i.e., *Gemeinschaft*) and "life in the world" (i.e., *Gesellschaft*). Life in religion involves not only retreat from the secular life but expectations regarding one's conduct, particularly exemplary behavior that functions as a model of the "morally superior" life. Thus, although the monk may only rarely, if at all, participate in the secular life, he clearly has an impact on the ideals held by those who do. Life in religion is typically life in a highly personalized community in which relationships tend to be face-to-face, and, following the *Gemeinschaft* model, participation in the religious life is an end in itself.[13] In addition to adherence to the norms of obedience to the sacred rules, e.g., the Rule of St. Benedict, the monk is bound to the monastery under the principle of *stabilitas loci*, which identifies him physically with a particular place. Since the whole of his life may be spent within the cloister, since it may afford him a livelihood through agricultural or other pursuits, and since it has a particular locus, the monastery approaches empirically what R. M. MacIver defined as a community.[14]

In contrast, the order that proliferated during the thirteenth century was an organization with a specific mission to perform. Although the members were bound to one another, it was more like participation in an association in which the organization was a means to another end. Relationships between members tended to be less intimate and personal, and more segmental, and there was greater physical mobility. Members tended to maintain residences in a variety of places over time depending upon the needs and goals of the order. Social control was, nevertheless, rigorous. Here is Francis's description:

> The monastic novice enters a specific monastery. During his training period he is systematically being reeducated and remodeled, above all by participation in the intimate life of the concrete, rather small, face-to-face group, by exclusive interaction with all its members, and by indoctrination with its group ways (or observances). Only after his *conversio morum*, that is, his complete conversion to the mores of this particular group, has been assured, is he received into it as a full member, a professed monk, and by his vows becomes an integrated part of the group, severing for his lifetime all ties with the outside world. Even today most of the members of the stricter orders (Trappists, cloistered nuns) after joining the organization are on principle not allowed to have any social contacts except with the members of their own community, and even these are rigorously restricted by such provisions as the rule of perpetual silence.
>
> In the Jesuit order, on the other hand, which is the most developed form of a typical order, the unit is not the local community but the order as such, which for administrative purposes is subdivided into provinces or territorial units. These include several local establishments, some of which are set aside for the specific purpose of training future members. These training centers, however, are not meant to become the permanent residence of the candidates; on the contrary, Jesuits may expect to be moved on short notice not only within their own country but literally to any spot on earth where the order needs them. *Any permanent attachment either to persons or places is definitely discouraged,* while mingling with the "world" is implied in the Jesuit's

life goal of active apostolate. Complete segregation from outside contacts is maintained only during training and the periodical retreats, which may last for as long as a month. Beyond this, withdrawal from the world is observed not by well-defined and integrated groups but individually, and this largely on a purely psychological level in the form of that inner "detachment" so greatly emphasized by St. Ignatius of Loyola. Membership in the Jesuit order and other organizations of the same type has thus an entirely different meaning from that in a Benedictine abbey. While monastic life is essentially a collective undertaking, the Jesuit type of order aims at the efficient organization of specially trained individuals as determined by utility and purpose . . . the other types of religious orders (e.g., Franciscans and Dominicans) represent intermediary stages between the extremes.*[15]

Monasticism, as a type of organization, was a total way of life, largely otherworldly in orientation, modeled after the apostolic pattern, relatively isolated from the secular world. The monastery was organized as a type of family, and distinctions of status and rank were supposed to be relatively amorphous, with one person, the abbot, elected by his brothers to a position above the others. Property belonged to the community, and personal status or asprations were proscribed. As in the case of the religious protestors of the later Middle Ages, to whom I referred in Chapter 1, the ideal for this communal pattern was, I repeat, derived from the *via apostolica*, the life-style attributed to the Apostles. Montalembert described the monks as the bearers of the true life of the Apostles and quoted from the New Testament as the source of this exemplary pattern: "And all that believed were together, and had all things common; and sold their possessions and goods, and parted them to all men, as every man had need. . . . And the multitude of them that believed were of one heart and of one soul; neither said any of them that aught of the things which he possessed was his own; but they had all things common. . . . Neither was there any among them that lacked."[16]

The discrepancy between the way the monastic life-style was supposed to be and the way the monks actually behaved seems to have become increasingly wider from the beginning of the establishment of the system. As links evolved between those who were accustomed to some degree of splendor and the monasteries, the vulnerability of the system increased. Monasteries required material support, and beyond the fees for penances and the relatively modest income from agricultural pursuits within the monastery lay the real wealth: lands, estates, endowments, and other direct gifts from the aristocrats who helped establish and maintain the system. The monks themselves, now having become conspicuously self-indulgent and wayward in terms of the ideals of the system, became the deviants and sinners in the eyes of the secular

---

*The italics associated with the statement on temporality of attachment are mine. I will review this aspect of the Jesuit pattern in the context of the abeyance process, below.

Christians. The Church, through its major organ, the monastery, had become corrupted. By the twelfth century there seemed to have been very few who doubted that reform was in order.

REFORM AND DECLINE.   Those monks who were well-connected, including those who saw the monastic life as a steppingstone to high position in the medieval Church, had little reason to renounce the pleasures afforded by the increasing affluence of the Church. It was the behavior of these monks as well as the conspicuous growth of material wealth that made the Church and particularly its central organ, the monastic system, vulnerable to attack.

In order to restore the primacy of their central function, propagation of the spiritual life, the monasteries attempted to reform themselves by divestiture of involvement in the secular world through rejection of "lay abbots . . . lay proprietors and even of bishops."[17] New, more isolated monasteries sprang up in the tenth century in an effort to provide uncontaminated settings for enhancing the ideal spiritual life. Among these was Cluny.

The efforts at reform during the tenth century, including Cluniac monasticism, though seemingly successful at first, failed. The failure of reform was a result of at least two major factors, one inherent to the monastic system and the other external. It is ironic that the success of the monastic system, both spiritually and materially, was a major source of its own demise. This is illustrated by the case of Cluny, although the pattern applies as well to a great many other monasteries.

Cluny, established in A.D. 910 as a reformist monastery, had a simple goal, "Back to St. Benedict."[18] Led by two famous monks, St. Berno and St. Odo, it soon enjoyed the acclaim of monks and laymen throughout France and, later, western Europe and England. Performing its dual role as absorber of aristocrats and leader of the spiritual life, Cluny soon attained that same power and wealth which had contributed to the corruption of many an earlier monastery. J. B. Russell describes the gradual process by which Cluny first contributed to the spirit and then succumbed to its own successes.

> The reaction of the feudal nobility to this foundation indicates that among even the wealthy laity who had most profited from the corruption of the Church, respect for the spirit was strong. Large donations of money and land flowed in, knights and great nobles came to make retreats at Cluny and to seek spiritual advice from its monks; and monks themselves were attracted in great numbers to the pure life . . . an enormous and elaborate abbey was erected; and the abbot of Cluny, now next to popes and kings the most influential man in Europe, there received in splendor the great and the powerful from all over Europe. By imperceptible stages, Cluny began to drift away from the strict observance of the rule and to prefer power and wealth to humility and poverty. In the twelfth century, it was itself the target for a new generation of reformers.[19]

When Cluny and the other monasteries were most influential in western European societies they served not only those who sought permanent engagement with the Church but sojourners as well. Associated with the monks were a great many persons, as I noted earlier, whose commitment to the monastic institution was less than total. But the monasteries absorbed them, nevertheless, in their role as hospitaler to the needy in both body and spirit. Because it was the dominant institution in society, aristocrats, too, sought affiliation with the monastery. Thus the personnel in a monastery, at any time, might typically include those who were committed for life and those who were sojourners. It was this capacity to include almost any Christian in some monastic activity which enhanced the monastery's capacity to absorb surplus populations.

Although the motives behind the establishment of the new reformist monasteries of the tenth century seem to have been primarily spiritual, these monasteries were available during the eleventh century when population expansion created an increased need for status vacancies. The period of Cluny coincides with the rapid expansion of population, on the one hand, and the beginnings of an urban-commercial expansion, on the other. Cluny's expansion, which took the form of the creation of new monasteries, particularly throughout France but throughout other parts of Europe as well, was a response to the rapid increase in population associated with this period. The equally rapid decrease in "eremetic foundations in France,"[20] "a mere half-century after the phenomenal increase" of these organizations, suggests that during those fifty years alternative positions emerged and those who might have been monastic sojourners were gradually integrated into other activities in European societies.

The decline of the monasteries was a result of a number of factors. By the late eleventh century, western Europe was experiencing an outburst of economic and other activities that created opportunities for many who only fifty years earlier might have been integrated into monastic activities. A surplus population arose in western Europe for the first time, but this did not aid the monasteries because alternative status vacancies simultaneously appeared.[21] Change was occurring in all parts of society, and this was no less the case for the monastic system. The economic depression that had begun in the third century, mitigated to some extent only by the agricultural productivity of the monasteries and their offshoots, had come to an end by the eleventh century. As noted earlier, population expanded, old towns grew and new ones emerged, and industry and commerce flourished. J. B. Russell writes: "The eleventh through the thirteenth centuries are a period of population and economic growth absolutely unparalleled in the history of the West until the nineteenth and twentieth centuries."[22] As the new urban phenomenon proliferated, the services performed by the monasteries were now offered by others. The newer orders established schools, in the world, where lay subjects, including those necessary to the new industrial and commercial enterprises, were taught; voluntary religious organizations emerged to care for the sick and indigent; and commercial lodgings now replaced the monastery as a haven for the weary lay traveler.

The role of the monasteries in providing monks as knights for the wars of the nobility, who in any case were often proxies, had also declined in importance, according to Cantor.[23] This, plus the general changes in society and the takeover of many of the traditional activities of the Benedictines by the secular clergy, created a crisis that led finally to the withdrawal of the monastery from engagement in the secular world and a reestablishment, on a much more modest scale, of the ascetic life. From the twelfth century on, the most dramatic occurrences in medieval Europe were associated with the Church's efforts to deal with the many reform movements both within (in the form of orders) and without (in the activities of varied collectivities of revolutionary millennialists). All of these factors contributed to the decline of monasticism.

POPULATION AND MONASTICISM.   It is very likely, given the data reviewed by J. C. Russell, that the increase and decline in monastic influence is *indirectly* associated with the increases in population beginning in the middle of the tenth century and continuing until the middle of the fourteenth, when the Black Death dramatically put a damper on an already declining rate of growth.[24] That the impact of increased population on monasticism was indirect is of great theoretical importance.

The monastic system became organized not under conditions of absolute population expansion in Rome and the Empire but under conditions of decline. Russell's data show that this decline characterized the period from A.D. 200 to 600. On the other hand, the *contraction* of the monastic system occurred under conditions of *expansion* of population. Thus there is, if at all, an inverse relation between population and monasticism. Russell's view is that "depopulation brought depression, economically, socially, and intellectually, and that these induced a stronger religious interest."[25] But this global view does not explain how this "depression" becomes transmitted and implemented by those in the population into a social pattern reflecting "religious interest." If this statement is plausible, it does not explain the very extensive involvement of wealthy people in the monastic system and other religious activities. What is more likely and to the point is that extreme *shifts* in population trends, upward or downward, are associated with involvement in religious activities during the medieval period and that the effect of these shifts is mediated by changes in *social structures*. It is the expansion and contraction in this aspect of societies that intervenes and impacts on organized group behavior. And this process may vary independently of population expansion and contraction.[26] What I am suggesting here is that a more sociologically conceptualized unit of analysis, status vacancy, is required if we are to understand how expansion and contraction of numbers of people impact on organized behavior in society.

Monasticism and Status Vacancy

There is consensus among historians of monasticism that the pattern which took form during the fourth and fifth centuries was a result of an exodus from the secular activities characterizing a recently Christianized but still essentially pagan Roman Empire. This exodus became channelized into a movement of large masses of Christians, both men and women, toward the more remote areas of what is now the Near East, North Africa, and Italy. When these masses became organized into communal settlements, the movement, as Francis reminds us above, ended and the monastic system was born.

I have noted that in absolute terms the population of the Roman Empire was on the decline at the time. Thus the rapidly proliferating masses who joined and formed monasteries and nunneries must have left existing positions in the secular social structures from which they came. They were not, in the sense in which I used the concept in Chapter 1, surplus populations. Nor were they marginal. The positions which they sought and which, finally, they occupied were statuses they created, as they created new organizations and the new institution. But once it was created, role expectations emerged, and, presumably, limits on the number of such positions became established. Conversely, if we were able to look back at the contexts these Christians had left we would find positions that were unoccupied, tasks left undone, and structures in increasing decay. More than one commentator has attacked monasticism for having siphoned off much of the talent and personnel who might have helped Rome defend itself against the barbarians as well as reform a way of life uniformly described as decadent.

Over the centuries the relatively small size of each monastery seems to have remained about the same. As new groups of zealots came together they organized new monasteries. And, since the monastic system was a major source of occupations, particularly for the nobility, there was little competition on the part of the monasteries for personnel to fill positions.

As I noted earlier, a substantial number of monks remained uncommitted to the goals of monasticism, and it is likely that these constituted the most vulnerable members for recruitment to other activities. By the tenth century, because of increasing commercial activity, urbanization, and secularization, activities of the monasteries were now, as noted above, in competition with alternative forms of activity in the secular world. Nevertheless, "a wave of enthusiasm for monasticism"[27] emerged, particularly in England, and the number of members swelled. As the numbers swelled so did the number of positions, thus expanding the monastic organizations. The impact of competitive occupations was most dramatic by the fifteenth century, in which, according to Hale, so many monks left the monasteries that the ones who remained found themselves filling increasing numbers of positions in order to complete those tasks necessary to maintain the schedule of monastic activities.[28] Expansion of opportunities in the secular world as well as other factors had drawn the marginally religious out of their retreats.

Like the millennial movements that reflect its failure, monasticism was a pattern that initially provided an outlet for individual expressive behavior. In the monastery the overzealous concern for holiness and purity was turned inward. It was channeled by a disciplined system of rites and regulations that were primarily directed to otherworldly pursuits. Only later did some of the monks turn back to secular society, proselytizing and insinuating themselves into powerful families and political positions. By the thirteenth century the Franciscans were bringing the spiritual life directly to the layman in a way that may well have been a direct antecedent to the Protestant emphasis upon a spiritual life for all Christians.

The effectiveness of this life of renunciation may well be best demonstrated by what did not occur during this long period of monastic siphoning-off of presumably dissident elements. The millennial movements of the late Middle Ages and the following two centuries, the sixteenth and seventeenth, occurred when the Church had lost its control over those in the population who were most likely to lead and participate in them. The monasteries themselves were now suffering anomic decay. "Lax discipline, the neglect of vows, concubinage, ignorance, domestic squabbles,"[29] and a transformation of some abbeys into settings that seemed more like baronial castles than religious centers characterized the situation.

"The causes of this decay were obvious enough. Men and women were admitted too easily and not instructed properly once they had entered; peasants sent their children for reasons of prestige, aristocrats treated monasteries and abbeys as privileged systems of relief from a too numerous brood. Yet in many monasteries the numbers had so dropped that most every monk was needed to fill some office and it was impossible to discipline them by demotion."[30] Added to this—or perhaps it is a major cause of it—the theological ignorance of the lower clergy contributed to the lack of adherence to religious disciplines. The increasing tendency for the children of the bourgeoisie to fill the limited number of status vacancies in the universities, many of which were intended for the poor, decreased the likelihood that a member of the lower clergy—recruited from the ranks of the poor—would have studied theology.[31]

The decline of discipline within the monastic system and the simultaneous blurring of distinctions between the secular and the sacred tended to deregulate the activities and orientations of those sectors of the population who were most likely to be overzealous in their spiritual perspective on life. The Protestant Reformation and the numerous millennial movements in Europe and England were at least in part enhanced by the declining control over those who would have been co-opted by an effectively operating monastic system.

At the latent level, not only was monasticism a pattern that provided alternative status vacancies and abeyance—since ultimately those who took positions of authority in the secularized Church came out of monasteries—it was an important social control mechanism. I suggested earlier that religious overzealousness was a serious concern for those Church leaders who held the responsibilities for continuity of the Church and its activities and possessions. It has, indeed, always been a problem for large organizations. We are not surprised, then, to read in Workman, "Monasticism arose at a time when we see in the Church a marked reaction against extreme views."[32] Harnack also perceived that the secularized Church co-opted the monastic movement rather than allowing it to develop as a separate system and thus cast doubt on the spiritual mission of the Church.[33] By siphoning off overzealous elements of Christianity, a central function of abeyance, monasticism allowed the Church to pursue secular activities and to appeal to and incorporate those populations whose adherence to scriptural prescriptions and proscriptions would be allowed wide ranges of tolerance and interpretation. This capacity of the Church was seemingly effective until the late Middle Ages.

The decline of the monastic system as an effective spiritual and political influence on the secular world coincides not only with the emergence of the Beguine and Beghard movements and their efforts to bridge the gap between monastery and town. All of these show marked decline as alternative status vacancies rapidly expand, particularly during the Renaissance.

The Renaissance was a period of explosive activity in economic and artistic spheres. Recovery from the various plagues was then a reality. The plague, "depression, and social dislocation" of the fourteenth century gave way to a period of "new European expansion"[34] in the fifteenth. The expansion was characterized by a rapid increase in status vacancies in the secular sphere and a contraction of monastic life. By 1540 monasticism in England, as a result of the dissolution of monastic holdings, was "virtually extinguished"[35] and still another surplus population was created.

That the expansion and contraction of status vacancies must be understood in abstract terms is best illustrated by reminding ourselves of the nonmonastic orders. The Franciscan and Dominican orders came into existence during the expansion of population in the twelfth century. Preferring to maintain discipline from within, the Church encouraged the organization of new orders. Although members of these orders occasionally became overzealous, and thus threatening to the delicate balance of relationships between the Church and the secular world, they nevertheless absorbed and placed under control the potentially dissident. When overzealousness, or laxity, became a problem the good soldier of Christ could then be sent off to a retreat for contemplation and discipline. And, as control was needed, new organizations could be formed.

Although the data on numbers of monks and priests in relation to status vacancies are far from adequate to test formal hypotheses, the pattern of expansion and contraction is reflected in the accounts of medieval Church historians and other scholars. A number also recognized the social control functions of monasticism and the orders. For example, John Stuart Mill observed: "The effect of such a bank of missionaries . . . must have been great in arousing and feeding dormant devotional feelings. They were not less influential in regulating those feelings, and turning into the established Catholic channels those vagaries of private enthusiasm which might well endanger the church, since they already threatened society itself."[36]

As a total way of life the monastic system functioned as an absorber of surplus aristocrats and others for the total life span. Other organizations, and monasteries too, also performed this function for shorter periods of time. Temporality, it will be recalled, is one of the variables that articulates the abeyance process.

Monasticism and the Abeyance Process

Since I have described the monastic system in general it is appropriate at this point to turn to the variables which help articulate the differential capacities of organizations to perform the abeyance process.

TEMPORALITY.   My choice of monasticism for the first case study was intended to reflect an underlying continuum which would include the organized pattern that has persisted longer than any of the others and

the one that involves the longest duration of membership as measured
by life span. Membership in monastic systems is not associated with a
particular period in one's life and is not expected to end short of one's
mortal end. More than a total institution, it is a total absorber of the full
longevity of a member, sometimes beginning in childhood, when some
children were given over to the monks for integration into their community. The perspective of the monk, furthermore, is that the relationship
between him and his community is permanent, as prescribed in the
principle of *stabilitas loci*.

COMMITMENT. Closely associated with the temporality dimension is
the commitment variable. In both the monastic system and the orders—
the Franciscans, Dominicans, and Jesuits, to name but a few—commitment is total and for life. As a number of observers have noted, celibacy
is a norm that proscribes any alternative commitment for monk, priest or
nun. From the very earliest, the period of formation of the monastic
system, the ideal of rejection of the secular world—of spouse, children,
and other kin—symbolized and helped realize the intense and pervasive
commitment to the religious life that Coser has associated with "greedy
institutions."[37] Men and women took vows for life, nuns symbolically
married the Church, and the intensive socialization and reinforcement
that was associated with the "life in religion," to recall Francis, provided
the discipline that tied behavior and sentiment together. But it is at the
same time important to keep in mind that the objects of commitment
varied for monks as opposed to members of orders. For a monk, commitment was to the monastic community, the particular group, in adherence to the principle of *stabilitas loci*. The member of an order, on the
other hand, was committed to the goals of the order, wherever their
pursuit might lead. Thus, to quote again from Francis, "any permanent
attachment either to persons or places [was] definitely discouraged."[38]
The function of such an attitude is to help sustain a readiness to move to
another location, according to the needs of the system. With respect to
locus then, members of orders are *under*committed. This, as I will show
below, is an important characteristic of intentionally organized abeyance
processes.

INCLUSIVENESS. With respect to abeyance, membership in monastic
communities, and in many organizations more generally, may be
thought of at two levels. There are, on the one hand, those who represent the relatively permanent core, whose involvement represents a life
or career commitment, and those who are akin to sojourners in that their
participation is relatively short-lived. It is largely for the latter that the
abeyance process in organizations works. The expansion-contraction of
an organization's personnel as the larger system requires absorption,
mobility, or expulsion involves primarily the relatively marginal mem-

bers. Thus the pattern requires great *inclusiveness* as the organization absorbs and greater *exclusiveness* as it expels or attempts to hold constant in number those who are members. During periods of absorption the criteria for membership remain loose and during periods of expulsion the criteria are more stringent. In the case of monasticism, criteria for core membership became stringent only after the fifth century, when the religious-movement phase declined and the organized, systemic phase began. Prior to this period, monasticism accepted almost anyone who wanted to participate in a life of renunciation and religiously defined work. The willingness to accept almost anyone was a characteristic of both the period of origin and the period of dissolution. In both cases there were many people relatively unattached to alternative structures of social control who were encouraged to attach themselves to the monasteries. Descriptions of the undifferentiated and ambiguously motivated mass who flocked to the monasteries and to earlier retreats are provided by Gibbon, Workman, Lecky, and others cited earlier. Hale, in commenting about the decline of monasticism, added this tendency toward inclusiveness to his list of "causes of . . . decay".[39]

Knowing that the monasteries were providing "learned bishops for many sees"[40] and that one of their functions was to provide a temporary retreat for all kinds of Christians, including the hospitality functions as well, the monks could hardly be choosy about who might be let in. But it is well to keep in mind that participation in the monastic life, even if only temporary, involved highly disciplined behavior, and thus socialization and reinforcement of norms for marginal or core members with concomitant social control.*

DIVISION OF LABOR.   In order to be willing to include almost anyone who appeals for either permanent or temporary membership, one must overlook the question of what special talents or capacities people have. Since the normative goal of a monastic community was spiritual rather than worldly, the nature of one's work while in the monastery was of relatively little importance. It will be recalled that performing penitential duties for others was an occupation that enhanced slothfulness. To be sure there were monks who were, upon entry—and others who became—highly skilled, but this was a matter of personal choice. It was both adequate and appropriate for members of the monastic communities to pursue relatively unskilled tasks, typically agricultural. Members perceived of themselves in relatively democratic terms. What was essential was that they be obedient to the rules, that they practice humil-

---

*Monks were likely to impose strict rules for guests, who, if they did not adhere to them, might be whipped. There are numerous examples and comments in the literature about the uses of whips for both lay and religious people who failed to conform to the norms of the monastery.

ity and perform their tasks as best they could. Had the monasteries encouraged the buildup of a division of labor, i.e., a network of interrelated specialized skills, it would have created an obstacle to the mobility potential for those who participated in the community. Although the core membership may have become dependent upon one another, this would not have been desirable for those earlier described as sojourners. As my subsequent case studies will further demonstrate, abeyance is enhanced when there are few inducements to remain tied to the organization.

INSTITUTIONALIZATION.   How effective an organization is with respect to its abeyance function depends in part on the capacity of society to motivate personnel to assume status vacancies. When the activities of an organization are legitimated by the normative system of a society, participation in these patterns is acceptable behavior. When these activities are considered *ideal*, participation is more than acceptable—it is exemplary—and it is likely to accord considerable prestige to the occupant of a status in the system. That monasticism was institutionalized, that the image of the behavior of the true monk, in contrast to the sojourners, was idealized, and that membership in a religious community during the medieval period was, because of its association with the aristocracy, highly prestigious is clear from the data above. When societal conditions were such that a shortage of positions in other sectors occurred, the monasteries could attract personnel without difficulty. When conditions changed, as in the tenth and eleventh centuries, and later, in the fifteenth and sixteenth, monasticism suffered a decline in the eyes of the mass of the people and it became increasing difficult to recruit personnel. It was to these conditions in the late fifteenth century that Hale referred when he said, as quoted earlier, that a shortage of monks in many monasteries made almost every monk necessary and hence impossible to discipline by demotion.*

What is central with respect to institutionalization is that it is much easier to get people to perform the activities that society needs at a given point in time under institutionalized patterns than under patterns which are not highly valued.†

---

*Hale was obviously referring to a monastery that was more hierarchically organized than what I appear to have suggested in discussing division of labor. To clarify, it is important to keep in mind that these necessary offices Hale refers to presumbly did not require the kinds of specialized skills that could not be relatively easily learned on the job. Thus it is not unjustified to suggest that the level of specialization within the monastery was *relatively* low.

†My definition of institutionalization is implicit here. What I mean, simply, is that the activities which are institutionalized are those which society, by relative consensus, recognizes as desirable and worthy as ends in themselves, i.e., necessary to maintain a given normative or factual condition.

STRATIFICATION. I have attempted to stress the importance of potential for physical mobility as an aspect of the abeyance process. In the sections on temporality and commitment the Jesuits were used as an example of religious who were discouraged from developing attachments to monastic communities or to particular retreat organizations. The Jesuits, Franciscans, and Dominicans exemplified those who were religious sojourners in contrast to those whose commitment was characterized by the rule of *stabilitas loci*. Although there were and indeed are hierarchies within the orders, the emphasis on avoiding attachments to place means that having a relatively higher position in a hierarchy does not make the priest more necessary in the maintenance of a community. Relatively low stratification implies relative ease in the process of replacing personnel in the system in much the same way as low division of labor. Furthermore, the potential for the emergence of career aspirations, which could be an obstacle to one's willingness to move as society requires, must be kept relatively low.*

In sum, the variables describe monasticism as a pattern characterized by high longevity of attachment for the monk and low longevity for what I have called sojourners; very intense and total commitment for the monk; high inclusiveness for sojourners and relatively higher exclusiveness for those accepted as monks; a relatively low level of specialized member skills; high institutionalization; and a relatively low level of social stratification within the organization.

When compared with the other patterns, monasticism was and remains the most complete in terms of involvement and social control of personnel. Its outline will become increasingly sharper as it is contrasted with the other forms. At this juncture it is well to note that the Beguines, to whom I turn in the next chapter, were closely associated with, but not part of, the monastic system and the religious orders.

---

*As I describe my other cases below, the stratification variable will be more sharply articulated.

CHAPTER 3

Beguines: Ambivalence and Heresy

"For there must be also heresies among you, that they which are approved may be made manifest among you."

—St. Paul

The thirteenth century, as I noted in the preceding chapter, was characterized by intense activity in the religious, economic, and social spheres. A surplus of population, i.e., more people than places, still existed even though status vacancies were on the increase. The urban-commercial explosion, colonization, and the military activities that were associated with aggressive ecological expansion and the Crusades siphoned off many of those who represented this increased population. Who, then, were these surplus people and what happened to them?

Medieval historians are inclined to agree on at least one demographic fact. Medieval society during the thirteenth century and for two or three centuries thereafter had many more unintegrated women than men.[1] Moreover, the unattached women tended to be concentrated in urban areas. What happened to these women is a story not unlike the one describing the gradual integration of unattached Christians into the first monasteries, and, at a later time, into the expanded monastic organizations of the tenth and eleventh centuries.

I have already suggested that during the thirteenth century the monastic system was on the decline and that the new orders, most notably the Franciscans and Dominicans, were gaining adherents. Not only were there movements for reform of the monastic system and the Church, more generally, but there were social movements, as well, that challenged the legitimacy of the Church as mediator between man and

God. The thirteenth century gave rise not only to relatively conservative movements but to radical ones as well. It was during this period that the best known of the many movements labeled heretical, the Waldensians and the Albigensians, began to threaten the Church.[2] The thirteenth century was, in short, characterized by religious fervor, and this spiritual motive moved women as much as men.

The growth of orders, armies, and some of the monasteries as well drained off substantial numbers of men who might otherwise have become mates for equally substantial numbers of women. This, as I will suggest again below, was a major factor creating the surplus of unintegrated women. Thus a great many women now became potential recruits for all kinds of religious movements, both radical and relatively conservative. It was under these societal conditions, particularly in western Europe, that a number of religious organizations for women began. Among these were the Beguines. In order to understand this particular form and its contribution to abeyance, it is important to understand first the situation of women in medieval society.

Medieval Women

Starting with the decline of Rome and the emergence of organized monasticism, women played an increasing role in religious and secular affairs.[3] Although some accounts suggest ambivalence in the prestige and influence accorded women, particularly with respect to their role as purveyors of wisdom and as good and evil witches, women gradually assumed more importance in a variety of social contexts. Although the alternatives were few and they varied for women in diverse social strata, the history of economic affairs, as well as religion, abounds with examples of women holding power and wealth on the one hand and leading religious movements for change on the other. Three alternatives appear to have been open to women. A woman could choose marriage, if she were also chosen; independence, thus risking becoming in the eyes of the community a "loose woman"; or she could select some type of religious life.[4] The position of women varied over time and region, and by class of origin.

The descriptive accounts dealing with the decline of Rome and the emergence of the monastic life include many examples of women who have inherited either their family's or husband's wealth and who, in a dramatic show of embracing the *via apostolica*, give away their holdings. That this occurred with some regularity indicates that women did enjoy whatever status was associated with wealth from the earliest days of the Christian era. Personal title to property was allowed women prior to the medieval period but it was especially during the tenth and eleventh centuries, when a number of societal changes drew men away from domestic contexts, that women's economic and social position was enhanced.

The development of the ideal of chivalry, "which seems to have restricted" the economic role of the husband, was an important factor in the rise to social prominence of women in France and Germany, where these ideals took hold.[5] Warriors and married priests generally needed to be freed from domestic obligation, thus enlarging the economic functions of women. And the physical mobility of the population, more generally, created status vacancies in the economic sphere that women filled. To quote Herlihy: "Among those social classes (such as the medieval warrior nobility) whose mode of life involves considerable travel and movement, the man is the family member most frequently absent from home, while the wife, physically less mobile, is likewise more capable of assuming a continuous supervision over the family's fixed possessions. Moreover, in a social situation involving emigration or exodus, whether permanent or temporary, from the older centers of population, men tend to leave earlier and in proportionately greater numbers than women."[6]

The good wife, at least in the propertied classes, could not only organize, supervise, and maintain her household but could also keep accounts; she knew something of agriculture, or whatever the family economy was based on, and she could supervise those who labored in the fields and carry on whatever economic activities were necessary to enhance and maintain the family's life-style.[7] To a more modest degree, this was also the situation of the bourgeois wife, who could, when widowhood occurred, carry on her husband's trade or even begin a business of her own.[8] To quote Power: "The lower we move in the social scale the more laborious, naturally, was the housewife's life, because she would commonly be obliged to help with her husband's craft or to carry on some by-industry of her own, as well as caring for house and children. Below the ranks of the gentry and the richer bourgeoisie few housewives were able to concern themselves solely with their homes, which were frequently supported by the earnings of wife as well as of husband. Most laborious of all was the lot of the peasant woman living upon the land."[9]

Thus women were very much engaged in the affairs of the real world, holding varying amounts of wealth and possessing, as well, diverse amounts of prestige. On the normative side, the conception of women was characterized by ambivalence. On the one hand woman was "the supreme temptress," an ever-present threat to the implementation of the ascetic life. On the other hand, she was the symbol of the cult of the Virgin, an aspect of the idea of chivalry. "The cult of the lady was the mundane counterpart of the cult of the Virgin and it was the invention of the medieval aristocracy. . . . In chivalry the romantic worship of a woman was as necessary a quality of the perfect knight as was the worship of God."[10] Women were, then, during the medieval period, simultaneously superior and inferior. They may have had wealth or power, but ultimately men determined their status in society. In the day-to-day behavior of medieval society it was the subjection of women that was most widely accepted.[11] We should not be at all surprised, then, that women played a prominent part in the many revolutionary messianic movements which sprang up in medieval Europe.

Die Frauenfrage: Too Many Women

Although it is clear that some women in medieval society often played economic roles in addition to domestic roles, the position of women was complicated by the fact that there were simply more women than there were status vacancies to absorb them. Time and time again the literature of the period describes an imbalance between men and women, particularly in the urban areas of Europe.[12] Among the problems assigned by commentators to women, then, was not only the ambivalence of attitude toward them but their existence as a surplus, marginal population. This situation cannot be attributed simply to individual choice.

I noted above that there were, for the most part, only a few alternatives to women in medieval society: marriage, independence, or some form of the religious life. But like all social choices these alternatives were limited by the woman's position in the social structure. Marriage required, first, an eligible male and, second a dowry. One of the ironies of life in medieval society was that those who could afford a dowry often could not find and hold an eligible male, whereas those who did have eligible and willing males often had limited dowries and, congruent with their low economic positions, males who could not offer economic security. I am describing of course, two extremes, the women in the relatively high ranks and those in the low.

On the assumption that marriage and family were the normatively dominant expectations for medieval women, a shortage of males at all levels of the socioeconomic scale appears to have been a critical factor in the creation of surplus populations of women. At the top of the system of ranks, it was the monasteries and Crusades that siphoned off males who would otherwise be eligible to marry. At the bottom were the ever-mobile seekers of economic opportunity and security, some looking for work in diverse parts of Europe and others looking for wars and the modest booty that soldiering would provide for them.[13] Bolton suggests that there was greater female longevity and "a masculine proclivity to death,"[14] as well, adding to this demographic imbalance between men and women.

It is important to note that the surplus of women during the twelfth, thirteenth, and first half of the fourteenth centuries can be attributed not to biological factors but to contractions in social organizations. The shortage of males who could assume statuses as husbands led as a necessary result to a contraction of status vacancies for women associated with the institution of marriage.

> But the large number of women following independent careers must be considered a very normal part of medieval life, caused by ordinary social circumstances rather than by unusual biological influences. Devotion to religious service in church or monastery naturally imposed a renunciation of family life upon large numbers of men. It is also possible that more women than men were involved in the general flow of population from the countryside into neighboring towns. Moreover, the economic life of the medieval town seems to have been favorable to the unmarried existence of women. Finally, specific religious and economic factors worked against matrimony.[15]

Many of those women whose husbands were "on the road" assumed economic roles; for others limited careers, as we noted above, were available; but for many others some form of the religious life became the selected alternative.

The religious spirit of the medieval period was, on the one hand, a contributing factor to the assumption of the status and role of wife and, on the other, a motive to reject the position and assume a life free of the demands marriage placed on the woman. That subordination to a husband and the bearing of children was expected of women has always been the case in Catholic doctrine. But in Bolton's view, the intense religious spirit of the age, and a growing emphasis upon piety and purity, "expressed through devotional literature," may very well have created in the minds of many girls an aversion toward marriage.[16] Thus, added to the factors of dowry and availability of males is the rejection of marriage as one of the alternatives from which the medieval woman might chose a future. Although I noted above that the position of women in Christianity had tended on the whole to improve, this was not always a uniform process.[17] Bolton and Southern emphasize the insecure position of women as a factor motivating them to select the religious alternative.

> Possibly this women's movement towards religion was stimulated by the disadvantageous position which they appear to have held in feudal society. Primogeniture became more usual and depressed the independent status of some aristocratic women in land-owning families. Nobles could no longer necessarily afford large dowries for their daughters. Such insecurity may

often have provided an incentive to enter a religious house or join a Beguine community. As a disadvantaged group in society women looked for any-thing which might improve their personal status. They turned to religion as nothing else was available to them. It is possible to argue that they might indeed achieve status through austerity in this world, or if not that, "what they cannot claim to *be*, they replace by the worth of that which they will someday *become*."[18]

But pursuit of the religious life as an alternative to marriage or inde-pendence was, similarly, characterized by finite opportunities. The con-straints of differential wealth and social position, generally, limited the opportunities to affiliate with religious organizations. And the degree of commitment associated with each of these organizations varied as well. For women of wealth there was of course greater choice, although this did not mean that access to positions in these organizations was without impediment.

Southern notes that status vacancies had to be created for those women in the higher ranks of medieval society who might remain marginal.

> The provision of a suitably dignified religious retreat for unmarried women and widows had presented a difficult problem for the aristocracy of the early Middle Ages. An unmarried woman was an anomaly in secular society. Girls were commonly married at the age of thirteen or fourteen, and widows were expected to marry again without undue delay. It was only in this way that the obligation of family policy and the military responsibilities of property could be discharged. Yet, unattractive though the position of unmarried women in society in many ways was, it had its alleviations. Great families felt bound to make provision for girls who could not *or would not marry*, and widows with important connexions and an established place in society could not easily be coerced into disposing of themselves and their property other-wise than as they wished.[19]

It was because of these factors that there existed a very large number of nunneries during the early medieval period. But it was for the wid-ows and daughters of "the great," rather than the multitude, that these organizations provided a retreat.[20] Not only were these nuns encour-aged to remember that they belonged to a ruling class; they were served by monks living in attached communities who provided "the necessary services of sacraments and temporal administration" for the nunn-eries.[21] In time, however, the position of women in the monastic system declined and male dominance was reasserted.

A clear example of the creation of status vacancies for women to compensate for the siphoning off of males is associated with Cluny, which I have described above. Hugh, abbot of Cluny, having encour-aged numerous married men to become monks, suggested the creation of a nunnery at Marcigny "for the special purpose of providing a retreat" for their wives.[22] Several centuries after the establishment of the nunneries described above, the decline in the esteem and power of the nuns was reflected in the organization of the community.

Social control appears to have been a major concern of Hugh and those who organized Marcigny, for the women no longer controlled their own affairs, nor did they preside over monks. The abbot created this "glorious prison" to provide strict control of the women lest "in appearing in the world they either made others desire them, or saw things which they themselves desired." The nunnery was to be "a place where mature women who were tired of matrimonial license might purge their past errors and be worthy of attaining the embraces of Christ. Noble women who had been freed from matrimony chose this place, resigning themselves more patiently to the loss of matrimonial joys as they discovered how short and full of sorrow are its pleasures."[23]

The motives of Hugh and his cohorts, as suggested by these comments, seem to have been less than religious. To avert the possible dangers seemingly inherent in the corruption of the souls of women and their threat to the stability of marriage and family relations, Hugh hoped to place unattached women under supervision. The literature of the period reflects great concern with 'the moral and social dangers of feminine wantonness."[24] It is clear that the nunnery provided status vacancies to control surplus women even though the personal motives of the women to join them may have included spiritual elements. But the nunnery, it is well to keep in mind, was for aristocratic women. What of those who were lower in the social scale?

The Beguines

Although the problems of the Church and some of the orders internally revolved about controlling those aristocratic women who had resolved that they would determine their own affairs, there still remained the many women of lesser rank who were similarly of concern to the Church. If there was a shortage of nunneries to absorb the women who could afford to buy their way into the monastic system—and wealth was indeed a prerequisite—there was an even greater shortage of positions for those women who were not aristocrats. During the twelfth and thirteenth centuries, with the rapid increase in population and the drain of men into activities that discouraged matrimony and the domestic life, the surplus of women, as I noted above, increased. It was at this time that numerous religious organizations, often informal in nature, emerged. One of these was the Beguines. Their importance lies in large part in the fact that they are an example of one of the alternatives available in the Middle Ages to those women of other than aristocratic rank.

The Beguines seem to have originated in the Low Countries about the middle of the twelfth century. Unlike the *Beguins* of Provence, to whom they apparently bear no similarity, the Beguines (*Beginen* in German; *Beginjenen* in Flemish and Dutch) did not share a particular religious doctrine. If they were to be considered heretics at all it was primarily as a result of their lifestyle rather than their beliefs. There was, however, among some Beguines an identification with the doctrines of the Brethren of the Free Spirit. They are more significant as organizations that provided status vacancies for women than as groups of religious dissenters.[25]

Although a seemingly small number of women who joined the Beguine communities were aristocrats, presumably because the monastic system could not absorb all who desired membership,* most of the Beguines originated in the relatively lower ranks. This included the offspring of the well-to-do burghers as well as those much lower on the social scale. Those Beguines who entered the organization with wealth provided, in effect, the endowment for the organization, including support for those with limited resources.[26] However, according to Martin Erbstösser and Ernst Werner, the Beguines were not organizations for the very poor women.[27] This assumption is plausible and consistent with what I have said above about participation in social protest movements, i.e., that those people at the bottom of the social scale† are less likely than those higher up to abandon their life-style. Similarly, since almost all of the religious protest and reform movements during the Middle Ages involved the assumption of the *via apostolica* and its concomitant, the divestiture of worldly goods, it is plausible that only those would participate in the pattern who had something to divest—and divest their property they did by giving it to the Beguine community. In any event, it is clear that unlike the monastic women, the communities of Beguines were heterogeneous in class origins. This heterogeneity was manifested in two ways. On the one hand, there were Beguinages whose members were of mixed class origins. On the other, there were houses, according to Phillips, that were established by the more affluent Beguines for the use of women in need of economic aid.[28] Thus, there was diversity of class origins within as well as between the houses.

Regardless of the diverse class origins of those who became Beguines, their new life-styles were normatively much the same. There was indeed a pattern of behavior that was deviant from the norms of both the larger communities and the Beguines themselves—to which I will devote more attention below—but in terms of its manifest ideals the Beguine movement was religious. In a largely religious environment in

---

*And, it is well to note, *would not*. The conflict over attaching groups of nuns to the various orders, particularly the Franciscans, Dominicans, and Cistercians, is well documented. See Bolton, in Baker, *Sanctity*, and Southern, *Western Society*.

†I refer to those whom Marx, for example, called the *Lumpenproletariat*.

which renunciation of the secular world and the opportunity for a religious life was now possible—i.e., one in which prayer, devotion, and good works could be pursued—many women shed their secular garments in favor of a quasi-religious habit* and a new, often elevated status. This status was enhanced not only by its connection with religion, the dominant institution in medieval society, but by its association in the minds of the multitude with the aristocratic women who became nuns and those who became their sister Beguines.

Who were these women and what did they do?

Beginning about the middle of the thirteenth century and lasting into the sixteenth century but dwindling rapidly thereafter, groups of women took up living together in houses called *Gotzhüser* in the Rhineland, *Beguinages* in France and parts of Belgium, and *Begijnhofen* in the Flemish and Dutch cities of Europe. Phillips provides an excellent analysis of the housing and ecological setting of the Beguines of Strasbourg, particuarly in the fourteenth and fifteenth centuries.[29]

Precise data on numbers of Beguines are lacking. Data on the number of Beguine convents are more accessible though incomplete. Both Southern and Phillips provide such data.[30] The data indicate the Beguinages varied in habitation from four or five occupants to some with a hundred or more. Southern's estimate for Cologne at the end of the fourteenth century, for example, is about 1,500 Beguines living in 169 Beguinages; this is out of a total population of approximately 20,000.

Concentrated in areas near the friar convents of the town, these *Gotzhüser* allowed for a direct religious impact of the Dominicans and especially the Franciscan friars upon the life-style of the Beguines. Providing physical and social security, convenience, and opportunity for religious devotion, the Beguinage simultaneously functioned as an organizer of unattached women, both unmarried and widowed, and thus provided control over their daily lives. Under the watchful eyes of the friars as well as their sisters in religion, the Beguines pursued a relatively conventional religious life. If there was controversy surrounding them it was more likely to be a result of their religious overzealousness than their diversion from the path of religious and secular norms.[31]

The seemingly harmonious life of the Beguines in Strasbourg, as described by Phillips, did not evolve without strain and conflict. Not only were there the ordinary strains associated with the ambivalent position of women in medieval society, but there was the added ambiguity of a claim made by these Beguines that they were a legitimate, acceptable part of the religious institution, the Church. Thus, they were

---

*The habit worn by Beguines was often a source of controversy because the Church authorities were ever on their guard lest the Beguines become indistinguishable from nuns. There was considerably less ambiguity about the status of nuns in the eyes of the Church when compared with the Beguines.

a potential threat not only as unattached, "wanton" women but as heretics. The heresy, as our story unfolds, can be located primarily in the eyes of the beholders.

It has already been noted that simultaneously with the increase of population and the largely urban commercial expansion there was a concomitant effort to reform the monastic system in particular and the Church more generally. The establishment of the Cluniac monastic pattern and its proliferation throughout France symbolized both the effort at reform and the difficulties of its attainment. The seemingly arbitrary rejection of the Waldensians and the acceptance of the Franciscans exemplifies the ambivalence that characterized the response of Church authorities to the numerous religious ecstatics who chose to abandon the secular life for a life in religion.

With the increase of population in general, and particularly in the cities, there emerged an increased demand for opportunities to express those religious sentiments that the Church, through its priests in the world, held up as the most worthy. Unlike the opportunities available to aristocratic women during the eighth and ninth centuries, when the demand created a supply of structures and status vacancies in the form of new nunneries, the opportunities for involvement in the religious life were now finite. The lid was clamped on the recognition of new orders by the Fourth Lateran Council (1215), assuring, in effect, that the movements for reforms which were to follow would be kept marginal to, if not outside, the Church and its discipline. The responsibility for countering the undisciplined pursuit of the religious life was placed on the Dominicans and Franciscans. The Inquisition, it may be recalled, was largely the work of the Dominicans.

Though we know that many men divested themselves of property to exchange their life-style for the *via apostolica*, there were clearly more women who sought the life of religion and poverty. And although there may have been frequent shouts of "heresy," on the whole both community and Church must have encouraged the integration of women into the Beguinages as well as other organizations. This support, for the most part, of the Beguinages was motivated by a desire to provide control over the many unattached women who now resided in the towns and cities. The Beguinages were family surrogates, and like the family they controlled their members and mediated between them and the larger community. Members were protected by being part of a unified body of *religiosi*, and they received economic support through the connections that the organizations maintained with the churches and other donors.

Although the women wore similar garb they only approximated the life-style and organization of orders of nuns. For one thing, they were clearly of the lay rather than ecclesiastical world. Secondly, they tended to perform occupations that were more menial than those of nuns, especially domestic tasks, and these were neither career-oriented nor were they seemingly perceived as permanent. Thirdly, the life of the Beguine was often perceived of as a temporary resting place on the way to other pursuits, including marriage. According to McDonnell, "The institution . . . tended to resemble a retreat for independent widows or superfluous daughters of well-to-do burghers or a refuge for the dispossessed."[32] Finally, whereas nuns took vows of asceticism and chastity for life, Beguines did not. Beguine organizations were abeyance structures, simultaneously controlling the behavior of members and providing status vacancies as other alternatives declined. As such they were also buffers against the effects of alienation from families of orientation.

Regardless of the diverse motives and structural factors that gave rise to the movement, the consequences were significant. By the organization of this largely unincorporated segment of the population, first into movements and secondly into town communes, a potential threat to Church authority was contained. As in a great number of movements that appear spontaneous and lacking in organization, the excessive expression of religious zeal in this case was channelized along clearly religious lines and according to norms associated with the prescriptions of the established Church. The system provided increased status vacancies, and in time the Establishment came to accept Beguines as somewhat less than religious orders but still legitimate members of the Church.

What were some of the concerns of the Establishment with respect to Beguines? Four appear to have been most prominent. *First of all there was the growing concern with heresy in general, which had, as noted above, become a preoccupation of Church authorities.* This was perhaps, at first, more a result of the surfacing of differences that had always existed in diverse parts of Europe than a manifestation of new challenges to Establishment doctrine. Substantial sectors of Spain, France, and central Europe had never become fully integrated into the Church. The Albigensians typified this source of concern. *Secondly, millennial movements, which were beginning to explode with increasing rapidity, threatened a Church which had directed itself to adaptation to and control over the secular world.* These movements directed attention to both the otherworldly dimension of religious belief and the doubtfulness of seeking wealth and security in the secular world. The Church had, of course, become the Establishment. *Thirdly, there was concern over the possible contamination of the monastic system in particular and the Church in general by all of these ideas, which ignored Church-promulgated prescriptions to remain in one's place, to accept "what God wills."* Finally, the Establishment was more generally concerned with deregulation of the society at large. During a period of great physical mobility, expansions and contractions of local populations, and commercial and urban expansion the authorities would need to maintain a watchful eye. The establishment of various groups of Inquisitors represented the most drastic reaction to the threats mentioned above. Thus it appears that more fundamental and long-range concerns underlay the earlier willingness to co-opt the Beguines and the later, more drastic step of pursuing heretics and witches. These boundary-maintaining efforts reflected the weakening of Church authority, which was already reflected in the decline of the monastic system.

Because the dominant institution in the Middle Ages was the Church, it was Church authorities who had to face the problem of alienation and social control. The Church attempted to secure conformity by many types of structures, some manifest and others latent.

The Beguinage as a mediating structure between the kinship institution and the religious institution exerted control not only over the expression of religious overzealousness. It absorbed unattached women, as well, and diverted their behavior from activities that might also have threatened the kinship system. Fewer women were likely to turn to prostitution and fewer women were available generally to challenge wives for the affection of husbands. Hence Beguinages ultimately received institutional supports from both kinship and religious systems.

In one of the classics on medieval religious movements, Herbert Grundmann describes two types of Beguines, a difference that helps explain the concern with social control. The contrast between the rootless, unregulated marginals and those Beguines who were housed was, according to Grundmann, not adequately taken into account by the public. Those who lived on alms and who were more prone to deviant behavior cast a stigma over those who worked hard and conformed to the ideals of the Beguine life-style.

Grundmann quotes from the poet Nikolaus von Bibra, whose biting satire articulates the difference between conformists and deviants:

Während die guten Beginen Tag und Nacht arbeitend, meistens spinnend, ein frommes und reines Leben führen, häufig zur Kirche gehen und die Mess hören, fasten, wachen und Almosen geben, heist es von den anderen: *sub falsa religione ocia sectantur et per loca queque vagantur,* und in der Beschreibung ihres zuchtlosen Triebens mit Mönchen, Klerikern und Studenten.[33] ("While the good Beguines work day and night, usually spinning, carrying on a clean and pious life, often going to church and hearing the mass, fasting, conforming and giving alms, as for the others: under false religion they very quickly gained followers and they wander everywhere. [They are] portrayed as undisciplined, fornicating with monks, clerks and students.")*

There are a number of suggestions in the literature that the Beguines were thought of, in the minds of the multitude, in a manner similar to

*The German translation is my own. I thank James Powell and Jerome Mazzaro for help with the Latin.

the characterizations of the hippies in the United States during the 1960s. McDonnell, for example, holds that the use of *Beguine* suggests someone who is less than religious. "The word *beguine* is deliberately opposed to *mulier bona*, a reliable devout woman," in one of his examples.[34]

Toward the end of the thirteenth century, when it became evident that regulations were necessary, the Dominicans in Strasbourg, through Friedrich von Ersteheim, formalized a set of rules for entering and sustaining membership in the group. In this case all the sisters pledged to accept discipline, and recruits who entered the sisterhood were similarly expected to take a pledge. However, the fact that it was stipulated that those who remained in a house for a year were, by their commitment, assumed to accept the code indicates that not all women who entered did make such a pledge.[35] Thus it is likely that some women viewed their involvement in the group as potentially temporary, and equally important, the group recognized that some women were only temporarily attached to the sisterhood. Like the situation associated with the monastic system, then, some participants were for the most part sojourners, laying over until another alternative came along.*

Regulation was one thing, but it was as a perceived threat to the Church organization that the Beguines were labeled heretics. Under attack themselves, the friars often turned to criticism of the Beguines and others who were ready bait for scapegoating. Although in some cases the Beguines accepted both the protection and the authority of the Franciscans and Dominicans, on the whole they did not accept the friars' organizational status. Thus the Beguines were feared as usurpers of the role that the friars played as mediators between the faithful and the Church.[36] But the attack on the Beguines was made easier by the close connection between some of the most conspicuous of them with the Brethren of the Free Spirit.[37]

THE BEGUINES AS HERETICS.   From the latter part of the twelfth century, when there is evidence of the Beguines in the Brabant (now part of the Netherlands and Belgium), the reactions to them as heretics were a recurrent issue.[38] The mixture of social change, increased populations, and dominance of religious ideas gave rise to many groups who, like the ecstatics swelling the hermitages and monasteries in the fourth and fifth centuries, chose the *via apostolica* as their dominant life-style. It is clear that for a while the authorities were willing to tolerate these self-styled and self-proclaimed *religiosi*. As mendicants and pseudoecclesiasts these people began to compete with the friars with their lay translations of the Bible and their freedom to pursue the religious life at will. Both lay

---

*One of the suggestions that emerges, then, is that the Beguinages must have functioned as hospices something like the YMCA residences in American cities.

opposition and attacks from the friars gave rise to a pattern of restrictive reactions, which were manifested at the Councils of Lyons and Vienne.

The Second Council of Lyons of 1274 is noteworthy for the acceptance of three tracts that were hostile to the Beguines.[39] Bishop Bruno of Olmütz, concerned only with discipline, "complained that men and women who belonged to no papally approved order still dressed and behaved themselves like friars, refused obedience to their parish clergy, and wandered about without discipline through the cities. A second report by the Dominican Humbert of Romans proposed that 'poor religious women' should not be tolerated unless they had the wherewithal to support themselves without begging or wandering."[40]

Gilbert of Tournai, a Franciscan, complained of the translation of the Bible into the vernacular and the reading of it, by some Beguines, in public. The deviations of the Beguines, it is clear, were not from the religious norms but from the expectations of both secular and Church authorities that religious appeals to the lay public would be made only by those formally recognized to do so, i.e., members of orders. Neither Bishop Bruno nor Brothers Humbert or Gilbert attacked the Beguines for heresy. On the contrary, conspicuous overzealousness was their error and the Council verbally reinforced the ban on new orders associated with the Fourth Lateran Council, "adding a corollary that all orders that had arisen after 1215 without papal confirmation were to be dissolved."

At the Council of Vienne, 1311–1312, the Beguines were almost proscribed from continuing their way of life.[41] Attacking them for failure to take "vows of obedience," give up their property, or adhere to "an approved rule,"—and perhaps more important, for wearing a special habit and spreading opinions that the Council rejected—the Pope issued a decree supported by the Council that forbade women from following "the Beguinal way of life."[42] However, an exception was made for those Beguines who lived in the Beguinages.

The fourteenth century was the high point of the Beguine movement. The Councils of Lyon and Vienne reflected the recurrent ambivalence associated with the diverse movements of piety that were less than heretical. The Beguines were sometimes persecuted but more often tolerated, and this varied with conditions having little to do with their behavior. Their behavior, for the most part, conformed to religious precepts and their presence in the midst of the secular world made it difficult for the lay public, who often saw them as little sisters, to accept them as a real threat to the social order. They were, nevertheless, not beyond suspicion, and the intrusion of Church officials into their activities, from time to time, helped reinforce the dissident labels attached to them.

"Suspicion of heresy combined with disciplinary proceedings helped to regulate them, cutting down the number of individual Beguines and small groups and driving them into larger Beguinages; at the same time the impetus to the Beguine life tended to fade. Their greatest days were over by the mid-fourteenth century."[43]

ABEYANCE AND THE BEGUINES.   It is clear from the data reviewed that the Beguinages emerged, grew, and were reinforced by women who were marginal to the existing institutions of medieval society. With fewer opportunities to marry, limited opportunities and, perhaps, will to join nunneries, and limited (though somewhat greater than earlier) choice for careers in the secular world, many selected affiliation with groups of Beguines. Avoiding vows for life, a characteristic of nuns, and participating in the secular world, the Beguines had no clear religious doctrine that differentiated them from orthodoxy or the diverse sects proliferating throughout western and northern Europe. Their character was thus, in my view, largely social. Their form was religious.

Like the recent hostels for women in urban areas, including the Young Women's Christian Association; sororities on college campuses; and other organized groups who provide a haven for the unattached, the Beguinages also exerted control over our seemingly most feared sex, women. From the point of view of the Beguine it is likely that donning the special habit associated with the sisterhood provided, in addition to economic and physical security, enhanced status. The women who joined Beguines were not typically revolutionaries; they wanted to attach themselves to a life-style that was associated with the dominant institution of the period.[44] But in a period of rapid change, where the future might offer even greater opportunity, it was good strategy to avoid marriage to the Church, to keep one's options open. Thus, one of the most important aspects of the Beguine pattern was the nature of its temporality.

TEMPORALITY.   In contrast to the monastic pattern, including the nunnery, affiliation with the Beguinages was assumed to be of relatively short duration. Although it is known that some Beguines continued to live in their own homes, participating in a more intensive religious experience than those women about them, it was the Beguinage that was for them the recognized center of activity. The requirement imposed by Friedrich von Ersteheim, and referred to above, that those women who remained in Beguinages for a year or longer must take a pledge to adhere to group norms indicates that many Beguines affiliated themselves with the group just long enough to find an alternative source of integration into the life of the larger community. In this respect many were like what I earlier called sojourners, and thus attached themselves temporarily to Beguinages in much the same way as those who were marginal to the monasteries and nunneries.

COMMITMENT.   What really differentiated Beguines from nuns was the limited degree of commitment to the group that characterized their affiliation. Not only was commitment of short duration for the sojourners, but the core groups as well might decide to leave the order at any time without approbation. For the widows and unmarried this allowed opportunity for future matrimony. For those who might chose careers in the expanding urban commercial economy there were no fetters to inhibit opportunities. In time the expansion of status vacancies elsewhere played a role first in the contraction of the Beguines and then in their demise. Southern's data on the Beguines in Cologne indicate that they had reached the high point of conventional saturation by 1310. From this date the number of convents founded began to decline.[45] Phillip's data on Strasbourg reflect a similar situation.[46] We do not know where the Beguines who left the convent went or what were the alternative sources of status vacancies that integrated medieval women who might have chosen some form of the religious life. We do know, however, that Beguines were not required to take vows for life and that this factor enhanced the process by which women could be freed or expelled as alternative positions that could absorb them expanded in other social structures.

INCLUSIVENESS.   Certainly, in contrast with the class exclusiveness of the nunneries, the Beguines were more inclusive. Here was a sisterhood of the socioeconomically heterogeneous. Here was also, as a concomitant, a group of diversely educated women from somewhat divergent regions and from diverse age categories. The only criterion which appeared to be significant was that the recruit aspired to a pious life and good works in the world. Although we know that, in fact, some who were called Beguines did not adhere to these norms, it is clear that most did conform. And it is this conformity which helped the Beguines survive the constant fluctuations in stance taken by those officials of the Church who saw them now as heretics and at other times as good little sisters who do the Lord's work. This willingness to accept and absorb almost any woman who would pretend to a religious life made the Beguinage a superb instrument for the societal functions of control and abeyance.

DIVISION OF LABOR.   Although the monastic system was characterized by a relatively low degree of specialized work, as compared with secular activities, the Beguines were even less specialized. Work, as such, was not an integral part of the Beguine organization. Though idleness is clearly proscribed, nowhere in the literature does one find reference to the specific kinds of jobs Beguines were expected to do. That they did domestic work, aided the ill and infirm, and occasionally assumed secular occupational tasks that provided income is known.[47] However, there is no special type of income-producing work which can be identified with the Beguines alone. In addition, participation in the Beguine life-style was apparently not perceived as a career, nor was it a training process en route to a career.[48] The Beguinage was an urban commune in which there was rough equality of status and productive capacity. Thus as a potential source of competition in relation to alternatives in other social structures or occupational pursuits, Beguines were low on the scale.

INSTITUTIONALIZATION.   If by institutionalization we mean more than the sheer persistence of a pattern of group behavior, we must place the Beguines relatively high on the scale but not at the top. The Beguines did persist for several hundred years. They were perceived as serving community and societal goals rather than personal aspirations. They were also recognized, for the most part, as worthy in themselves rather than as instruments for other goals. But neither lay nor Church officials, nor the public for that matter, perceived them to be a necessary part of society. Nor did they mandate support of the Beguines or the Beguinages in which the women lived. More important, however, the constant ambivalence in the relationship between the Beguines and the Church made the continued existence of the sisterhood, at a given moment in time, precarious. Nevertheless, the incorporated Beguines were not deviants, and although they were less institutionalized than monastic foundations they were generally tolerated and recognized as an acceptable form of religious expression.

STRATIFICATION.   As suggested above, the status relationships within the Beguinage tended to be egalitarian. Unlike the nunneries of the eighth and ninth centuries, to which I referred above, and in which nuns who were originally of aristocratic birth were encouraged to conduct themselves in manners reflecting their origins, the Beguinages were relatively unstratified. To be sure there were included, in contrast to those nunneries, women of diverse status origins. However, the fluidity of membership tended to inhibit the emergence of an articulated system of stratification within the group. This was, of course, an enhancement to the process of abeyance and aided mobility from membership in the Beguines to affiliation with other organizations. In short, other than membership in an organization that might yield some increase in status for some Beguines entering from relatively low strata, membership offered few social rewards that would encourage too strong a hold on those who might be recruitable for alternative status vacancies.

The Beguines emerged at a time when the capacity of the monasteries to control dissidence was in decline. Not only was there an absolute increase in population, which began about the eleventh century and continued until the fourteenth. Expanding urban centers were now the recipients of rural migrants, and a greater number of these, as I have noted, were women. The increase in urban populations—and, more important for my purposes here, the imbalance between the sexes—was a result of more complex phenomena than an increase in birthrates or greater longevity of women. A number of institutional factors, including economic factors, shrank the number of traditional status vacancies which women would ordinarily have occupied, and this, more than anything else, had a greater influence on the surplus of women that has been noted by medieval historians and others concerned with this period.

The Beguines effectively attracted and held thousands of women who might have otherwise added to the swelling ranks of revolutionary millennialists about whom Norman Cohn wrote. More recent scholarship has shown that there were more women participants in the religious protest movements of the medieval period than men.[49]

The Beguinage performed the societal functions of abeyance and control, though this may not consciously have been a factor in the motivation of those women who assumed roles as Beguines. As Bloch noted, everyone below the ranks of the aristocracy was economically exploited, and women more than men. Many women joined protest movements because their property rights were being jeopardized, and rather than give property to the Church they gave it to alternative religious groups, including the Beguines.[50]

Though the Beguine pattern was religious in form, its functions were social. Another form that has always appeared exotic and has nevertheless provided status vacancies for surplus populations, and thus abeyance and control, is bohemianism. I turn to this pattern next.

CHAPTER 4

Bohemians: Vagabonds and Aesthetic Pretenders

"Crime is the price society pays for creativity."
—Émile Durkheim

Women were not the only ones who needed to be kept under watchful eyes and social control. Wanderers in general were a perceived threat to society, and among these were the minstrels and troubadours we Westerners have romanticized, as well as scholars, actors, and artists. All of these occupants of relatively exotic statuses contributed to the model of what came to be called "bohemian." And the selection of that term to describe itinerant outsiders was probably a result of a concatenation, in the popular mind, of that ubiquitous symbol of the vagabond, the gypsy, with that frequent perpetrator of what was perceived to be heresy, even into the Renaissance, the Bohemian. For even after most of the millennial movements of central and western Europe had waned, the direct and distant descendants of Jan Hus in Bohemia continued to challenge Church authorities.[1] That the Hussite rebellion was, according to Cohn, largely a result of a surplus population in urban areas, created by an influx of people from rural areas and a simultaneous lack of status vacancies to absorb them, is important.[2] But it is as a source, in part, of the term and model for nineteenth- and twentieth-century bohemianism that we remind ourselves in this context of those fifteenth-century rebels.

The concern with vagabondage, particularly in England, was a result of two factors. Although there was a shortage of labor in England during the end of the fourteenth century, there was a normative element that proscribed free mobility. Although societies in general require that people be integrated through occupancy of some position, and thus remain under control, medieval society seemed to be somewhat more concerned than most about this matter. In medieval society a person's status was ordained and typically permanent. As E. K. Chambers noted, "It was part of the mediaeval [sic] conception of things to assign to every individual a definite function in the social organism and to expect from him the regular fulfillment of that function. To such a theory the migratory beggar and the masterless man were naturally repugnant."[3] The laws associated with vagrancy, as discussed by Tawney,[4] were dealt with above. But the concern with vagrancy was directed not only to the poor who became marginal as a result of Enclosure. In sixteenth-century England all manner of men, including "juglers, pedlars, tynkers and petye chapmen . . . fencers, bearewardes, comon players in enterludes and minstrels," were placed under suspicion and statutory control.[5] Although the actors and minstrels may have been the victims of an overzealous Parliament, who in this case decided to throw them into the same category as ordinary tradesmen, they were clearly recognized as a threat to the prevalent moral order. For the tradition of using their art to criticize both sacred and secular authority had long been associated with some of the troubadours, minstrels, and actors. It was in England and in Germany that formal social controls were most vigorously imposed on potential dissidents. But the idea of freedom to express an unpopular view gradually came to be associated with particular roles that were present in all Western societies.

Travelers

Though the ideal norm in medieval society required holding one's place socially and physically, it is clear that a great many people were on the move.[6] Not only were there those looking for work—the professional soldiers and itinerant artisans referred to earlier—but there were others whose movement was recognized as legitimate and desirable. There were pilgrims constantly on the road winding along the way to Rome and Jerusalem. Crusaders passed through en route to the Middle East. Later, when England became Protestant, religious exiles could be found wandering. Students from all over Europe, and from England as well, traveled to and from Italy and France pursuing the many masters of the medieval and later period. And the masters themselves, including such eminent scholars as Erasmus, were often itinerant as well.[7]

The more flexible and tolerant the region, the greater the chance that wanderers would be observed either passing through or as integrated members of society. Such was the situation of the minstrels and troubadours in Provence, who were sometimes in one place but often on the move. Whether itinerant or attached to a given court, the troubadours were typically integrated and under the surveillance and control of the authorities.[8] The minstrels tended to be less integrated.

Provençal society during the Middle Ages was probably the most open and tolerant sector of France, and perhaps second only to the north of Italy in its acceptance of diverse life-styles. Exposed to many cultures, including Arabic and Jewish, Provence was "regarded by the Church authorities as breeding grounds for heretics,"[9] including the Cathars and Albigensians. It was in this context that the troubadours took hold and proliferated, simultaneously exemplifying the connection between artistic activity, social protest, and deviant behavior *within* rather than outside of a relatively conventional society. And like a number of other innovative groups who emerged with that same expansion of population which impacted on the monastic system, the troubadours and their more popular, lower-status compatriots, the minstrels, attained wide acceptance during the twelfth and thirteenth centuries.

Just as medieval women developed alternative religious forms to provide for those who were not aristocrats and thus could not become nuns, troubadours and minstrels represented similar roles in diverse status contexts. The troubadours were largely from high-status contexts and were associated with court life, whereas the minstrels, who preceded them, were lower in status, primarily entertaining the masses. That they were perceived differently by Church authorities, and that the activities of the lower-status entertainers were more likely to be labeled deviant, is notable.[10] The process of defining in-group activities as virtues and out-group activities as vices worked in this context as well.

The troubadours seem to have grown out of the traditions of the minstrels, whose traditions, in turn, grew out of earlier forms.

> The medieval minstrel has been described as a cross between the court bard and singer of the Dark Ages and the agile mime of classical antiquity. Even after the theater, as it had existed in pagan Rome, had been banned by the Church and classical culture had all but disappeared, the descendants of the old mimes continued to travel about Europe entertaining the masses with their rough, uniliterary and unsophisticated art. There are references to them in Gallo-Roman times, and they were especially numerous in Germanic countries. Until the ninth century they had little or no contact with the court singers or bards. . . . Even though these court singers of heroic lays do not seem to have enjoyed much prestige, and few of their names have come down to us, they held themselves aloof from the popular entertainers, who were considered no better than "rogues and vagabonds." Singers and minstrels of every kind were attacked by the Church. Charlemagne's court theologian, Alcuin, declared, "He who brings actors, mimes and dancers into his house is forgetting the host of devils that he lets in along with them."[11]

That the mimetic pattern is suggestive of a "subterranean tradition,"[12] even though it reflects the behavior of adults as well as youth, is important. For the connection between the drama, music and musical entertainment, art, and intellectual activity which characterized the bohemianism of the mid-nineteenth century in France is an emergent of a pattern of norm evasion that was and is, for the most part, tolerated. In every social context with which we are familiar the mime, the musician, the artist, and the intellectual are perceived as more or less deviant in life-style but are nevertheless allowed to pursue a more unconventional life-style than others.

The troubadours provide an interesting example of patterned norm evasion.[13] Apparently beginning with Guilhem VII of Poitou the troubadours espoused a doctrine of romantic love outside of marriage as the ideal relationship between man and woman.[14] Although the ideal of marriage was not challenged, romantic love was held to be impossible between husband and wife. Thus the "natural order" of social life was supported by both Church and troubadour, contributing to the maintenance of the status quo. Since the troubadour seemingly threatened nothing of importance, as viewed by the authorities, his encouragement of love outside marriage and his occasional (typically subtle) songs of protest were tolerated. As pressures to curb heresy increased, during the latter part of the medieval period, the troubadours, too, were increasingly attacked. As the Inquisitions against the Albigensians and other Provençal sects increased, so did the songs of protest sung by both troubadours and other minstrels. By the fifteenth century the troubadour had slipped from the scene, and only the minstrel and mime seemed to survive. The minstrel continued to cater to the classes who were unable to share in the news conveyed by the novel printed page, and the mime began to organize, with his peers, the theaters—which, from the time of Shakespeare onward, were to structure and control his wanderings and utterances. As a visitor to the court the artist was now primarily an entertainer, and only secondarily a conveyor and creator of history and news.

THE MINSTRELS.   To suggest that a wider range of tolerance was enjoyed by minstrels and other artists when compared to the mass of the populace is not to hold that their life was without strain. Though their popularity had increased during the eleventh century, thus allowing them to more easily survive, "the history of minstrelsy [up until then] is written in the attacks of ecclesiastical legislators . . . and in the notices on monkish chroniclers."[15] A number of statutes were designed to discourage public performances by the minstrels, and some citizens, particularly clerks, were held to be commiting sin if they attended these rallies. But why the great concern on the part of the ecclesiastical authorities with the minstrels and their performance?

Although the minstrels were relatively controlled wanderers, it is clear that they developed a base of power as a result of their popularity

with the masses. It is likely that no small amount of jealousy motivated
many a bishop to be wary of the influence of the minstrels upon his
flock. In addition the minstrels were responsible for composing and
performing songs that were critical of particular causes and personalities, often subtly challenging those in high positions.[16] But part of the
reaction to the minstrels is reminiscent of the response to the Beguines,
who flourished at the same time.

Though the range of toleration of the relatively unconventional life-
style of the wandering minstrels was relatively assured at first, the cloak
of immunity from authoritarian reaction was soon donned by others
whose motives and bearing diverged from those of the committed minstrels. As in the case of the Beguines and the monks, there can be
distinguished a core membership and sojourners. The core included the
household minstrels, who, like the integrated troubadours, were for the
most part attached to the courts. The wandering minstrels, on the other
hand, were relatively lower in status even though they enjoyed many of
the same privileges as their household brethren. But the circumstances
of allowing a category of wanderers a wider leash among the masses
soon became an attraction for those who used this relative immunity to
cloak their deviant behavior. What became evident was that there were
serious minstrels and those who were only pretenders. Like the distinction between the "good" and the footloose Beguines, noted in the preceding chapter, the recognition that all minstrels were not the same led
to a contraction of liberties for all who claimed to be minstrels.

In 1315, "a royal proclamation had considerably restrained the liberty of the minstrels. In view of the number of idle persons who 'under
colour of mynstrelsie' claimed food, drink, and gifts in private houses of
prelates, earls and barons none resort to meate and drynke, unless he be
a mynstrel."[17] It appears that the proclamation was directed to those
minstrels who did not enjoy the protection of persons of power, which
entailed legitimation for their wanderings. By the middle of the fourteenth century, in England at least, there appeared the beginning of
legislation against vagabonds and beggars, a late version of which Tawney refers to in his discussion of enclosures. This early legislation, the
Statutes of Laborers, was directed primarily to the rootless mass of the
population but imposed great constraints upon the minstrels. The flexibility that had allowed even the monasteries to enjoy the minstrels, in
spite of normative regulations opposed to this practice, hardened. And
the Church, too, made a distinction similar to the one made in relation to
the Beguines—between the deviants and the tolerable wanderers. Those
who haunted taverns, who sang "loose songs of love and dalliance,"
who indulged in wine, women, and dice, were distinguished from minstrels who were honorable.[18] The latter were attached to the powerful
and the former remained unattached, and, as a consequence, un-

protected from those who would impose sanctions on them according to formal or informal norms.

But both the statutes and the co-optation of the household minstrels and troubadours soon imposed a pattern that contributed to the demise of the minstrel. The minstrel of honor, now under more direct surveillance and control in the household, tended to be more compliant than his predecessors and his counterparts on the road and in the streets. The increasing press of the authorities, both Church and secular, made wandering a more precarious activity. And if these constraints were not enough, the printing press now deprived the wandering bards of one of their functions, the reporting of news and the retelling of the deeds of admirable and evil men and women. The minstrel movement, like many others that provide opportunity for a critical stance in relation to authority, must have required opposition in order to flourish. Once the troubadours came into being and once the more skilled minstrels became co-opted, those who might have been most adept at negotiating the rivers of tolerable dissent joined those who would have been the objects of satire and probing song. Like the "good" Beguines, the "good" minstrels diverted their critical stance to one that was supportive of authority. Institutionalization, again, sapped the vitality of the deviants, and constricted the range of critical behavior.

By the fifteenth and sixteenth centuries the "medieval form" of minstrelsy began to disappear. "The mimes of course endured."[19] The minstrels had little more to do, since they were more than entertainers. Some of them became integrated into the newly emerging tradition of the drama. And some, along with the mimes, carried on the subterranean tradition of criticism of authority within the boundaries of tolerable reactions.

ACTORS.   E. K. Chambers refers to a "mimetic instinct, which no race of mankind is wholly without [and which] appears to have been unusually strong amongst the peoples of the Mediterranean stock."[20] When Christianity arose, with its "prejudice against disguisings," it came directly into conflict with a well-established pattern that had proliferated throughout the known worlds of Greece and Rome. But the mimetic pattern and the diverse forms of entertainment more or less associated with it were already viewed by authorities as a less than honorable activity. From the very beginning, those who engaged in performing for the masses were denied the civil rights associated with other citizens of Rome. And this perception of the mime as being somewhat outside of conventional society, in a parallel caste, has been passed on to us even into contemporary Western life.

The existence of prejudices against performers, even among the pagans, provided opportunities for the Church to exert controls over the mimes and their associates. And early on in the life of the Church the capacity to simultaneously tolerate and control dissidence, which is without doubt one of the factors aiding the survival of Roman Catholicism, was demonstrated in its relationship to the performers. But this capacity seems to have derived from the ambivalence of the Roman emperors, associated with the strong will of the masses to be entertained, and the pressures of the Church to curb all kinds of performances, particularly on Sundays and during holy periods. Negotiating between these competing demands helped establish the earlier--described traditions of toleration as a counterpart to the subterranean tradition.

By the time the minstrels and troubadours began to decline in popularity, the "mimetic instinct" was being incorporated into organized groups of actors; some of them toured within and between the countries of England and the Continent, and others, like the "minstrels of honour," were established in place. The distinction between the vagabond actors and their less mobile colleagues is reminiscent of the differences between those Beguines and minstrels whose life-styles were tolerable and those whose behavior was perceived as deviant. This distinction reflected similar problems from the perspective of the authorities, and the range of tolerable deviance constricted and expanded, *in part*, as differences among actors and pretenders became blurred.

That the social-control reactions of the authorities were responses only in part to problems of maintaining order is critical to an understanding of efforts to control dissidence. The efforts to curb dissidence by constricting vagabondage were also motivated by economic factors. According to Chambers, "it was primarily a shortage of labour towards the end of the fourteenth century which brought about the first serious endeavor to check vagabondage by legislation, and to compel the able-bodied vagrant, through the machinery of local government, to return to the village of his domicile and there take up again the service which he had abandoned."[21]

The interconnection between status vacancies, range of tolerable deviance, and social control, more generally, is evident in this case. The use of law as a device for attracting and repelling personnel in relation to status expansions and contractions probably began at this point in history, in England and in relation to those whose attachment to discernible, stable social structures was weak and remote. The vagabonds of all kinds were merely performing roles in a vast, amorphous abeyance structure. Their life-style was viewed as tolerable when they were a surplus but benign population and intolerable when their labor was necessary to maintain the economic system. Actors were among those whose liberties were threatened when labor demand increased.

The history of the rise of the theater in Tudor England is again a story of the constriction and relaxation of liberties, especially those associated with diverse categories of vagabonds. But in general the theater tended to enjoy official and public support as long as actors recognized and adhered to a tolerable range of unconventional behavior. No one expected theater people to behave like the rising bourgeoisie or like members of the aristocracy, but there were limits to what would be tolerated. And to ensure that these boundaries would not be violated, actors, like the minstrels preceding them, were the wards of the powerful. Accordingly, as "servants," they carried passes that simultaneously vouched for their identity and recommended them to other noblemen or gentlemen. Protected by this kind of relationship, they were excluded from the category of "masterless men" that made the vagabonds vagrants and thus vulnerable to pressures to return to their villages or become integrated into the labor force. Thus even under conditions of increased constraints upon wanderers the actors enjoyed greater latitude in their behavior.

The rise of the Puritans, however, put greater pressures on actors. By the middle of the sixteenth century in England the reactions to wanderers became more intense. In 1547 a statute was passed that called for branding vagabonds and putting them "to forced labor."[22] This statute was directed to all wanderers who were not under the protection of a patron, including actors. But even with the license to travel and to perform the Elizabethan actor was under control.

> The players had no free hand to play just when and where and what they liked. They were subject to certain conveniences as to times and seasons and localities, to precautions against breaches of the peace and dangers to public health and safety. Above all, in a time of political and ecclesiastical ferment, the sentiments of their plays had to be such as would stand the scrutiny of a government by no means tolerant of criticism. On these matters it was not, except in so far as heresy was constituted by Acts of Uniformity and the like, with statutes that they had to deal, but with the administrative regulations of the local and central executives. All over the country there were bodies charged with a general responsibility for public order, public safety, and public decency, as the Elizabethans conceived it. In the rural districts there were the justices of the peace, with powers more considerable than clearly defined; in the towns there were mayors and corporations, also acting as justices, but armed with a further authority derived both from custom and from charters, and with a very clear intention to use this authority to the full in the government of their communities. The regulation of amusements had always been regarded as falling within the scope of municipal activity, and in the end it proved a fortunate thing for the players, in London at any rate, that the central authority found itself driven by the pressure of circumstances to take over a large measure of the responsibility for stage control from the hands of the corporations.[23]

By the 1570s the Protestant counterpart of the medieval Catholic concern with public performances became strikingly evident. The moral tone associated with Puritan efforts to control personal behavior and sentiment was reflected in statutes regulating the performance of plays. The focus was clearly on sedition and moral impropriety, and the emergent policy was directed, according to Chambers, to "a complete suppression of the stage."

The following twenty-five years was a period of great proliferation of theaters and plays and an effort to segregate public performances by first pushing the open theaters out of the centers of cities (particularly London) to the suburbs and later eliminating the performances altogether. Much was made of the disorderly audiences and the spread of "lewd" plays. Writers, including Ben Jonson, were constantly being intimidated. Some were thrown into prison, while others found themselves on the run, fearing the worst at the hands of the magistrates.

The issue of the control of the stage again became entangled with the intolerance shown by the authorities toward wanderers. In 1597 a new Vagabonds Act directed toward distinguishing between the deserving poor and the idle vagrants cast a sufficiently broad net to include performers as well. This was an inadvertent result of a more humane Elizabethan poor-law policy, which, ironically, prescribed severe treatment for vagrants including whipping as well as more excessive punishment for those unfortunate enough to be designated felons. Greater constraints were placed on those who licensed and sponsored itinerants. By 1648 the suppression of public plays was complete. Parliament held that " 'all stage players, and players of interludes, and common playes, are hereby declared to be, and are, and shall be taken to be, rouges . . . whether they be wanderers or no, and notwithstanding any license whatsoever from the King or any person or persons to that purpose.' "[24] The range of flexibility was thus—again—contracted, and the bearers of the subterranean tradition moved underground. And what this meant was a more limited audience, confined largely to the household. This was possible because the patronized players, like the household minstrels, had become a recognized occupational category: co-opted, institutionalized, and under control.

That the theater was already an underground phenomenon of a sort had been evident for some time. Criticism of authorities, public figures, and public policies had always been associated with the mimes. With respect to the issue of social control, however, the question was not whether plays were critical of the behavior and mores associated with a given period in history but just how conspicuous or subtle the writer and the performers might be in delivering their message. By the seventeenth century it was clear in England that one took great risks in writing or performing what the authorities might designate lewd or seditious plays. Thus it is likely that those who tended to survive the onslaughts of the heretic hunters were those who developed the artistic capacities for subtlety and surreptitiousness that have come to be associated with sophisticated drama.

William Shakespeare exemplified, perhaps better than any other playwright of the English language, the genius required for an artist to be critical yet tolerable in relation to the authorities. Though pressures to avoid criticism were not as intense at the time he wrote as they were half a century later, concern with subversion on the part of the dramatist was still great. That Shakespeare's critiques were subtle is evident in the debates among scholars regarding the issue of dissent in his works. Thomas H. Jameson, in *The Hidden Shakespeare*, presents an analysis of some of Shakespeare's plays which leaves little doubt that he was, like a number of other playwrights, a subtle critic of Tudor authority.[25] Shakespearian plays include, among other themes, critiques of the concept of a "just" war, of attempts to justify the slaughter and starvation of civilian innocents in war, and, more generally, of Tudor repression at home. Shakespeare, in short, was an exemplar of the artistic dissenter who manipulates his medium within the range of tolerable deviance.

Bohemianism

The connections over time between diverse groups of performers is extremely difficult to document, particularly when the aspect in which one is interested deals with a theme like tolerable dissidence. Thus the connections between Greco-Roman views on performers and those of the Church and the Puritans in England are not as clear as a scholar would like. But given my goal here, to throw light on the emergence of a kind of bohemian model that has been emulated in nineteenth-and twentieth-century Western societies, the remoteness of phenomenal connections is subordinate to the development of the theme. In addition to this problem the interest in structural factors, such as the interplay between status-vacancy expansion and contraction and dissident behavior and control, forces the analyst to seek examples of illustrative phenomena rather than test hypotheses by representative samples. Developing a typology and a set of sensitizing concepts is what this study is all about.

The leap from seventeenth-century England to late-eighteenth- and nineteenth-century France, then to ninteenth- and twentieth-century America involves no small amount of arrogance if one is a social historian. For the theoretical sociologist, however, whose goal is conceptualization of categories of events, this need not be a problem. So long as the data used reflect the same kinds of phenomena, conceptually, the diversity of temporal circumstances and institutional and organizational contexts is less important. That this type of argument is rejected by the historian is acknowledged. I imply no less respect for the historian's craft or quest by suggesting that the sociologist's interests are markedly different.[26]

My thesis, it is well to restate, is that societies must provide sources of integration and social control in order to persist. Surplus populations are created not only by increased birthrates and survival rates but by contractions of positions in organizations that force formerly integrated people into marginal relationships. Such people are more likely to participate in collective protest. Elites recognize this and legislate in order to integrate and control the potentially dissident. But more subtle societal processes operate, as well, to absorb surplus populations. The expansion of commerce and industry, the outbreak of war, the undertaking of Crusades, and other phenomena are easily recognized. But the emergence of organized patterns that effectively absorb personnel also occurs unintentionally, at least with respect to the social-control function. This was true for the emergence of the monastic system and the Beguinages. The motives for participation in these patterns were surely complex, but it is clear that from the point of view of the actors the motives did not include efforts to control one's dissident tendencies. That those in power both in the Church and the community realized that surplus men and women could be brought under control through religious participation is clear from my earlier analysis. But it was largely the participants themselves who made choices that led to their integration and regulation. The degree of regulation as a reflection of the processes associated with societal flexibility varied with historical conditions. But some roles emerged in society that allowed for more latitude in behavior than others. Thus the various mimes, minstrels, and other performers were recognized as more prone to deviance than monks or Beguines. This reflects a pattern of norm evasion that is tolerated, a tradition that, although reaching back into history, is less than institutionalized but nevertheless organized and persistent. Thus all societies recognize certain groups—what I have called "parallel castes"— as being somewhat outside of conventional society, and so long as they do not pose too great a challenge to the behavior or mores of those in authority their ways will be tolerated.

Because it is understood that some people in society can "get away with more" than others, there is a tendency for pretenders to seek the cloak of protection associated with those committed to the tolerated lifestyle and thus derive sensual or material gains from this association. This was, as I have shown, true of the Beguines and minstrels, and probably of the itinerant monks as well. Throughout the historical literature there is a constant pattern distinguishing between the genuine adherents of a protected life-style and the pretenders. The pattern protrudes, as it were, out of the printed page toward the reader. In contem-

porary American Society bohemianism is a pattern that allows pretenders to enjoy the leeway accorded the artistic and literary cadres. But even
though it includes pretenders it functions in a manner similar to that
associated with the monks, Beguines, minstrels, and actors. That is, it is
characterized by self-regulation of behavior through participation in organized groups.

THE FRENCH REVOLUTIONS.   I am not the only sociologist to recognize
the connection between marginality and bohemianism. Cesar Grana
noted the connection between the contraction of certain status vacancies
resulting from the French Revolution and the creation of a surplus population of, among others, ex-aristocrats who invaded the many garrets
and other cheap rooms in Paris, establishing a colony of intellectuals and
artists.

The French Revolution and the subsequent dissolution of the social
structure created new masses of rootless, undirected, and uncontrolled
wanderers, including the *sans culottes* and migrant poor. In an earlier
period the lack of opportunity for intellectuals was a factor in the outbreak of the Revolution. Particularly in Paris the roving intellectual and
the spurious artist and writer were both ubiquitous and conspicuous,
due, in no small part, to their relatively great numbers and suddenness
of appearance. According to Grana: "Through the gathering of a large
marginal population in a great city, the scarcity of 'honorable' occupations, and the professional ambiguity of the new literature, that peculiar
version of the self-made man, the roving intellectual, had become a
permanent feature of Parisian life."[27]

The pretenders had little difficulty passing themselves off as artists
or intellectuals, since the forms of art and writing were, concomitantly,
in a state of flux. The new patron of the arts was the bourgeoisie, but a
mass audience, more generally, emerged after the French Revolution,
enhancing an enormous expansion of literary and artistic effort—and
ultimately income, too, for those whose output attracted the new
consumers.

The situation of the artist both under the Old Regime and after the
Revolution was unpredictable. Though some support, in the form of
free accommodations in the Louvre, was provided during the time of the
monarchy, this was limited to a very small artistic elite. Later Napoleon
expelled the artists from the Louvre. In general, enthusiasm for art was
not great, and the artist both painted and behaved in a conventional
way. But the rebellious posture associated with youth following the
Revolution was soon reflected in the attitudes of young artists. Several
simultaneous processes gave rise to the bohemian pattern, the changes
in the conception of art, the drawing together of artists and writers, and
the general idea that all creative people should assume a rebellious

posture in their public behavior. But the idea that artists and other geniuses should be appreciated while nevertheless being kept apart from polite society persists. And no less a writer of prominence than Honoré de Balzac provided the lines that reinforced the idea of tolerable dissent for some members of society.[28]

Influenced in part by Saint-Simon, who included painters, sculptors, muscians, poets, and novelists in the category "artist," Balzac viewed the artist as a martyr, an unhappy servant to the cause of community. As such, the artist was to set himself and adhere to the highest standards.[29] Balzac was thus inevitably inclined toward a somber view when it came to assessing the many pretenders and inept aspirants who haunted the bohemian paths of Paris. But he was no less hard on the genuine artist. In *The Human Comedy* he suggests that artists can be merciless and that they "do not understand the true meaning of love."[30] And further, being a successful artist may mean being a failure as a person. This characterization, which, I feel, lends itself to reinforcement of the image of the artist as outside conventional society, is reflected in the following lines: "We women ought to admire men of genius as one enjoys a play, but live with them—never!"[31] And this view that the artist should remain apart from society is reflected in Balzac's reminder that the artist should remain unattached to the social and political theories that flooded the Parisian intellectual scene during the early and mid-nineteenth century. The real artist, in short, works in solitude and avoids the drawing room and the salon. But Balzac was aware of the emergence of a new alliance among the diverse artists—a response to the need to organize, to assume power over the creative process, and to establish and monitor what they alone determined to be the highest standards of artistic output. Thus the circumstance of increasing numbers of aspiring artists, marginal pretenders, and an exploding market triggered by the rise of the bourgeoisie provided for the emergence of exclusive groups of productive artists. These became the core groups, and those who were not let in remained sojourners. The sojourners were essentially bohemians, and one of their attributes was a tendency to include rather than exclude marginal youth.

The most conspicuous characteristic of bohemianism is the pattern of imitation of the life-style of the artist. The poverty associated with the art student and the struggling artist was romanticized. The wearing of garish clothes, the midnight and early morning antics associated with the Left Bank, the bizarre behavior in general—all of these became part of the image that more conventional society conjured up when thinking of bohemians. And all of this behavior was possible because the degree of tolerance for deviant behavior was greater for artists and performers than it was for others in the community. The pretenders, who were for the most part not artists, gained from the wider latitude allowed the genuine artists.

The writer who probably had the greatest impact on the formulation of a bohemian model was Henri Murger. His *Vie de Bohème*[32] and other writings romanticized the life of the Montmartre and Left Bank artists and pretenders, and influenced, among others, Giacomo Puccini, whose opera *La Bohème* is a direct adaptation of Murger's story. Murger, sometimes called "the poet of youth,"[33] recognized the bohemian lifestyle as transitory, as a youthful interlude on the path to success as a genuine artist or even in the commercial world. Being young provides the rationale for the direct and immediate gratification of impulses. It is important to enjoy oneself in youth, for by age thirty the bohemian garment must be shed and the struggle with the real world, if it has not already been overcome, must commence. Bohemia is a way station on the road to success as an artist. He who remains "too long in Bohemia is doomed, or can escape only into the neighboring Bohemia of crime."[34]

When Murger himself attained a measure of success he began to write justifications for the bohemian style. To make Bohemia appear respectable he traces the pattern, much as I have attempted to do here, to the "unconventional and vagrant personalities in art and literature: Homer himself; Villon, 'poet and vagabond *par excellence*' . . . Molière and Shakespeare; Jean-Jacques Rousseau," and others. He describes three types of bohemians: "the dreamers, the amateurs, and the stalwarts—or 'official' Bohemians. Each class is described in detail. As to the first, Murger has more scorn for its conceit than pity for its sufferings; nothing but contempt for the second; and a real admiration for the third."[35] He, of course, includes himself in the third category.

The bohemian was, then, a pretender rather than a genuine artist, although some who participated in the bizarre behavior of the Left Bank and Montmarte youth later made their way into the cadres of genuine artists. But the latter, as both Balzac and Murger viewed them, were not idlers. Bohemianism was an imitation of what many youths thought was the artistic way of life rather than the pursuit of artistic activity. And the amorphousness of what was *creative*—and what was feigned reflection and ritualistic effort as differentiated from what was accepted by others as genuine art—enhanced tolerance for the behavior of many a pretender. But for the genuine artist, the admonition to abandon the bohemian way by age thirty involved constraints that required an unambiguous response. Was he to pursue the life of relative isolation, hard work, and insecurity that is associated with the quest for success as an artist or to find a place in the conventional world? Most chose the latter. And the pattern of choosing the "straight" world after sojourning with other youthful bohemians has persisted into the present century.

That the bohemians were perceived as being outside society, in a parallel caste, is clear. In commenting on the way journalists were viewed, during the Second Empire in France, Theodore Zeldin provides a telling observation. "They were condemned as bohemians, who were redeemed only by their wit. They were placed on the same level as actors 'whom people both despise and envy.'"[36] The bohemian pattern was associated not only with painters and sculptors, but, as we know from Murger's own life, with writers, actors, and others whose efforts were directed to public response. As performers of one sort or another their eccentric behavior did not go unnoticed. And because the distinction between the fake and the genuine remained blurred, those who sought to enjoy the benefits of greater license adopted the trappings of the artist's life-style. That conventional society allowed youth to experiment, to find their way, enhanced involvement with the tolerable deviants but only for a limited time. And this has been a characteristic of the abeyance processes associated with times of rapid societal transformations. If the pattern became institutionalized, as in the case of the Beguinages, it was possible for a sojourner to become a core member. If the pattern remained only marginally associated with society, the sojourner was much more likely to seek reintegration into more conventional sectors of society. Bohemianism became, and for the time being remains, a pattern that is uninstitutionalized but persistent, in relation to which the expectation is that it will lead only to a return to more "serious" life pursuits rather than to a new life-style.

CONTEMPORARY BOHEMIANISM.   The amorphousness associated with distinguishing genuine artists or writers from pretenders was a result of the romantic revolution led earlier by Victor Hugo. The idea that literary and artistic activity no longer required the old disciplines provided impetus to those with little or no talent to attempt to join those who were genuinely creative. To be sure, some without talent or skill may have been convinced that they might attain success in the arts. But others could participate in the life-style of the artist for other motives.

Hugo's message was dramatic: "Tear down theory, poetic systems. . . . No more rules, no more models. . . . Genius conjures up rather than learns. . . . For talent to surrender . . . personal originality . . . would be like for God to become a lackey."[37]

By the 1830s the artist as well as the pretender had a rationale for rejecting conventional life-styles. The talented needed to be organized into a movement that would oppose, on intellectual and aesthetic grounds at least, the rising bourgeoisie and the remnants of the Old Regime. And in order to articulate the differences between young and old, and between those who create and those who attempt to control society, artists and pretenders together dramatized their divergent posture. Clothing styles became bizarre, public behavior became boisterous and impulse indulgent, and the atmosphere around the Left Bank and Montmartre was like the carnival, or Mardi Gras, rather than a work setting for serious students and aesthetes. And this model, adhered to by artist and pretender, persists to the present day.

Richard Miller, in a recent book on bohemianism, attempts to tie the bohemian pattern to political activity.[38] Although those youth who were involved in the unconventional behavior patterns of Paris in the 1830s and later were undoubtedly more prone to political activity, this tendency was not and is not inherent in the bohemian ideal. It is Murger's model of bohemianism which has persisted to the present, and this image of the bohemian proscribes direct political activity. The artist and the bohemian both must influence society through creative activity rather than battering the barricades. That political activists associated themselves with artists and the bohemian life-style and that some men of genius participated directly in revolutions and what they perceived as "just wars" is true. The Revolution of 1830 and the Spanish Civil War of the 1930s attracted a number of prominent writers and artists. But it is more likely that their personal sensitivity to the political issues propelled them rather than adherence to bohemian patterns. An example from the 1960s may be instructive here.

It probably is no accident that the radical youth of the 1960s adopted, at least superficially, the life-style of those bohemians called "hippies." It is also likely that calling themselves "Yippies" was contrived as a device for obscuring the difference between those whose protest was social and symbolic (hippies) and those whose goals were political, directed toward altering the basic structure of the state (the Yippies: Youth International Party). Adhering to a similar life-style and choosing to be called by a similar name was strategically important. The movement for political revolution could then appear to the rest of society and to potential rebels as involving many more supporters than it actually did. Like the pretenders in France who used the greater latitude accorded artists to pursue their own goals, the genuine revolutionaries of the 1960s, in the United States, hid under the cloak of permissiveness alloted those youth who were sojourners, i.e., only temporary dropouts from conventional society.* The hippies, like other bohemians, tended to be apolitical.

What was the nature of bohemianism following its rise in France and its diffusion in the nineteenth century to the United States? The French were not the only ones who read and found romance and inspiration in Murger's *Vie de Bohème*. Though a goodly number of young writers and

---

*The suggestion about the use of the hippies as a device for pretending to have larger numbers was made by my friend and colleague Charles Willie in an informal discussion some years ago.

aspiring artists of all sorts were already following a life-style similar to that of the French bohemians, it wasn't until some of them had been to Paris and others had read Murger that they began to call themselves bohemians. In contrast Edgar Allan Poe, the most notable of those following that life style, adopted by American bohemians as a member of their special world, had seemingly never heard of Murger and the French bohemians. Yet his own life-style—his poverty, drinking and attacks on the Establishment of the time—provided a model for the *misérables* who aspired to great art while enjoying their collective poverty. The bohemians of Greenwich Village, beginning with a group who began to meet at Pfaff's, a saloon, claimed Poe as one of their own, as they were later to make honorific profit out of the brief involvement with them of Walt Whitman. Though Poe could be used to legitimate the Pfaff's group and the others to follow, he could not obstruct the Murgerian impulses reflected in the gaiety and romanticism of the Villagers. For Poe's somberness, morbidity, and pathological tendencies could only be romanticized, and perhaps ignored, up to a point. His influence as a personal model was, ironically, greater on an important Frenchman than it was on the Americans, and this influence impacted upon other Europeans as well. Baudelaire's succession to the mantle of morbidity passed on by Poe fostered a shift in posture among the continental bohemians. From a lighthearted and chiding approach to criticising the bourgeoisie there was a change to bitter, snarling attacks. Even the Russians (as the work of Dostoevsky, for example, shows) were influenced by Poe and Baudelaire in their morbid soul-searching and their concern with evil.

The lighthearted form of bohemianism prospered in both the United States and France during the nineteenth century in spite of some fluctuation resulting from expansion and contraction of the labor force. As the diverse cadres of immigrants arrived, they too developed their own bohemian enclaves. And these prospered and waned as opportunities for integration into the new society fluctuated.[39]

From the mid-nineteenth century onward, Greenwich Village remained the model for bohemianism everywhere in America. Boston, Chicago, and other cities to a lesser extent all had their bohemians and Bohemias. But Chicago by the turn of the century suddenly gained preeminence through the sheer brilliance of those who assembled and established themselves there as artistic and literary figures.

New York's bohemians, after the turn of the century, began to drift toward political rather than symbolic-artistic rebellion. Marxism, according to Parry, became the vehicle for the anti-bourgeois youth of Greenwich Village. This contrasted both with the historic thrust of the Village bohemians and with the rebels who were assembled in Chicago. In the view of the latter, the battle against the philistines was to be fought over free verse and similar issues rather than free speech or political economy.[40]

Ben Hecht and Maxwell Bodenheim exemplified the light and cheerful tone of the Chicago experience. They and many others, including Carl Sandburg and Sherwood Anderson, came to be recognized as genuinely creative artists, and as such they legitimated the activities of the Chicago bohemians. In time Chicago became part of a shuttle from the Middle West to the East, conveying many of the great and aspiring-to-be-great to and from the Near North Side and the Village. By the 1920s hegemony over American bohemianism shifted back to New York, and the Village again became the undisputed leader of the war against the philistines.

Malcolm Cowley, one of the many writers who participated in and observed the bohemianism of the 1920s, described the two kinds of rebellion alluded to above.[41] Side by side were those whose commitment was to political radicalism and those whose attack was primarily on what Cowley dubbed "puritanism."[42] During World War I the Village was denuded of young men. Bohemianism, at least in terms of active engagement, was on the wane. But the return of Cowley, and others like him, from Europe provided a marginal population that might have helped replenish the remnant groups of artistic rebels. Bohemianism and its ideal had become diffused through American society by that time, but it was only a small minority living in the Village who still thought of themselves as bohemians. The two cultures, the political and the aesthetic, survived the co-optation of ideals and symbols by the bourgeoisie. But the intimate connection between the arts and rebellion that was romanticized by Murger, and nurtured by the denizens of Pfaff's and those who dwelt along the streets adjacent to Chicago's Water Tower, was severely strained. Bohemianism was to become, for the most part, detached from serious artistic aspiration, only to appear and reappear as an amorphous alternative behavior pattern capable of enhancing permissiveness for the middle class without direct involvement with art or artists.[43]

What were these ideals which, for the most part, became part of the subterranean tradition?

1. The idea of salvation by the child. Each of us at birth has special potentialities, which are slowly crushed and destroyed by a standardized society and mechanical methods of teaching. If a new educational system can be introduced, one by which children are encouraged to develop their own personalities, to blossom freely like flowers, then the world will be saved by this new, free generation.
2. The idea of self-expression. Each man's, each woman's, purpose

in life is to express himself or herself, to realize full individuality through creative work and beautiful living in beautiful surroundings.

3. The idea of paganism. The body is a temple in which there is nothing unclean, a shrine to be adorned for the ritual of love.

4. The idea of living for the moment. It is stupid to pile up treasures that we can enjoy only in old age, when we have lost the capacity for enjoyment. Better to seize the moment as it comes, to dwell in it intensely, even at the cost of future suffering. Better to live extravagantly, gather June roses, "burn the candle at both ends."

5. The idea of liberty. Every law, convention, or rule of art that prevents self-expression or the full enjoyment of the moment should be shattered and abolished. Puritanism is the great enemy. The crusade against puritanism is the only crusade with which free individuals are justified in allying themselves.

6. The idea of female equality. Women should be the economic and moral equals of men. They should have the same pay, the same working conditions, the same opportunities for drinking, smoking, and taking or dismissing lovers.

7. The idea of psychological adjustment. We are unhappy because we are maladjusted, and maladjusted because we are repressed. If our individual repressions can be removed—by confessing them to a Freudian psychoanalyst—then we can adjust ourselves to any situation, and be happy in it. (But Freudianism is only one method of adjustment. What is wrong with us may be our glands, and by a slight operation, or merely by taking a daily dose of thyroid medication, we may alter our whole personalities. Or we may adjust ourselves by some such psycho-physical discipline as was taught by Gurdjieff. The implication of all these methods is the same—that the environment itself need not be altered. That explains why most radicals who became converted to psychoanalysis or gland therapy or Gurdjieff gradually abandoned their political radicalism.)

8. The idea of changing place. "They do things better in Europe." England and Germany have the wisdom of old cultures; and Latin peoples have admirably preserved their pagan heritage. By expatriating himself, by living in Paris, Capri, or the south of France, the artist can break the puritan shackles, drink, live freely, and be wholly creative.[44]

That these ideas had already become part of the world view of portions of the middle classes is not at all surprising. World War I had, for the first time, brought Americans into closer direct and indirect contact with the Continent. Some had gone to France to serve in the armed forces, while others received news and other descriptions of life abroad from those most directly involved. And, instead of the spread of a cosmopolitan view among the wealthy alone, the middle and working classes now developed a broader perspective on behavior than had hitherto been the case. Although they might have benefited in this regard from the many immigrant cultures that prospered in the large cities of the United States, this was not likely to be the case. For the immigrants were outsiders whose ways were to be changed or, more simply, ignored.

In addition to the greater contact, under war conditions, which allowed for more deviant behavior patterns, the increasing prosperity and movement within the United States dislodged the traditional patterns of conformity to older norms. These patterns need not be accepted as reflective of what Americans did in private, because deviant behavior is always present in society, but now there was an increase in general in the range of tolerable deviance observable in public. The 1920s, in short, was a period of change in public behavior and the bohemian ideals tended to be compatible with these new forms.

But the toleration of behavior by the middle classes, the guardians of American virtue, that had formerly been associated primarily with those who were at the edge of conventional society deprived the latter of an important source of distinction. And this distinctiveness, which helped articulate and maintain the boundary between the bohemians and the bourgeoisie, ultimately lost its association with those who protested against the middle classes. The ideas that Cowley described had gradually diffused throughout American society. Some of them are clearly recognizable today.

If the doctrine which provided articulation of the differences between the bohemians and the bourgeoisie was no longer capable of doing so, what was to happen to bohemianism as Murger knew it?

The post–World War I behavior patterns represented a sojourner phenomenon. The movement of people from positions in rural areas, out of the armed forces, and away from conventional settings generally provided American society with a large marginal urban population. The previous sources of social integration—whether family, army, or occupational statuses—were no longer capable of holding personnel and regulating them, or had thrust out their occupants, as in the case of the armed forces. The 1920s in the United States is a period during which behavior patterns were, in some institutional contexts, anomic. And as in the past, whether it was the decline of Rome or the transformations of the urban commercial patterns during the eleventh and twelfth centuries, older social forms had to expand or new forms emerge in order to provide a place for the marginal populations. As in the early and middle nineteenth century, to be more specific, many unintegrated people chose the bohemian setting and pattern as their way station en route to success in the arts or as a temporary opportunity to sow their "wild oats." Again, it is possible to observe the increase of amorphousness that accompanies the efforts of pretenders to squeeze under the cloak of tolerable nonconformity. The boundaries between the core members and the sojourners become blurred, at least in the eyes of the outside observer.

The careerists and commercialists began to move in on Bohemia, opening stores and small shops that featured avant-garde styles and *objects d'art*. This was as true of the Village as it was of the Chicago Bohemias, as Caroline Ware and Harvey Zorbaugh have demonstrated.[45]

The bohemianism of the Village had for a long time been detached from artistic activity. By the 1920s the creative artists, according to Parry, only came by to make an appearance among those who, more than others, idolized them.[46] The pattern of voluntary poverty that characterized the early monks and Beguines, and that Murger had romanticized, seemed to give way to a pattern of impulse indulgence more typical of the bourgeoisie than those who, in principle, opposed them. Had the Depression not arrived a decade later, the poverty aspect of bohemianism, voluntary or involuntary, would have disappeared.

Bohemianism had, in sum, become a pattern that was shared by many urban Americans, some of them not even pretending to create art. By the 1940s and the 1950s the pattern became well organized and lodged in urban communal activities. In the 1960s the communal thrust, under the pressure of very large numbers of marginal youth, was directed to the rural setting of America.

COMMUNALISM. The idea of the "crash pad," as it was referred to in the 1950s and 1960s, had been part of Murger's legacy. The poverty-stricken bohemian, whether his condition was voluntary or imposed by genuine destitution, could hardly refuse to share what little he had with his anti-bourgeois brethren. For it was the bourgeoisie who were the materialists; it was they whose consciousness was dominated by their possessions. The quest in common to present to society at large a higher set of standards unencumbered by sham morality and customs, as suggested by Balzac, made it impossible for the bohemian to refuse to share what little he had with his fellows. From the very beginning, bohemians in France, and later in America, lived communally both in cities and in the country.

But the pattern of communal living was distinctly bohemian, rather than a pattern associated with creative artistic activities. For, as we noted above, the serious artist required solitude. This was particularly the case when he was engaged in intensive work. Bohemianism, being a highly social activity, was an obstructive pattern when genuine work was required. Because the communal life was detached from the life-style of the artist, it too assumed a pattern of its own independent of creative activity.

The diffusion of some of the avant-garde ideas associated with the bohemians of Malcolm Cowley's era, coupled with the increasing institutionalization of the arts in America, enhanced the separation of lifestyles noted by Murger and others in France half a century earlier. By the late 1920s and 1930s America's artists declined for the most part to identify themselves as bohemians. The federal writers' and artists' projects of the Depression era were an aid to this tendency, but Cowley had already noted that many of the creative artists had begun to reject any connection with the bohemians.

The communal setting became still another home away from home for the middle-class youth of urban America. Whether their homes were on the other side of the city, or "uptown," or in small-town rural America, the bohemian "pad" could provide a temporary resting place away from the dependence and pressures to conform to middle-class norms at home. Whether through advertisements in newspapers or by word of mouth, young people who wanted to avoid the YMCAs and other settings that seemingly constricted their range of behavior found the way into urban bohemian enclaves in or near the Village in New York City or on the Near North Side of Chicago.*

Caroline Ware noted the pattern in her study of the Village.

> Certain houses, owned by a landlord whose reputation for befriending bohemians was known from coast to coast, housed most of these, although some were scattered in the garrets of unremodeled houses. In these apartments, no one was put out for failure to pay the rent, but was simply moved to smaller quarters or put in with another occupant. The landlord even went so far as to help out his tenants with money or food when they were badly off, or lent them typewriters. He recognized that many were shiftless and took advantage of him, that others lived from drink to drink, while others were really struggling and devoting themselves to artistic or literary pursuits. This group drifted in and out, but some members stayed on for years. The type and its habits remained constant from the earliest days of the Village until 1930, though the proportion whose artistic pretensions were real appeared to have dropped, and the homosexual types became somewhat more prominent.[47]

What was important about these face to face groups living together was their willingness to accept almost all who wanted to share in the bohemian life-style. This inclusiveness was enhanced by the very high mobility associated with these youths and by the prescription, passed

---

*In my own research on bohemians in Chicago during the late 1940s and early 1950s, I found that several of the eighteen youths living in the particular house I studied had responded to an advertisement in the newspaper.

on from Murger, that Bohemia should be a temporary resting place and by age thirty the life-style should be abandoned.

The pattern of physical mobility and provision of lodging noted by Ware in the 1920s persisted through the 1930s, when destitution was real rather than pretended, and it became an important part of the bohemianism of the 1950s and 1960s. The "crash pad" was only another version of the communal thrust that had characterized Murger's era in France.

But unlike the boehmians of France, the Americans developed a pattern more in tune with the times. Not only were there those who made a full-time commitment, for the duration of their typically short stay in Bohemia, but there were the part-time adherents as well. Called by Ware the "pseudo-bohemians," these became the weekenders of the post–World War II period; they included, as well, the "teenyboppers" of the 1960s.[48]

Under the cover of literary and other aesthetic interests, the part-time refugees from what was to them a constricting, conventional life-style made excursions on weekends and midweek evenings to the Bohemias of New York, Chicago, Boston, and San Francisco, to mention only the best-known centers. The loci of poetry readings, lectures, discussions, and art shows were sometimes the unambiguously commercial restaurants and bars of Bohemia, or they might be a studio that sought voluntary contributions from those who entered. Under the guise of aesthetic pretensions, the adventuresome, the lonely, and the naively romantic aspirants to inclusion among the community of urban artists congregated. Both verse and sexuality were loose and free, and it is probable that the latter represented a stronger motive than the former for engagement with those who pursued the joyous and abandoned life of the part-time bohemian. The old norms were being strained by excessive changes in society and the economy, and individualism was now a publicly rationalized, legitimate posture even if it was only practiced on weekends. Everybody under age thirty was welcomed, and sometimes even those who were older might be included. All that was required was willingness to share the pretense that art was everything, that materialism was not only nothing but that it was a threat to the pursuit of genuine human values. Under the conditions of rapid social change, the affluence of the post–World War I years, and the destitution of the Depression there was what Durkheim described as a concomitant of the anomic phenomenon: "a search for the bizarre and novel."[49] The search required little effort, for the pattern of bohemianism was readily available, and the cadres of the full-time swelled to include the sojourners.

By the advent of World War II artistic activities had become further institutionalized. Foundations that had emerged in the 1930s—including, for example, the Ford Foundation—were now supporting artists, some of whom had been discovered by the federal artists' and writers' projects. To a greater extent than at any other time in American history youth became integrated into a vast organization for waging war. Bohemia, as in the period associated with World War I, was again denuded of youth. And it was not until after the war that reconstruction occurred.

BOHEMIANISM AFTER WORLD WAR II.   The dislocations that impacted on American society following World War I were repeated in the late 1940s. The sudden return of some ten to fifteen million men and women, and the contraction of certain kinds of industry and expansion of other kinds of activities, contributed to the existence of a massive surplus population. With increasingly rational awareness of the potential societal problems that could emerge under these conditions, political leaders forged the GI Bill. Diverse educational organizations would be created and expanded to absorb the ex-GIs. Employers would be pressed and subsidized to "hire the vet." The abeyance process was now, perhaps more than ever before, necessary to soften the impact of these massive numbers on society and to extend over time the process of reintegrating the now-surplus personnel into occupational and kinship structures.

Schools and colleges of all kinds emerged and expanded, ranging from technical training institutions to those providing a traditional academic program, and also including music and art schools. GI benefits were liberally applied for tuition and personal support, thus allowing not only for instrumental and academic education but for programs that enhanced efforts to pursue artistic studies. And many of the ex-servicemen selected the latter, seizing an opportunity that was unlikely to occur under ordinary circumstances. The cadres of all kinds of students expanded, and among them were included those who might now aspire to artistic success. With artistic aspirations extant in a greater portion of the student population than ever before, it was not surprising that the numbers of those who took on the bohemian life-style increased. Bohemianism during the postwar period proliferated through the urban areas of the United States, first in its relatively traditional form, at least manifestly associated with the arts, and later in a form that was more independent of aesthetic creativity or pretension.

In Chicago, to use one notable example, bohemians concentrated in lodging houses all over the city rather than in the locus of the earlier bohemians, the Near North Side. For the area adjacent to the Water Tower had become, like Greenwich Village, commercialized and too costly for those of limited means and others who preferred voluntary poverty to the bourgeois life. Reminiscent of the houses described above by Caroline Ware, these tended to be like boardinghouses that catered to aspiring artists and to the sycophantic pretenders who were ever-present.*

But the many small groups spread about the city were not segregated from one another, not autonomous, and not without allies in their symbolic battle against the bourgeoisie. At a community art center in one part of the city, the South Side, and a commercial setting downtown (which on Saturday nights could be transformed into a large salon featuring African dance, avant-garde jazz, poetry readings, and similar activites), the representatives of la vie bohème congregated, communicated, and became integrated into a larger body. And though the walkers in the streets of downtown Chicago might appear quiet and restrained, those upstairs at what was called "The Gaffers," overlooking the Chicago River, were happy and boisterous, Murgerian. Some were bedecked in bizarre costumes, and others, though identified as bohemians and residents of the houses described above, dressed in expensive evening clothes or in the uniform of those in voluntary poverty: old clothes and blue jeans. To the observer, the bohemianism of Murger's era had surely been resurrected. To the prophet, this was the thin facade of a pattern that would soon give way to a different form—a form that would nevertheless perform the same function. The bohemians would become the "beats," who would in turn give way to the "hippies."

I refer again to the abeyance and control functions to which bohemianism as a pattern has, from time to time, contributed. The surplus populations of the late 1940s and early 1950s were made up of (1) those ex-GIs who were continuing on in school or who, for diverse other motives, had not yet become integrated into the existing social structure and (2) more youthful cadres who were for the most part unattached to kin and peers other than the bohemians. Of those I observed in Chicago, many were from the small towns and cities of the Midwest. And their engagement with la vie bohème was temporary and somewhat fortuitous.

Some of these youth were also students, although not on the GI Bill, and others were merely finding a resting place on the way station to a career, although they were unlikely to admit that the goals of the straight world had any meaning for them. Still others might be called contemporary "remissions men" and women, sent away to seemingly far-off places—modern counterparts to the British son who was shipped out to the colonies and provided with a stipend so long as he remained out of parental sight. Among these were some homosexuals whose be-

---

*These statements are based on the observations referred to earlier. Included in these studies was participant observation among a group of eighteen residents of one of these houses and observation of the activities of associations of groups from the Chicago area. The latter were carried out in large settings allowing for the forging and reinforcement of a large subterranean community.

havior must have been perceived by the folks back home as a threat to the family's status.

The rooming houses, both communal and individual, helped keep them in place, off the streets, and, if only modestly, under surveillance and control. The bohemian life provided some degree of status and a feeling of being in a community. But because these groups were relatively deviant, they required rationalizations for their behavior and some degree of adherence to the ideologically based prescriptions that provided them with a rasion d'être. The Murgerian code of anti-materialism and anti-philistinism provided the anti-norms to which all were expected to adhere. Though strong commitment to the group and weak commitment to particular members was expected and adhered to, the tie between the member and the group was of relatively short duration. Bohemians over age thirty were rare, and of these there were at least some who seemingly did not fit into the larger society. Others were indeed aspiring artists, but those who were most adherent to the bohemian pattern seemed most equivocal about their commitment to creative activity.

Sexual behavior, as in the earlier days of bohemianism in the United States, was relatively free. But adherence to the group's expectations involved avoidance of exclusive sexual access to a particular partner. As Coser suggested in *Greedy Institutions*, commitment to a particular group member might intrude on and weaken one's commitment to the group itself. This was illustrated time and time again when I observed that visitors to the group I studied in Chicago were allowed access to another's usual sexual partner without competition, and seemingly without jealousy.

This principle is illustrated also in an observation made by Laurence Veysey in a study of 1960s communal groups.[50]

On one occasion an authoritarian leader of a rural New Mexico commune, ever watchful over group discipline, pressed one of the females into a public sexual act to which she submitted. His motive? She had been developing too strong and too exclusive an attachment to one of the other male members. The drama was played out to symbolize commitment only to the commune at large and not to particular people.

That this principle became one of the cornerstones of modern bohemianism should not come as a surprise. Possessiveness and uniqueness are, after all, associated with the bourgeois life and are therefore taboo. The corollary paradox that artistic activity in the West has in recent times, at least, been directed to the uniqueness of one's creative acts is interesting in this context. For the idea of *Gleichheit*, or commonness of production, the extreme opposite of the bourgeois thrust toward uniqueness, is best exemplified in what is called "socialist realism." The bohemians in America, particularly those following the Murgerian prescriptions, seem to have fallen short in their anti-bourgeois communal thrust, particularly in the sphere of the arts.

But as something to do while one decided where and how to become integrated into the larger society bohemian activity functioned as it did during Murger's time. Verbally decrying careers in the straight world, and enjoying sexual latitude and romantic attachment to what appeared to be aesthetic activities, the surplus youth of the post–World War II decade simultaneously remained out of competition for a relatively limited number of status vacancies and under the controls associated with deviant-group membership. For, it is well to keep in mind, discipline is an important characteristic of deviant groups, as Veysey, for example, has shown.[51]

Discipline is, however, simultaneously a source of control and a precipitant of group dissolution, and the strain between these two attributes is one of the factors that enhances mobility between bohemian groups. The middle-class youth who flee to Bohemia are, in part, motivated by a desire to avoid regimentation, but attempting to survive as a group in a hostile world requires solidarity and boundary maintenance. Given the ephemeral nature of group attachment and the absence of early socialization into the norms and social roles associated with bohemianism, external means become the primary source of group cohesion. Common verbalized antagonism toward the bourgeois world becomes a major vehicle in this case. And, because members are for the most part temporary exiles from a life-style into which they have been socialized, they must make an extra effort to avoid behaviors that might reflect the norms and values of "the straights." Bohemians have always been in a small minority, deviants in the midst of a society in relation to which they are ambiguously tied. And this ambiguity requires an ever-watchful eye over one's own and others' behavior lest it backslide into conventional paths. So bohemianism provided a temporary resting place and an opportunity for middle-class youth to sow their wild oats before joining the competitive world of conventional aspirations, kin obligations, and the diverse accoutrements of life in the now-proliferating suburbs.

By the early 1950s the older bohemian forms were beginning to change. A joining of the bohemian life-style with the now-diffusing jazz culture and the language that characterized the subgroups of musicians provided the style which became known as "beat." The beatniks, led by Jack Kerouac and Allen Ginsberg, emerged on the scene in San Francisco as a parallel form of bohemianism—a curious phenomenon in the view of the Village and the Near North Side bohemians. Through the 1950s they expanded slowly, developing a communal life-style on the beaches and in rural areas and a distinctive type of literature.[52] The Beat Generation was the disillusioned generation. The communal life-style now, for apparently the first time in the history of bohemianism, included the widespread use of drugs, one of the attributes of the life-style of the jazz musician. But drug use served not only as a means of dealing with the apparent disillusionment of the Beat Generation. Sociologically it functioned as a source of group integration, since it was experienced not in solitude but in common, reminiscent of the usages found among some of the North American Indians. And it served also as a symbolic means for distinguishing between the world of the "squares," or "straights," and those who were soon to be referred to as "hip." The "squares" were distinguished by their usage of alcohol in more and more exotic, mixed-drink, forms.[53]

The life-style of the beats was less cheerful than that of the Murgerians, due, probably, to the combined soporific effects of drugs and a burdensome outlook on the mordant aspects of life in the larger society and world.[54] These were the first bohemians to face the truly great transformations that had occurred in Western societies and the attendant outcomes of bureaucratic impersonality and mass murder. On the whole, beat humor was eclipsed by the rising tide of alienation rhetoric, which received an extra boost from the square intellectuals both inside and outside academia. Civil rights, Nixon, and disaffiliation from American society became issues that made it extremely difficult to concern oneself with humor, except in the form of satire or sarcasm. The solution was to "drop out" of the square world, to rebuild a society on the basis of love and egalitarianism. The vehicle was to be the communal settlement, including the "crash pad," which could provide for the itinerant youths.

By the 1960s, when the youth population in the United States swelled, during a lag in the expansion of status vacancies in colleges and in the occupational structures, the beats had become transformed into "hippies." Many thousands of youths now took to the road, not unlike the wanderers of medieval Europe. And though the vast majority of them later became reintegrated into the straight world, some remained and still remain today in communal settlements, both rural and urban.

The hippies were different from the beats in important ways. The Kerouacs, Ginsbergs, and Ferlinghettis who were now idolized by the younger bohemians, the hippies, had demonstrated intellectual and literary inclinations. Unlike the beats, the hippies contributed finally to the complete segregation of art from bohemianism. The "flower children" were for the most part anti-intellectual and anti-artistic.

The use of drugs, which in the beginning simulated the Indian style and involved the sharing of a largely social experience, became more and more directed to what was called a "cosmic" experience. Though drugs continued to be taken in groups, the inner experience was directed to a mental fusion with nature rather than with one's fellows. The shift from marijuana to the use of LSD and other laboratory-created drugs was associated with a shrinkage in group size. Instead of passing around a "joint" among his or her "tribe," the drug user increasingly participated in two- and three-person groups.

But the most significant change, from my perspective, is the dramatic divergence from the earlier bohemian forms. By ignoring art, the umbrella that allowed for greater tolerance of life-style, the inclusion of some of the square segments of society in the bohemians' activities became more difficult. The weekend visitors to Bohemia were now either out-and-out tourists or the very young. For the duration of their brief movement the hippies were in all-out war against the rest of American society.

The pattern of voluntary poverty that had surfaced during the rise of Christianity was now resurrected. And the costumes that became de rigueur were reminiscent of the ones worn by the early Christians and others who pursued the *via apostolica* in medieval Europe.

As to the nature of the communal group, Lewis Yablonsky's description of the small groups that characterized the hippies lends itself to the perspective being developed here. Using the provocative but largely ignored concept of "near-group," which he had formulated some years before in a study of gangs in New York City,[55] Yablonsky contrasted hippie groups to "true groups." The near-group was placed, conceptually, midway between an "ill-defined mob of youths" and a cohesive group and had the following properties.

(1) The roles of members were not precisely defined; (2) the organism had limited cohesion and tended to be impermanent; (3) there was a minimum consensus among participants about the entity's norms; (4) the members and participants were constantly shifting; (5) leadership was often vague and confused. *All of these factors are applicable to the smaller group organisms found in the overall hippie movement.*

Another dimension of the near-group concept applicable to the hippie scene is the fact that there are differential levels of commitment to the movement. There are core participants (complete drop-outs), and *marginal* participants (partial drop-outs).

Most true groups have a greater consistency of commitment. Members are clearly committed and belong to the group. In near-groups there is a greater allowable range of involvement or commitment. In the near-groups of the hippie movement core or central participants would include the "high priests" and "novitiates." In a more *marginal* part of the group would be teenyboppers and hippie fellow travelers.

Members of the movement can be recognized or placed at different levels of commitment to the movement and being dropped-out from the society. For example, high priests are totally involved in the movement and totally dropped-out of American society. Novitiates, even though they are living in the movement, are still emotionally working out their status in their "new" and "old" world. Teenyboppers and fellow travelers are physically and emotionally marginal participants living both in and out of the movement.[56]

The remarkable similarity of conceptual scheme to the one I have been developing in this study, including the terminology, reflects the similarity of outlook that characterizes sociological perspectives and also the generality of the phenomena that I have chosen as my focus. Edward Shils's perspective, alluded to in the analysis of the Beguines, similarly uses the concepts "core" and "periphery" with respect to centrality and institutional dominance.

What is similarly interesting is Yablonsky's usage of a religious mode in describing degrees of commitment. He has, in effect, made the connection for me between the differential nature of group commitment *within* groups and the similarities *between* seemingly divergent forms: hippie groups and the religious organizations with which I dealt earlier.

Although I heartily affirm Yablonsky's view of the hippies at an organizational level, I do not readily agree with his perspective on individuals and his explanation for their involvement in the hippie "movement." His view that "personality structure" is an important factor in the drift toward participation in the near-group can help explain some but not all of the motives for participation. If those who have joined the movement have "limited social abilities to perform adequately in the inclusive society,"[57] then what has happened to them since the 1960s? Surely thousands of those who were hippies have been reintegrated into the square world from which they emigrated. This is not to deny that the bohemian umbrella, to which I have often referred, provides a haven for those who do not fit into the conventional society. But it is necessary to explain the fact that the dropout phenomenon is a temporary one for most hippies and other bohemians. If we could trace their movement into another inclusive organization in which role performance was similarly undemanding, we would find the personality explanation more plausible.

Though the colleges and universities do provide an alternative structure within which deviant behavior, to some extent, is tolerable, they, too, are only temporary havens from the demands of middle-class society. And, in addition, certain kinds of discipline are clearly required. Some former hippies did return to school; others took jobs that allowed a greater latitude in behavior than most jobs, including human services in the United States and abroad; and some have remained dropouts. But the majority are now older, adherent participants in the conventional world—more "hip" in their views on life in society, perhaps, but integrated into the middle-class pattern much in the same manner as they would have been had the revolutions of the 1960s not occurred. But what of bohemianism in the 1970s?

Youthful bohemianism declined with the relative expansion of colleges and universities during the 1960s and 1970s; simultaneously there were an increasing number of youths who could be integrated into higher-educational activities. As the abeyance function of formal educational organizations increased, their standards for admission and continued engagement in these activities declined also. Grading became easier, and a degree was consequently less difficult to attain. To be sure, there were ideological elements to justify this greater latitude. But, as I shall emphasize in the following chapter, the system of formal education reached out to these surplus youths and brought them under greater discipline, surveillance, and control.

Since the colleges and universities now lag behind the contraction of the youth population, there are more status vacancies than personnel to fill them. But the imbalance has now shifted to the youths of the 1960s who have followed the path of formal education and are now a new surplus population, overeducated for the limited number of available positions. Society at large shows little concern with them, for they are relatively few as compared with the many uprooted youths of the 1960s, and they seem to pose no threat to the more conventional segments of society.

Bohemianism now resides in the ever-present core group in the Village and Soho (New York City's new residence for artists and pretenders), in San Francisco, and (in lesser numbers) in other places, including rural New England and the southwestern United States. The pattern remains, available for the next invasion of surplus youth, in the possession of the guardians of the Murgerian spirit. The rapprochment between the aesthetic creators and the pretenders is underway. The capacity of the bohemian umbrella to justify deviant behavior assures the persistence of the pattern.*

Abeyance and Bohemianism

The somewhat greater latitude in behavior associated with the itinerant outsiders rests on the functions performed by their patterned activities. Whether these functions were consciously perceived, latent elites and masses have been willing, for the most part, to tolerate deviant behavior among actors, minstrels, troubadours, and other performing artists. While often berating these performers in public, elites have, for example, tolerated their behavior because they were reluctant to risk challenging the masses by depriving them of an important source of entertainment, as well as a safety-valve for letting off steam built up by pressures associated with Church doctrines. Itinerant outsiders have also been tolerated because they seemingly offered no competitive

*I have tended to ignore the economic aspects of the interplay between the core bohemians and the sojourners. It is well to keep in mind that the weekend and evening bohemians, many of them affluent, are an important market for the aspiring artist. The relationship is symbiotic, the bohemian artist providing the social pattern and inclusion of the temporary émigré from the bourgeois life and the sojourner providing the funds for the marginal artist's survival.

threat to the existing social structures that enhanced making a living. And they have been tolerated, too, because if the community could find no use for them, they could easily be encouraged to move on.

In the examples we have chosen, the strictures against wanderers have come from two sources, one normative and the other manipulative. The medieval inclination to expect that there was a proper status and locus for everyone influenced suspicion and concern about all manner of people who were not clearly integrated into a discernible social structure. This impacted on the religious outsiders, including the Waldensians, for example, and the Beguines as well as the minstrels and troubadours. To the extent that it was clear that these people were more or less integrated and under control, they survived to test the winds of fluctuating freedoms. But it was also the case, as Tawney and others[58] have suggested, that more devious motives often lay behind the intolerance shown wanderers. The various regulations against vagabondage seem to have been correlated with shortages of labor, in England at least.

On the whole, the occupants of the statuses associated with the performing arts have enjoyed a greater range of tolerance of their behavior, than others in society. Those who are designated as guardians of the sacred symbols and rites of a society enjoy, in contrast, considerably less personal freedom. Teachers, religious functionaries, and government officials are not only expected to lead exemplary lives but are also expected to be sanctioning agents for society in general.

Bohemianism is a special phenomenon, but its contribution to society is nevertheless general and significant. Growing out of the greater range of tolerance associated with the arts, it became patterned and imitated as a sometimes closely attached concomitant of the life-style of the artist, and, more recently, sometimes detached from that life-style. Thus bohemianism, following Murger's model, has become primarily a Western phenomenon that provides both transitional and abeyance functions for middle-class youth. It is not typically a political phenomenon, although it is often the case that bohemians verbalize relatively radical viewpoints. It has become an alternative to what, in the past, was associated only with the well-to-do, who could travel in style, seeking experiences in foreign places, and sometimes casually pursuing formal education while deciding where to direct their adult lives. Thus it is another temporary holding pattern keeping young people "out of trouble." Like the monastic system and the medieval Beguinages, bohemian patterns provide opportunity for expansion of status vacancies when a surplus of youth emerges and contraction when alternative status vacancies become available. Among the alternative status vacancies are those associated with formal education, which will be discussed in the following chapter. At this point, it is well to review the phenomenon of bohemianism and its predecessors in the context of my analytical scheme.

TEMPORALITY.   The temporal norm associated with Murger's model for true bohemians had clear implications for the organization of these itinerant outsiders. The prescription that the genuine aspirant to creative productivity should consider age thirty as the upper limit of engagement in the bohemian life-style assured weak social organization. Bohemians were and are expected to be on the move and to attach themselves to an abstract, largely symbolic, cadre of youth. When organization does emerge, as in the case of the urban or rural commune, it is either excessively tight or, more typically, excessively loose. Either one gives up one's individuality and autonomy to a leader, as in some contemporary cults,[59] or one maintains a careful guard over his or her rights and prerogatives. The pattern of subordination to a leader is normatively incompatible with the Murgerian creed, but it demonstrates an effort to deal with a serious problem faced by communal bohemian groups: their tendency to dissolve after relatively short duration.* This tendency is a direct result of the extreme sensitivity of bohemians to involvement with organized groups, which might conflict with their intense commitment to democratic, noncoercive social relationships. It is escape from the coercion of the bourgeois life-style, after all, that bohemians claim is a major motive for their involvement in bohemian patterns. Thus, although the pattern has evolved over hundreds of years, any particular group of bohemians experiences a relatively short life. This is reflected in the extreme rarity of second-generation bohemians. Bohemians do not seem to beget more of their own kind.

In sum, bohemian organizations are relatively low on the temporality scale. When there is a surplus of youth, particularly middle-class youth, the pattern is available to justify nonadherence to normative expectations in the conventional world, in which, more often than not, there is a shortage of status vacancies and concomitant opportunities for societal integration. In marked contrast to the monk, for example, the bohemian's engagement with other itinerant outsiders is relatively brief. *La vie bohème* maintains its attractiveness for only a moment *in the life course* of the middle-class adherent.

COMMITMENT.   Since bohemianism is perceived by its adherents to involve only temporary relationships, commitment to the associated communal groups is relatively weak. The expectation that physical mobility

---

*Since this writing Benajmin Zablocki's *Alienation and Charisma* (New York: Free Press, 1981) has appeared. This extremely well-done and extensive work provides systematic data on some of the issues raised here. A number of communal groups which are relatively longer-lived are treated in that study. My comments are limited, of course, to *bohemian* communes while his study deals with a broader spectrum.

will be frequent similarly weakens commitment to particular groups. The bohemian is the sojourner par excellence, in trite parlance, the "rolling stone that gathers no moss." With the exception of a relatively small group of intensively committed artists who participate in a relatively free life-style, the bohemian is a pretender whose commitment is limited and of short duration. After experimenting with behaviors that are, to the conventional youth, exotic, the bohemian is relatively smoothly reintegrated into straight American society.

Because of a tendency toward undercommitment to the bohemian life-style on the part of youths who assume this role, it functions well as an abeyance structure. The cadres expand and contract with relative ease as alternative status vacancies become available. A major alternative dating from the 1960s has been the system of formal education, but some ex-bohemians who have already completed their education have joined the Peace Corps, have taken jobs working with the underprivileged, and have gone into politics as a means of attempting to influence social change. The vast majority have become indistinguishable from the millions of others in their age cohort who never strayed from the conventional career pattern.[60]

INCLUSIVENESS. Anybody can become a bohemian and almost anyone in the appropriate age category can find a group that will accept him. Though bohemianism is largely a middle-class phenomenon, there are no barriers against those in relatively lower or higher classes. With respect to the lower classes in particular, and the ethnically and socially stigmatized, there is, furthermore, a definitely favorable bias based on a romantic orientation to those whom conventional society has rejected. By tradition and by deed, bohemians have welcomed other youth so long as they verbally espoused criticism of the bourgeoisie and made some pretense at being artistically inclined. That both of these postures reflect pretense rather than reality is demonstrated by the short duration of commitment and the relative ease with which ex-bohemians become reintegrated into the straight world.

DIVISION OF LABOR. Like the monks and Beguines, bohemians tend to be unspecialized in their work. Pursuit of a career, except in the arts, was and is proscribed. Rather than pursue a task that might fit in with the extant system of productive labor, the bohemian attempts to create his own unique and innovative place in society. Since he typically has little or no training in artistic activities, he typically meanders from one art form to another. The bohemian who does in fact commit himself to a more serious pursuit of creative activity soon begins to drop out of the group's more sociable activites and assumes greater solitariness.

The discipline, furthermore, associated with creative artistic effort seems to be in short supply among the more typical bohemians. It is almost a matter of definition that those bohemians who become dedicated, disciplined, and skilled workers pass from the role of bohemian to that of artist.

With respect to the more conventional society in relation to which the part-time bohemian may be integrated, the division of labor is again low. The part-time bohemian, if he is not engaged in full-time career activities in the artistic sphere, tends to seek those jobs that provide little more than subsistence. Thus the typical bohemian who works in the straight world will hold a menial job, preferably one that is associated with the romanticized lower classes and castes. If a job should become linked to a career, the part-time bohemian risks rejection by his fellows.

INSTITUTIONALIZATION.   Bohemianism is low on the institutionalization continuum. Although it has been a clearly articulatable pattern for the past 150 years, it has remained outside of the normatively prescribed organization of Western societies. It is a *tolerable* life-style rather than one to be encouraged. Unlike the monastic and Beguine patterns, it does not benefit from its connection with a dominant institution. It is not a legitimate life-style and it is not manifestly perceived as being necessary to society or serving the public good. In short, bohemianism is a deviant pattern.

But bohemianism illustrates well what is meant by patterned norm evasion. It is nonconforming behavior which is recognized by participants as within the range of tolerable deviance. The degree of stigmatization, in sharp contrast to that associated with the criminal or homosexual, is very low. Bohemians shuttle between the straight and deviant worlds with relative ease.

The committed artist, however, though not perhaps viewed as a participant in the mainstream of life, is nevertheless not thought of as a deviant. Unlike the bohemian, the artist adheres to the work ethic and has some tangible product to legitimate his efforts. Art has, furthermore, become institutionalized in Western socieites. Not only is there private support by patrons, as in the past, but foundations—and, as I will demonstrate below, governments—provide funds and facilities to enhance genuine artistic efforts. And the distinction between what is "genuine" and what is pretense is often tantamount to the distinction between artists and bohemians.

STRATIFICATION.   The stratification pattern among bohemians is similarly weak. Bohemians are ranked by their manifest connections with artistic creativity and by their adherence to the ideals of poverty and anti-materialism. But poverty alone is insufficient for high rank. It is the poverty endured by those who dedicate themselves to artistic creativity which counts. The poor immigrants or the *lumpenproletariat* do not rank

high except in a romantic sense: they symbolize the greed and materialism of the philistines.

Edgar Allen Poe, who never was or thought of himself as a bohemian, was adopted by the nineteenth-century bohemians as a model
because he suffered great deprivation while struggling to produce his
writings. The characters in Murger's novel and Puccini's opera starve,
steal, connive, and suffer tuberculosis all for the sake of art. These are
the prototypes of the high-ranking bohemian.

But it should be kept in mind that since involvement with the bohemian groups is typically short-lived, there is, accordingly, a fluid system
of ranks. By the time one attains recognition, it is often time to move on,
and, more significantly, often time to return to the conventional world.
So there is little to be gained from status attainment among bohemians
and this enhances the abeyance process. With little to encourage strong
and lasting attachments, the bohemian returns with ease to the unfinished business of finding a place for himself in conventional society.

Albert Parry holds that bohemianism began in France because industrialization came more slowly to the French and the need for "bright
young men as managers, engineers, clerks, or entertainers" was less
than in England, America, or Germany.[61] Cesar Grana, writing about
the period following the Revolution of 1830, suggests that it was the
surplus of young, educated aristocrats who provided the personnel for
bohemianism.[62]

Bohemianism required and continues to require suplus youth if it is
to prosper. And these youth do not emerge on the scene simply as a
result of biological factors. They become surplus because status opportunities contract or organizations fail to expand in time to absorb them.
Bohemianism, growing out of the amorphous attitudes of tolerance associated with the surveillants of artistic performers, is especially well
suited to absorb for relatively short periods of time those youth for
whom there are too few places in society.

A pattern that emerged at about the same time in England and the
United States, rather than France, is mandatory formal education. It is to
this structure and process that I now turn.

CHAPTER 5

Compulsory Apprenticeship and Education: The Quintessence of Control

"The London Bridewell (around 1619) had thus two distinct functions to perform. On the one side it was a House of Correction, on the other it was a technical school for young people."

—E. M. Leonard

The bohemian commune as an organized pattern contributing to the abeyance process and social control evolved out of the life-style associated with bohemianism. As a form that absorbed those who joined voluntarily, the commune had much in common with the Beguinages, which encapsulated medieval women. As in the case of the Beguines, the bohemians tended for the most part to subordinate themselves to control and surveillance by their peers. Under some conditions, it will be recalled, the Beguines did subjugate themselves to external authorities, but the ambiguity of their status within the Church allowed them greater ranges of toleration than the members of orders or monasteries.

Another organization that contributes to the abeyance and control process is the school. This form, growing out of compulsory apprenticeship, is especially important because it represents the first major effort to use statutes to legitimate the incarceration of formally nondeviant persons in society. Participation in supervised activities for a substantial portion of the life of the child and youth is thus made legitimate and mandatory. Unlike the situation in earlier centuries, where and under what conditions young people outside of the family are placed is not left to chance. The State now intervenes to assign and assert control, for specified periods of time, over its youth. How has this pattern come about and in what ways does it contribute to the abeyance and social-control process? To understand these developments we must first glean some understanding of the attitudes held toward vagrants and others who were marginal to societies in the past, as well as the behavioral reactions to those people who were not "in place."

Vagrancy and Idleness

The ubiquitous and intense concern with vagrancy, whatever the motives of those who sought to control it, reflected on many segments of the unattached in society. There was interest in the lack of societal place not only for troubadours, minstrels, actors, and other performers, but for anyone who might either engage in idleness or request alms by begging or placing himself at the mercy of the Church or the community at large. The fear of the vagrant, or "the tramp," as Tawney was earlier quoted as describing him, was thus moral, political, and economic.[1]

Morally, idleness was anything other than virtuous. Both the Old and the New Testaments provided ample guidance on the virtues of hard work and the benefits to be derived from it. The idea that work is virtuous, as an end in itself, was hardly discovered by John Calvin, to whom social scientists pay homage as the purveyor of the central values associated with the Protestant Ethic.[2]

Politically the unattached were recognized as a potential tinderbox, vulnerable to unrest and perhaps available to participate in revolutions against those who reigned. General disorder and rebellion was commonplace in England and on the Continent throughout the Middle Ages. Again, it will be recalled from the quotation above, Tawney held that the statutes directed toward control of vagrants were not only economically motivated, they were "police actions."

But though social control as an end in itself was a major motive for onslaughts against those who were unattached, it is well to recall that economic factors also played an important role in this process. Particularly after the Black Death (1347–1350) attacked the populations of England and Europe, the shortage of certain kinds of labor threatened disaster for the economies of Western societies. Keeping workers on the land or at their trades at home became difficult because opportunities expanded elsewhere. It was, at times, a seller's market, and what was being sold was labor. The anti-vagrancy laws were used to curb mobility by discouraging those who would leave home for more fertile pastures and by coercing those who had left to return to their homes and, presumably, prior obligations.

The intrusion by statute of the authorities into the affairs of the ordinary citizen, thus formally limiting his freedom, represented the beginning of intentional, formal, structured control of the potentially dissident. At the level of the emerging nation-state the authorities were now codifying what had been practice in and between communities for some time earlier, particularly in England.[3] Among the structured activities that the state now imposed was work in houses of correction and systems of compulsory apprenticeship and education.

Compulsory Apprenticeship

Formal apprenticeship, at least in London, was by 1300 a well-established pattern. An early reference, dated 1261, "fixes a term of service at seven years . . . forbidding one master to entice away another's apprentice from him."[4] By 1450 apprenticeship was a feature of most English guilds and towns.[5] By 1562, with passage of the Statute of Artificers, what had been a largely local, voluntary system resting on guild authority now became a national, compulsory system formally administered by the Crown and its subordinates. All who wished to engage in a trade or craft were now required to serve an apprenticeship. Apprenticeship had become "transformed into a national institution."[6] Although it is clear that this statute was simultaneously intended to deal with vagrancy, poverty, and internal control by the masters of guild and trade affairs, it is also clear that it was a social-control and abeyance device.[7] And it is clear, too, as Davies notes, that the institutionalization of compulsory apprenticeship in the sixteenth century had its counterpart in the institutionalization of compulsory formal education in nineteenth-century England and, I should add, the United States.[8] Moreover, though it is clearly the 1652 act that was central to the establishment of the compulsory apprenticeship system, understanding its role as an abeyance and control pattern and as a precursor to compulsory education requires linking the act to the Poor Law of 1601, which attempted to deal with other aspects of unattached populations.

Apprenticeship had been a long-established pattern by the time the Statute of Artificers was passed. As I suggested above, local communities had been engaged in a voluntary, informal (though legally supported) system from about the thirteenth century onward. Advantages accrued to the community, parents, and masters when a child was bound, and it was these gains that enhanced the diffusion of the pattern. For the community, a potentially idle set of hands could be put to what was recognized as good use. And an apprentice was on the way to becoming a self-supporting member of the community rather than a pauper. As the responsibility for paupers shifted from the monasteries to the secular community, responsibility for the poor became a matter of intense concern.

For the parents, particularly those whose own resources were limited or those who could provide only meager opportunities for their offspring in family enterprises, apprenticeship meant that one or more of their own would be more likely to find security and status in a world of fluctuating status and economy.

The security and status that was enhanced by bondage to a master reflected the advantages accruing to both master in particular and guild in general. Control of quality of work was central to control of the quality and reputation associated with the produce that guild members alone created and placed on the market. More important, perhaps, was control over the numbers of persons who could engage in producing or marketing a product. Control of numbers of status vacancies and the flow of personnel into them was, so long as the system of compulsory apprenticeship lasted, one sure way to hold down competition and control the flow and price of goods and services.

Because of these advantages the pattern spread in both England and on the Continent. By 1562 the number of specialized statutes dealing with aspects of employment in England had accumulated into a motley mixture of ineffectual, useless, and useful directives. It was at this point that the Statute of Artificers was codified and passed.[9] Dunlop, coupling the Statute of Artificers with the 1601 Poor Law, recognizes the broader social intentions associated with these acts.

> These Acts comprise within themselves the Elizabethan remedies for the social and economic troubles of the time, the decay of towns, the social unrest, with which went the instability of the rural population, the increase of pauperism and unemployment, and the diminution, actual or feared, of industrial skill. Apprenticeship, which is dealt with in both Acts, was one of the means they employed to remedy these evils.[10]

From the perspective of the Crown an important element in these acts, reflecting concerns beyond pauperism and unemployment, was emphasis on a principle that is reminiscent of monasticism. Although *stabilitas loci* was earlier associated primarily with those who entered monasteries, resonating also to the lay population in medieval society, the decline of Church authority and the rise of the secular state did not completely erase this principle from the lexicon of societal constraints. Whether "it was firmly believed that the duty of the agricultural laborer both to God and to the nation was to remain on the soil and so keep up the strength of the military class," as Dunlop holds, or whether the motives were more rational than normative, the concern with holding a person in place, particularly the one "in which he actually found himself," was genuine.[11] In addition to what may have been a lingering normative motive for people remaining in place there was awareness that wealth required social stability, "whereas a population in a state of ebb and flow was regarded as productive of pauperism and unemployment."[12]

Though it is well to keep in mind that there were diverse motives underlying the acts establishing apprenticeship as a recognized national institution, the concern with idleness was nevertheless of great importance. That the guilds recognized their broader role as a social-control and antipoverty institution is reflected in the following rule promulgated by the weavers of Bristol in 1562.

> Item that for-as-much the poverty within the City daily increaseth and the number great of idle young boys within the City which wander and range abroad and about the City for want of Masters, and are not placed into service to some trade or occupation whereby to get their living and keep them out of idleness. It is therefore now provided and established that no Weaver or Craftholder of the Company shall from henceforth take any apprenticer into his service but such as are born within the City and liberties thereof.[13]

In the event that my earlier reference to the voluntary aspects of apprenticeship prior to 1562 misled the reader, it is well to keep in mind that the Crown, and probably lesser authorities as well, were inclined to bind youths into apprenticeship regardless of their personal desires. This was typically in response to the dual concern with vagrancy and poverty. Both Henry VIII and Edward VI, had prior to the 1562 apprenticeship act, directed that vagrant children between the ages of five and fourteen were to be bound apprentice. A later policy held that sons of vagrants might be apprenticed until twenty-four, and daughters until twenty. Punishment for rebellion was slavery.[14] The 1562 act gave to lesser officials—justices of the peace and officers of the towns—power to bind the unemployed. The 1601 act added the authority to bind children of paupers and vagrants as well as children in families judged to be unable to support their offspring.

These efforts to restrict the freedom of youth in general, and more particularly, workers' freedom to move about at will, are significant primarily because, as far as I know, they represent the first major statutory intrusion of a national state on the personal rights of the citizen.

Strangers have always been objects of suspicion and have been coaxed to move on. The same is true for paupers. Lepers and others who seemingly possessed contagious diseases have also been moved along. For a long time, inducements to leave and outright attacks on the undesirable were the result of routine, spontaneous actions on the part of insiders, who assumed, presumably without serious reflection, the role of informal sanctioning agents. The acts of 1562 and 1601 now shifted the responsibility to the more formal organs of the community, now backed up by whatever might the nation-state possessed. Outright manipulation of the potentially dissident masses was now a legitimated activity.

That deprivation of a youth's opportunity to select idleness, pauperism, or perhaps even a type of occupational pursuit was not simply accepted by the masses is clear. Denial of freedom must have been perceived as denial of one's God-given rights long before the modern age. Both the Old and New Testaments provided bases for anti-bondage attitudes in the story of the Israelite exodus from Egypt and a great many other biblical incidents. The system of apprenticeship, which bound the apprentice for seven years, required a coercive arm legitimated by statute.

Because the statutes were often violated there emerged a new role, that of the professional informer and prosecutor; like some of the statutes predating the 1562 act, this role had already come into existence prior to the involvement of the Crown into what had been relatively localized affairs. The professional informer and prosecutor made his living from portions of the fines imposed on the violators of the apprenticeship laws, and, no doubt, from bribes and out-of-court settlements.[15]

But it is essential to keep in mind that enforcement of the apprenticeship rules, though cloaked by reference to the immorality of idleness, vagrancy, and nonadherence to a morally binding agreement to remain in bondage for seven years, was based on economic motives as well. Whereas the professional informer gained from the ready availability of deviants, a condition that certainly enhanced his economic posture, the nonprofessional informer saw the nonadherents as a threat to the very foundations of his economic well-being. The latter, usually engaged in business himself, viewed the unapprenticed as business competitors. Thus the informer whose livelihood was derived from business was more likely, according to Davies, to push for prosecution of violators.[16] The professional informer, in short, gained most from the process of pursuing and exposing the violator, while the nonprofessional informer tended to gain more from the ends of the process, the extrusion of illegitimate competitors from the business life of the community.

The case of apprenticeship is, thus, an example of the interplay between the diverse motives that underlay efforts to control surplus populations. The moral concern with idleness and the more social concern with control of the sources of livelihood were intertwined. That they represent alternatives to the type of social control exercised by monasticism, the Beguinages, and organized bohemianism is clear. But there is a critical difference between compulsory apprenticeship and also compulsory education as opposed to the patterns with which I dealt earlier. Compulsory apprenticeship was formal, legally sanctioned, and officially enforced. Control of potential dissidence was in the hands of the nation-state, and this pattern was the harbinger of later forms of social control, particularly compulsory education.

Beggars and Pauperism

The apprenticeship system absorbed thousands of young men and women, training and keeping them under watchful eyes for some five or six centuries. The formal system, initiated by the Statute of Artificers in 1562, came to an end in 1813. But repeal of the 1562 act, although it removed the legal necessity to serve in bondage in order to pursue a given occupation, did not eliminate the system altogether. The various functions that apprenticeship performed, as described above, still required some pattern for their fulfillment. And until alternatives emerged or dramatic changes in society occurred to provide for the simultaneous training of youth and prevention of pauperism, on the one hand, and control of vagrants and potential dissidence, on the other, some form of occupational integration was necessary.

With respect to the demise of compulsory apprenticeship, however, it is likely that the system was the bearer of its own seeds of destruction. The emergence of industrialization and widespread adoption of the factory system was clearly a factor contributing to the shrinking value of formal apprenticeship. So, too, was the rise of the laissez-faire orientation toward commerce and industry. But it was probably the pattern of exclusiveness that most directly influenced the dissolution of the legally mandated system. In addition to the preference shown for the offspring of those who were already masters or on their way to full membership in the guilds, there was already, by the sixteenth century, a policy that attempted to reserve apprenticeship places to freemen and the sons of freemen.[17] Other obstacles, including heavy admissions fees, contributed to limiting the number of places and the count of how many could be absorbed. Thus, among other factors, the system's unwillingness to absorb large numbers of youth—particularly since there were few public schools and few other abeyance patterns—cost the support of communities and the larger society that it had earlier enjoyed. The principle of exclusiveness limited the capacity of the guilds to control potential vagrants and dissidents and to prevent pauperism. But other status vacancies were created as a result of the increasing intrusion of the State into these affairs.

The topic of concern about beggars was dealt with in Chapter 1. Tawney, it wll be recalled, noted that in England this concern was responded to by anti-vagrancy activities at both the local and national level. In order to fill the unusually large number of status vacancies resulting from the Black Death, Parliament in 1388 passed regulations restricting the movement of both beggars and laborers. These were part of the numerous efforts, referred to in Chapter 4, to control wanderers of all kinds. But once the population had recovered from the depletion associated with the Black Death, the surplus shifted from too many status vacancies to an excess of personnel. By the sixteenth century, about the same time that apprenticeship was becoming mandatory, beggars became a more serious problem. The surplus resulted from a number of factors, some of them impacting on other Western societies as well, and these factors explain the existence of vagrants and others who remained marginal to conventional society.

Both in England and on the Continent the sixteenth century was a time of rapid transition, eliminating some of the older occupations.

> The feudal society of the Middle Ages was giving place to the modern industrial and commercial community. War, public and private, and service with great nobles had formerly occupied large members of the male population. But the fifteenth century had witnessed the growth of central authorities strong enough to preserve order and to control the power of the great lords. . . . Order had given place to disorder, lawsuits had succeeded private wars. The power of the nobles was no longer maintained by force; they had no longer the need of many followers to fight their battles.[18]

This was the period I described earlier, quoting Hale, when soldiers traversed the continent seeking wars to occupy them. And the number of ex-soldiers could not have been small. Sir Thomas More in *Utopia*, for example, takes note of the problems in France resulting from professional soldiers no longer being occupied. He notes also that they often became thieves or starved.[19] Thus, in terms of my theoretical perspective, contraction of an important source of status vacancies was a factor in the creation of the sixteenth-century surplus population.

A second factor was the insecurity associated with the increase of manufacturing. Although in the long run greater employment opportunities became available, in the short run a contraction of jobs occurred. The preindustrial situation of the craftsman producing for a limited but stable market varied little as compared with the sixteenth-century expansion of marketing and marketing centers. "In bad times the craftsman might get a little less work, but he was not thrown utterly out of employment."[20] Fluctuations in demand, and now employment, became enmeshed with occurrences that were external not only to the craftsman's local setting but to conditions within the nation as well. As manufacture for export became more widespread, intranational and extranational factors increasingly influenced the size of the surplus population.

The rise of prices for the necessities of life, resulting from an "influx of silver from the New World," was a third factor contributing to the increase in vagrants both in England and on the Continent.[21] The poor were, of course, most directly affected.

And, fourth, a contraction of positions for agricultural laborers and small yeomen helped create the large mass of vagrants in sixteenth-century England. Since England was now the great wool-producing country of the Western world, it became more profitable to breed sheep than to plow the land. Those who cultivated the soil now became increasingly superfluous at a time when alternative opportunities, i.e., status vacancies, were scant.

The number of vagrants who begged and stole—and, more important, I would hold—swelled the ranks of potential dissidents and revolutionaries increased in the sixteenth century. In Tawney's terms they constituted a "tinder box" for rebellion. To this situation the Crown responded with the anti-vagrancy acts, described by Tawney as a "police action." But a more effective and direct device for the control of the unattached began to take form at this time, and it, too, accepted the mandate to provide training while supervising formerly unattached youth.

The dissolution of the monasteries, described in part in Chapter 2, resulted not only in creating a contraction of positions that could incorporate the potentially dissident but in dissolving a vehicle for the care of the poor. Distribution of poor relief was now transferred from the monks and nuns to a more amorphous body, the community and society at large. Public annoyance with the increasingly likely prospect of beggars accosting them in the streets and pursuing them to their doors lent support to the emergence of a new institution, more than a hospital and only a trifle less than a prison: the workhouse. And it was this new institution, best exemplified by Bridewell in England, that became the model for what we Americans now call the public school. Here emerged compulsory education in a structured setting, with a legally mandated length of engagement based not on the tasks to be mastered but on the age of those required to participate.

Bridewell was organized to incorporate vagrants and untrained youths rather than the unemployed who had worked and who continued to seek work. It was an institution chartered to provide relief for the poor and training for the young, but the latent motive was to repress beggars and punish idlers. It is thus interesting to realize that the first public organizations for the training and education of youth were, in fact, prisons.

Like the hospitals, to which those vagrants who were genuinely ill were directed, Bridewell and the institutions modeled after it performed public rather than private functions. All were supported by public funds, since their collective raison d'être was now service to the community rather than to a more limited sector. And the first service was repression of vagrants, in general, and beggars, more particularly.

Thus under the guise of relief of the poor, which was undoubtedly a manifestation of moral mandates as well, the authorities created still another device, in hand with apprenticeship, to hold personnel in place. And this time it was in the form of a custodial organization directed simultaneously to social control and education of the young. The institution of Bridewell was the ultimate step in the coercion of the least powerful, and it reinforced efforts to control, by law, individual freedom. That the systems of poor relief played a role in preventing more serious social disorders than those experienced by the British was noted, among others, by a visiting Frenchwomen, Louise Michelle, who said of the Bridewell that "a like system in France would have prevented the French Revolution."[22] Although apprenticeship, and other patterns used by elites to manipulate the unattached, surplus mass were major factors in the prevention of disorder it was the tendency to incarcerate "the most difficult class of vagrants" in total institutions which most effectively accomplished that goal.[23]

The Rise of Compulsory Education

By the time the Bridewells became institutionalized, public training and education of the young in England was becoming increasingly popular. But the emergence of a system of universal public education, recognizable in today's terms, did not occur in England until the nineteenth century. And it was no accident that the rise of compulsory education occurred relatively soon after the formal demise of compulsory apprenticeship in 1813.

As noted above, the decline of the apprenticeship system as it was constituted during the medieval, Elizabethan, and Tudor periods in England was a result of a number of factors. But while it lasted, and in spite of the many violations of the 1562 statutes, as reflected in the growth of the system of informers and enforcement, a great many youths, both males and females, were kept under control. Through the sixteenth, seventeenth, and eighteenth centuries in England apprenticeship was *the* legitimate pattern for transferring control over the child from the family to the community at large, and, indirectly, to the nation-state. But the growth of commerce and the emergence and expansion of industrialization, and, more particularly, the factory system proved too much for the continued support of apprenticeship.

The laissez-faire ideology, by encouraging the free movement of the laborer, advanced efforts to fill the increasing need for factory workers, especially those without the kinds of training that could become an obstacle to the relatively simple but arduous tasks associated with factory labor. Efforts were now being made by the elites of the nation-state to encourage concentration of populations in factory towns, as exemplified by the later enclosures. Now that children and youths were free to take jobs without training, their freedoms proclaimed by the new ideology, they became an even more valuable commodity. Families did not have to simply give them away to be bound as apprentices; they could now be used as wage earners to support their parents. And this encouraged the growth of larger families.

Young people now became increasingly more valuable, and, simultaneously, independent. As they became more desired by employers than their elders they began to cast off the subordinate status formerly associated with childhood.[24] Thus the status and freedom of young people increased at the same time as they became more numerous in the general population, a potentially dangerous situation for those who feared the specter of an unattached horde of unemployed vagrants. And their fears were not unwarranted.

When a product is overproduced in a market economy, either the price of the product may be expected to decline or it may be stored up as inventory until demand increases, or the surplus may conceivably be destroyed. All these alternatives have been used at one time or another to influence the supply and price of a market product. If the over-produced commodity is a person, however, it is quite a different matter, requiring a more complex response. So it was in nineteenth-century England.

Because children could now be sent into factories, sometimes alone and sometimes as part of a whole family working in the same setting, they became increasingly valuable. The more children, the greater the potential family income. Thus, I repeat, families produced children to meet the demands of the factory. But as the vicissitudes of the international and national market economies impacted on the factories, the demand for workers fluctuated. In addition to market factors, constantly changing technology in the nineteenth century sometimes lowered the demand for workers. The great "industrial" reserve army of the unemployed, as Marx referred to them, was a result, in large part, of those same conditions that contributed to the demise of the apprenticeship system.[25] The surplus populations now increased as a result of an increase in population intended to fill an anticipated increase and sustenance of status vacancies. The surplus resulted as well from a failure of the apprenticeship system to expand and absorb an increasing number of potential trainees. The result was an increase in idleness, vagrancy, and crime.[26] Thus the system of apprenticeship began to lose its capacity to attract youths just as its potential value as an abeyance pattern should have increased. The stage was set for the organization of a new pattern to control the increasing numbers of unintegrated, footloose youths: mandatory education.

Although children may be perceived in economic parlance as a commodity, they could not simply be treated as such in the moral environ-ments of nineteenth-century Western societies. Their increasing eco-nomic value was not the only factor that enhanced the status of the young. The impact of the values emanating from J. J. Rousseau's and John Locke's views on the importance of educating the young, whatever the differences between them, conveyed the idea that the young were both different from their elders and important. Whereas Rousseau em-phasized the advantages of slowing the arrival of maturity, Locke's em-phasis was upon encouraging youth to imitate and engage in conversa-tion with their elders.[27] These notions, singling out youth for attention and concern, enhanced their positions as persons to be treated with dignity rather than as things to be manipulated at will.

The ideals of the French Revolution, impacting on nineteenth-cen-tury England, also contributed to reinforcing a moral context that made it difficult to treat children (and adults, as well) as mere commodities. Men now had "inalienable rights," in the words of the former colonials encased in the Declaration of Independence of the United States. And these "rights" were no less the property of the English at home.

Adolescence, a time of postponed maturity, was invented in the latter part of the eighteenth century. And it is probably no accident that the emergence of the idea and its proliferation throughout Western so-cieties came at a time when there were more children than there had been earlier. Child mortality rates had declined and the numbers of young people who were physically capable of assuming employment increased accordingly. By the latter part of the eighteenth century the demand both for factory laborers and for what we now call white-collar workers increased. The advantages of having more children, suggested earlier, coupled with the lower mortality rates encouraged the growth of population.

But the devices for injecting or holding back personnel from the occupational market—particularly apprenticeship, as noted above—were now incapable of controlling the process. Men could no longer be detained by those who wanted to restrain their movement. Statutes to encourage mobility to places where labor was needed now had to attack the matter in oblique and surreptitious ways. The later Enclosure Acts forced people from the land and into the cities by contracting oppor-tunities in one sphere while advertising the availability of others in another setting.[28] The era of Bridewells and anti-vagrancy statutes was coming to an end.

The idea of adolescence was timely. Here was an abeyance device that could be used to control the flow of personnel into the market. With apprenticeship on the decline and no other alternative holding system in sight, creating a new conception of the person provided the start of a more subtle device for social control. And this idea, probably more than any other, provided legitimation for the emergence of the new system to withhold or infuse society with personnel as status vacancies expanded and contracted.

Schools have existed from before the time of recorded history. Groups of children and youths participated in collective education in Greece and Rome, and among the wandering tribes who together were called Israelites, to select a few of our forebears. During the medieval period group learning was fostered by the monasteries for the Christians and by the sometimes peripatetic and sometimes established rabbinic councils for the Jews.

Education for the common man was extremely rare before modern times, at least in Western societies. The monks and priests, and later the secular teachers representing a given group of relatively private citizens, generally served a very limited, special segment of the population. Though a child might, during the period of ascendence and dominance of the monastic system, be taken in and taught by the monks this was relatively rare. Learning was the responsibility—to the extent that there was such a feeling—of the family or of very special groups in the community.

The lack of consensus on collective education is exemplified in the writings of Rousseau and Locke, mentioned above. Domestic education, directed by parents rather than servants, was Rousseau's ideal. Locke's choice of teacher was the well-educated and well-bred tutor. But the schools, catering primarily to a very select segment of the offspring of well-to-do families, were clearly not an established organ of the community at large.

Establishment of schools that would accommodate children from all social classes and were the responsibility of the community as a whole was a nineteenth-century phenomenon. During the medieval period popular education, i.e., secular and pragmatic learning, was carried on outside of what were designated as schools. The educational system was directed primarily to an intellectual elite, for whom a general education was perceived as being a prerequisite to professional studies. For the theologian, the lawyer, and the physician, emphasis on reading, writing, and arithmetic was judged to be too narrow. But the press of commerce required that some people read and write, and above all deal with numbers. The utilitarian forms of learning were, nevertheless, taught in parish schools as a responsibility of the priesthood. And this schooling, it is important to keep in mind, was supposed to be provided without charge.

Others learned what their families deemed important from private tutors in their own homes, or they might be sent off to serve in another's household, acquiring in the process whatever education their actual or anticipated status required. In all cases, however, there was one guiding principle, according to J. W. Adamson, that was subtle but pervasive: "every type of human capacity calls for cultivation."[29] This principle has clearly had its impact on education in modern Western societies, if only as an ideal toward which societies have striven. This ideal, plus the norm that education should be free to the student and the responsibility of some segment of the community larger than the family, also contributed to our more modern conception of popular education. And it also provided a rationale for encouraging, at first, and requiring, later, that every child spend time in school.

The nineteenth century was a period of industrial expansion, technological advances, and an increasingly large surplus population. The enclosures of the late eighteenth century continued to impact on the market for agricultural labor by shrinking the need for youth. The need for young people and others in factories began to decline, relative to the vast army of excess population created by the circumstances described above. By the middle of the nineteenth century, it was clear to a substantial sector of the elites and the public at large that children needed to be treated better than they were when they worked at their benches in the factories.

Placing children in schools, under the watchful eyes of designated sanctioning agents, i.e., teachers, was destined to become the most effective form of direct social control ever evolved in a formally democratic society. Here was the institutionalized control form par excellence! Children and youths could not only be required to do what was now morally correct—improve their minds and technical skills—but could also be socialized and disciplined in the virtues required by an industrial society. Secularized versions of interpreted religion emphasizing acceptance of a subordinate position in the present in anticipation of rewards in the afterlife; the virtue of diligence; hard work as an end in itself; and regularity of habits—all these could be taught in the context of learning a skill, whether it be intellectual or technical; and to make participation in the system mandatory, according to age, was sure to relieve the pressure of the many on relatively fewer jobs.[30]

Musgrove notes that in England there was a slight decline in the proportion of young people under the age of fifteen "before the 'slight dose of compulsory education' introduced by the Education Act of 1870 and the more effective Education Acts of Sandon and Mundella in 1876 and 1880."[31] And although the number of employed people in England and Wales substantially increased between 1861 and 1871, the number of those employed who were under fifteen years old increased only modestly.

This is not because a greater proportion was attending school. What alarmed investigators in the sixties, and provided powerful arguments in the campaign for compulsory education, was not only the apparent decline in the proportion of children attending school but a decline also in the proportion at work. The consequence was an increasing proportion of young people in the very margin of society, outcast and neglected. . . . Compulsory education was a necessity by the 1870's not because children were at work, but because increasingly they were not.[32]

How were these marginal young people occupied if they were neither at work or school? James McCosh, in an 1867 article quoted by Musgrove, provides a reply to his own question. "They are idling in the streets and wynds; tumbling about in the gutters; selling watches; running errands . . . cared for by no man."[33] With few organized patterns for integrating the large numbers of young people, regardless of their decreased proportion in the total population, England was again faced with a surplus population problem. But this time the surplus was not created to encourage people to assume positions that the elites wanted filled, e.g., factory jobs. This excess of personnel was unanticipated. And although the surplus was unequally distributed, some cities like West Riding still demanding more youthful laborers, a way had to be found to soften the impact of this nineteenth-century version of vagrancy.

But the evolution of compulsory education in England as one means for sustaining social order did not occur without substantial resistance. And this was in no small part due to more general issues associated with mass education, some of them reflecting the most profound differences in conceptions of how societies function. One of these issues is central to this study: the connection between the degree of knowledge and/or ignorance required at the motivational level of behavior for the fulfillment of those activites that must be performed for society's presumed welfare.[34]

Those who promoted the idea of mass education were clearly a minority at the beginning of the nineteenth century, struggling against an entrenched aristocracy and widespread conservatism, both of which were reinforced in reaction to an increasingly self-conscious, emergent working class. England was still a society characterized by an estate system of stratification, loose as it may have become since the seventeenth- and eighteenth-century impact of commerce and industry. The aristocracy, and other relatively high-stratum groups, were not at all willing to risk losing their authority over those lower in the hierarchy. Mass education might, from the point of view of many in those higher strata, encourage the lower classes to reject their subordinate positions; and, of particular interest now that the Establishment saw the advantages of industrialization, education might make the masses unfit for the occupational roles that the economic system required.[35]

Those who opposed mass education "hearkened back to the writings of Bernard Mandeville and Soame Jenyns, who attacked charity schools and argued for the necessity of an ignorant labor force."[36] Those who advocated mass education based their arguments on the sermons of the eighteenth-century Anglican preachers, who struck out, at that earlier time, for charity schools. The ideas of the latter prevailed.

The arguments for mass education both in England and America emphasized collective rather than personal goals. The reduction of poverty and crime and "increased economic productivity" were stressed rather than intellectual growth or personal advancement.[37] "Education for social stability and for the enhancement of the industrial enterprise was the major thrust of the advocate's argument. Mass education was justified by such notables as Malthus, Smith and Bentham "in order to rescue a brutalized working class from vice, overpopulation and antagonism toward the upper classes."[38]

But the opponents of mass education did not give in easily. Postulating a condition of full occupancy at the top of the social structure and a shortage of personnel for the more menial jobs, they railed against the creation of a surplus population of aspirants to high position. A zero-sum situation was envisioned, using modern terms, in which a gain for the newly educated would be at the expense of the already ensconced upper strata. Furthermore, the opponents of reform argued that "mass education would lead to disorder."[39] People who could read would reject what was formerly their God-given place in the scheme of things. Sedition, vice, and religious dissent were the anticipated outcomes of mass literacy.

Ironically the reformers continued to push a conservative line: mass education would increase social stability, not disruption. They eventually won the war against the Tory–High Church coalition on a platform that their opponents prized: "stability, deference and discipline. Education would prevent rebellion by humanizing the workers, whom industrialization had turned into savages . . . education would reduce crime. Prevention was better than punishment and cheaper. *Wherever schools were opened, prisons would be closed.* In addition to the moral training they provided, *the schools' custodial function was important: they would reduce crime and vagrancy simply by getting children off the streets.*"[40]

Thus the arguments raised the latent processes of social control by educational organizations to a manifest level, i.e., a pattern that was recognized and intended by those who were its advocates. The legitimation of the new system was not sought through rhetoric extolling the virtues of personal development and exemplary behavior—or, as was to occur later and especially in America, the success ethic—but through claims that reform was desirable and necessary for the collective good.

Even in the United States, where a separate battle was raging over mass education, and even in the absence of an entrenched hierarchy, advocates stressed that social stability would be the outcome of mass education. Personal development or opportunity to improve one's station in society was not a major concern. The ideology of equality and the rationale for education as a means by which Americans could achieve higher rank and its corollaries, important though it was to become as part of the moral mandate to attend and perform in school, was to take form later in the nineteenth century.

Mass education, and the important appendages making it compulsory in England and America, was a recognized device for controlling potentially dissident youth. With its emergence in the latter part of the nineteenth century it assured American and English societies that those who might become vagrants, beggars, criminals, or competitors for relatively scarce occupations would be under direct surveillance and control. And, by making attendance compulsory, the new system was more effective than the more oblique methods associated with the anti--vagrancy laws. The mandate was now clearly prescriptive, and the custodial process could be subjected to planning, could be expanded or contracted, as societal conditions required.

But unlike the other organized patterns described earlier that performed abeyance functions, formal education in the United States came to be valued both as a means and an end; and, more important, it became *morally* mandatory. Going to school and being in school has, for many decades, been what a child or youth should and must do. And in · the relatively higher classes in American society the mandate has extended to education beyond the public schools. Thus the appropriate place for the youngster is not at work in industry or commerce but in school. And the moral mandate reinforces, and is in turn reinforced by, statutes which require that persons of prescribed ages will participate in those directed and supervised activities which are called educational.

The American Experience

The differences between the English and the American situation are noteworthy. Although in both settings there was concern in varying degrees with a rebellion of the masses, the anti–mass education posture associated with the Tories was only faintly echoed in the United States. And "unlike the English Tories, Conservative Americans generally advocated schooling for social stability."[41] Rebellion was most likely to be, according to the Americans, an outcome of ignorance rather than morally sound education. But the Mandevillian notion that an ignorant mass was necessary in order to perform many of society's most important tasks did prevail in some sectors. Overall, however, according to Kaestle, the Tory view did not summon much force. And with respect to the slaves, the justification for keeping them ignorant was based not on an American version of the Tory position but primarily on "racial grounds."[42]

The anti–mass education theme did not travel well to America. Without a nobility or a High Church establishment there was no effective, organized source of resistance. But there was, in America, a widespread concern with rebellion and sedition and a view that mass education would enhance stability in general and mitigate class conflict more particularly.

The underlying concern was, nevertheless, with unattached and unintegrated youth. The traditional apprenticeship system in the United States, as in England, began to contract during the early nineteenth century, just as the cities began to expand. In addition to the rural migrants, immigrants from Europe now contributed to the vast numbers of new urban dwellers. Compulsory attendance at school was one sure way to organize and indoctrinate these potentially wayward youth, and the ubiquitous rationalizations for mass education enhanced the process. Even before attendance at school became compulsory, a Massachusetts law was passed making truancy an offense punishable by incarceration in a state reform school. The lag between laws, in this case two years, suggests that it was concern with dissidence that prompted compulsory education laws, another version of the anti-vagrancy statutes of sixteenth-century England.[43]

The reform school, America's version of the earlier Bridewell, was an exaggerated form of the ordinary public school of the time. And, although it was a total institution, in which a young person was lodged and regimented around the clock, it highlights what compulsory education was all about. If the family or an alternative group could not provide control over a youngster, the community now could by using some form of schooling. If the public school was ineffective in keeping a youth out of mischief, the reform school provided even more surveillance. And all of this was supported by an ideology of virtue, formulated to help rather than hinder the future adult. As the following quotation from a nineteenth-century New England document shows, it was felt that delinquent youths could be transformed through labor into independent, useful citizens.

> Labor, to employ the hands, and busy the mind, and awaken ingenuity, and produce results, is a demand of our constitution; is needful to the maintenance of virtue; and surely is needful to the recovery of the dissolute and vicious. Without this, the other means of discipline would fail, or would only half complete their work. The health of both body and mind is dependent on the purpose and the exertion of labor. And the habit of industry, nurtured and strengthened by years of trial in our institution, will not only be a

safeguard to the youth when he goes forth from us, but will be his assurance
of independence and position in his after life.[44]

That liberal education, as we know it today, was not one of the
emphases of the reform school should come as no surprise. For the
issues over the nature of the curriculum had not yet been resolved for
any of the public schools, let alone the reform school. But no matter;
what was important was getting youth off the streets and into organized
activities. What they would learn was, as is typically the case, determined by the elites. But the substance of the educational experience, like
the issue of mass education, was, as Michael Katz has suggested, not
decided without a fight.[45] Apparently extraneous factors associated
with matters of social stability and differential advantages for the various social classes ultimately determined what the curriculum would be.
Because the most urgent concerns were with actual and potential dissidence, academic matters were secondary to the creation, spread, and
reinforcement of this new institution for social control. The more manifest issues associated with compulsory mass education were and have
always been residual matters.

ABEYANCE AND SOCIAL CONTROL.   Joel Spring has held that "the American Revolution replaced the use of force with education as a means of
maintaining social order."[46] Citing the Northwest Ordinance of 1787
and the 1789 Massachusetts law establishing school districts, he has
noted that providing for the establishment of all kinds of schools was a
recognized means for helping train young Americans for disciplined,
conforming behavior, thus ensuring a low probability of chaos and rebellion.[47] Spring quotes Horace Mann, who argued that all forms of
social control "except education" had failed. In an 1848 report to the
Massachusetts State Board of Education, Mann wrote that "all means
and laws designed to repress injustice and crime, give occasion to new
injustice and crime."[48] A universal system of education would, Mann
held, end immorality.
    E. A. Ross, one of the earliest American sociologists, devoted a con-
siderable amount of attention to the use of education as an instrument of
social control.[49] Social control, particularly during the Middle Ages,
according to Ross, operated in two ways, one direct and the other indirect. The direct means, coercion, was delegated to the State, whereas
influence through education, the indirect means, was practiced by the
Church. "The contrast . . . was symbolized in the maxim that the state
has to do with the body, the church with the soul."[50] Even higher
education during the Middle Ages, which was originally free of intrusion by State or Church, came to be regulated by both civil and papal
authority through various "bulls," i.e., charters or licenses to teach.[51]

Protestantism required a reading knowledge sufficient for a biblical religion directed toward rejecting traditional authority, and this gave added impulse to elementary education for the masses. And though this may appear to have been liberating, the content of the educational thrust still enhanced social control. At no time since the Middle Ages, at least, has the substance of education been ignored by authorities.

Both classical learning, which stressed idealization of the past and acceptance of the status quo, and sharply contrasting education, which stressed progress and change associated with the Enlightenment views espoused by the French in Europe and Jefferson in America, were carried on under watchful eyes. In Ross's words,

> The avowal that free education is "an economical system of police" sounds rather brutal in this smooth-spoken age. It shocks the public and chills teachers. But now and then the cat is let out of the bag. . . . Napoleon said frankly . . . "I feel called upon to organize a system of education for the new generation, such that both political and moral opinions may be duly regulated thereby. . . . It seems to me that the special and the private schools ought all to be united, and brought under the cognizance of the education corps, which body ought to be so constituted as to have under its eye every child from the age of nine years."[52]

And, later, Ross quotes from Daniel Webster's 1847 speech on education, in which Webster holds that the public schools are "a wise and liberal system of police by which property and the peace of society are secured."[53] Education as the means for indirect social control, according to Ross, has continued to evolve as a State rather than Church responsibility. "Step by step with dis-establishment of religion proceeds the establishment of education."[54] In short, secular public education, as a functional alternative to Church-controlled education, continues to indoctrinate and educate in ways that enhance the regulation of behavior in society.

But what of education as a *direct* rather than *indirect* method of social control? With the initiation and extension of compulsory education, both aspects, coercion and influence, can be and indeed are embodied in the same institutional processes. Through the required commitment of increasingly greater amounts of time and an ever-increasing portion of their life span, the relatively young in England and America have been placed under more direct controls. School personnel supervise their charges directly. Like prison guards, custodians in mental hospitals, and other formally designated sanctioning agents, teachers have increasingly come to perform policing rather than intellectual tasks. And the extent to which one rather than another of these two aspects of the teacher's role dominates is primarily a function of the school's contribution to the abeyance and social control demands of the society and community at a given point in time. When the numbers of unintegrated, temporally marginal youths increase, the schools respond by performing the abeyance functions. As the numbers of marginal youths decline, the schools tend to emphasize their manifest functions, the education and training of their clientele. This expansion-contraction process and an organization's capacity to contribute to it may be better understood by focusing on the variables that help articulate the theoretical perspective being developed here.

TEMPORALITY.   That both the compulsory apprenticeship system and compulsory education today are characterized by clear-cut regulation of the temporal dimension is important. And that the unit of determination of length of engagement is age rather than skill, for the most part, is equally noteworthy. The length of attachment in the apprenticeship system was typically seven years, but the range of years selected included those that we now assign to youth or young adulthood: fourteen through twenty-one. From the control point of view these have been and continue to be the age categories within which the tendency toward undisciplined behavior and potential for dissidence has been greatest. I am not unaware that typical length of life has changed over the centuries and thus youths at an earlier chronological age were once treated as more mature persons. But throughout the ages the Western age curve for deviant behavior suggests that the high points occur somewhere between fifteen and twenty-five.*   When direct usage of compulsory apprenticeship to control vagrancy was implemented, the age span was increased to include children as young as five and adults as old as twenty-four. That slavery was the prescribed punishment for rebellion against imposed apprenticeship suggests that the latter was considered to be a less stringent form of control. But it was, nevertheless, a form of control.

The pattern for compulsory and voluntary higher education is similarly interesting, although somewhat more veiled and intangible. Although the creation of the concept of adolescence was an abeyance device, making it easier to hold youths in a dependent position, the ideational element was not sufficient to hold them in place physically. What was necessary was a structure that would keep young people from idling in the streets. That their idleness was already a result of a relative shrinkage of status vacancies in the economic sphere clearly ruled out formal work as an alternative. The school provided status vacancies that, for a given amount of time, could relieve the pressure on a limited

*Although this is only a speculative hypothesis, many studies tend to support it. The delinquency-crime statistics for the United States do bear this out. For an example from the historical files, see Natalie Z. Davis, "The Reasons of Misrule: Youth Groups and Charivaris in Sixteenth-Century France," *Past and Present* 50 (Feb. 1971).

number of jobs. As industrialization expanded, so did the population of youths and adults, including immigrants. As the ratio of personnel to status vacancies increased, so did the length of time required to stay in school. The spread, by age, of the employed in the United States, for example, indicates that the spectrum has been shrinking. Young people have been kept out of the labor force until they are older and adults have been encouraged until now to retire at earlier ages. With encouragement of higher education through subsidization, youths are kept out of the labor force until their early twenties.

Thus compulsory as well as voluntary education, in the form of college and university; have in effect extended time of engagement, and, consequently, attachment of youths to an organized system of social control. As an alternative to formal work, some form of school watches over young people for a substantial portion of their lifetime. But the school performs an abeyance function, it is well to keep in mind, and it can expand and contract in response to a surplus or shortage of personnel in society. When it is an absorber the school places less emphasis on intellectual tasks and greater emphasis on custodial responsibilities. When the school is an expeller of personnel, academic tasks assume greater importance.

COMMITMENT.   Though it is true that the school engages its clients for a long duration, *no one* is expected to be a student for life. To be committed to school as a lifelong vocation is appropriate only to those for whom education has become a career. The consumer of education, his supervisors, and his family and peers assumes that involvement in school is a temporary, preparatory activity in anticipation of relatively independent, permanent adult responsibilities. Commitment to the school as an organization is, accordingly, relatively low in contrast to the monastery or the Beguinage. Although for the teacher the school tends to be a greedy institution, it is not so for the student.[55]

INCLUSIVENESS.   As noted earlier, one of the factors that inhibited compulsory apprenticeship from contributing to the abeyance process was a tendency toward exclusiveness in membership. Rather than absorb large numbers of surplus youth the medieval guilds took a protectionist stance, limiting membership by diverse criteria including residence and kinship. When the need for social control became unusually intense, the English Crown and its supporting elites passed regulations that forced youths into apprenticeship, but the guilds tended to pick and choose rather than absorb anyone who was unattached. The Bridewell system provided an alternative absorptive organization, as did encouragement for migration to diverse parts of the colonial empire.

When compulsory education emerged during the early nineteenth century, the need to absorb large numbers of unattached youth was there. And the only way to effectively perform the abeyance and control function in English and American societies was to accept everybody. By its nature the public school, as we know it in the United States, is one of the most inclusive organizations in society.

DIVISION OF LABOR.   The modern public school is one in which students perform tasks that are, for the most part, similar. Though there are some differences in curriculum, the main thrust of the program is to prepare all of its charges to live and participate in a society that requires some degree of literacy, some capacity with numbers, and some general awareness of the norms and goals that are, seemingly, shared by the majority. At a latent level the school attempts to socialize its clients to adhere to those disciplines that are deemed appropriate by those who determine what goes on in school: middle-class parents and middle-class professionals. Thus the curriculum and other activities tend to emphasize what students should share in common rather than those aspects of education that would lead to specialization. Specialized training and education may be provided in some schools, but it is more typically the college that manifests a more pronounced division of labor. Thus, adherence to the requirement that one spend time in school is enhanced by low expectations regarding the development of special skills.

INSTITUTIONALIZATION.   Education is highly institutionalized in the United States. Whether Americans view education instrumentally, as a means toward other ends, or as worthy in and of itself, contemporary values emphasize the need for some kind of schooling. If a problem requires solution, some appeal to human rationality, in the form of education, is assumed to be a viable means. As my earlier analysis suggested, education was assumed to be an effective way, by those who advocated public schools for the masses, to help youth stay out of trouble and off the dole. An ignorant mass was considered a dangerous mass, and schooling was supposed to eliminate ignorance.

The institutionalization of education and the enhancement of both the abeyance and control processes has not emerged without opposition. Although the early-nineteenth-century advocates of mandatory publicly financed education finally won out, it was not without conflict. Even today there are some, like E. G. West, who oppose the kinds of mandatory systems existing today. To bolster his position, West draws together data on crime and delinquency, on the costs of education to English society in particular, and on the feasibility of state intervention into the rights of individuals to chose whether, how much, and what kind of education is desirable.[56] But West has missed the point. Institutions are not based on rationality but on belief and sentiment. Rational assessment of the cost of meeting the implementation needs of an institution is largely irrelevant. The Americans and the English believe that schooling is desirable and necessary; and the means that we use to fulfill these value commitments—the school—are for the most part institutionalized as well. Thus, from the control point of view, the Americans and the English encourage and insist on behavior patterns for their youth that make it easier to maintain order.

STRATIFICATION.   Within the school there is much stratification, both social and academic. But I hypothesize that when the abeyance process is impacting with the greatest intensity on the school, academic stratification is relatively weakly supported by the students. This is consistent with the highly inclusive nature of the school as an organization under conditions of absorption pressures.

Activities within the school, including the maintenance of academic standards, are all affected by the abeyance function. Standards for remaining in school decline, as reflected in grade inflation, and the whole system tends to become more flexible. The impact of a kind of Gresham's Law on performance and grades affects other patterns of status attainment. Among these, as James Coleman has shown, are popularity and athletic achievement. But these status hierarchies are most conspicuous during the period when the school's major responsibility is toward abeyance and control.[57] When the external pressures subside, I would hold, academic performance becomes the most pronounced basis for status among peers and teachers.

Herman and Julia Schwendinger have held that the marginalization of youth is a result of economic factors associated with a capitalistic economy and that alteration of the economic structure is the solution to this problem. The authors suggest, much in keeping with my own posture, that in diverse economic classes there is differential opportunity to use "absorption mechanisms" to mediate the impact of surplus youth.[58]

Although I do not reject their analysis in general, I would like to stress that problems of marginalization and delinquency often have their sources in substructures of society other than the economy. That the school is an important absorber and socializer of potentially marginal youth does not make it the sole abeyance device. Nor is the economy the only potential source of status vacancies to absorb marginal youth.

If a social structure is to be reorganized to bring together people and positions, planners might well consider alternative social structures to attract personnel and provide meaningful activities. The economy, I would hold, is only one such alternative. The school, the monastery, the urban or rural commune, and government-sponsored structures may also be consciously adapted to this task.

That more conscious efforts to co-opt and control marginal populations have been made in modern societies is exemplified by my final case study, the federal artists' and writers' projects of the 1930s in the United States. It is to this study that I now turn.

CHAPTER 6

Co-opted Aesthetes and Aspirants: The WPA Writers' and Artists' Projects

"What! A young knave and begging? Is there not wars? Is there not employment? Doth not the king lack subjects? Do not the rebels need soldiers?"

—*Henry IV*, Part 2

The direct intervention of the State into the process of placing temporally surplus populations under surveillance and thus control by requiring school reflects concern with specific sectors of the population rather than everyone. That unintegrated youths were particularly vulnerable to dissident behavior seems to have been clearly understood in England as early as the sixteenth century, when compulsory apprenticeship was used as a response to vagrancy. As a large cohort, young people are much more likely to be liberated from social-control structures than are those in other age categories.

By the time that compulsory education became a reality, in England and the United States, the capacity of the family to control the behavior of its younger members had diminished. With the increasing value placed on youth, both in the industrial setting and in society at large, it became more difficult for parents to tell their offspring what to do. Compulsory education took up the slack and a major part of the responsibility for social control was shifted to the school and its agents, further weakening the family's responsibility and capacity for overseeing the activities of its younger members.

The school thus integrated, at least for the period prior to their being thrust on the market, those who were the largest potential source of tinder. Marginal youths could touch off the flames of collective protest in particular and a wide variety of deviant behavior more generally.

But another potentially vulnerable population, although much smaller in size, has been that motley category of marginal people that includes intellectuals, artists, and other aspiring aesthetes. As I noted in the chapter on bohemianism (Chapter 4), a tradition of social criticism has been associated with these sectors of Western societies for at least two thousand years. Collective protest against authority required some kind of rationale, and it was the actors, troubadours, and minstrels who were the bearers and justifiers of the secular critical traditions. In the sphere of religion some of the relatively loosely integrated monks and priests broadcast the ideological components of the anti–Church hierarchy postures. With the invention of movable type, the proliferation of the mass media, and the increasing importance of art and music, intellectuals and artists assumed greater importance and thus greater influence on the masses. These traditionally marginal members of society were now more capable of impacting directly on the masses and indirectly on the powerful and wealthy.

The tradition of subsidizing and protecting artists and intellectuals that emerged among the aristocrats of Europe may not have been a result of conscious efforts to co-opt these intellectuals and aesthetes, but the consequences were much the same. Patronage is reflected in the descriptions, earlier in this study, of troubadours, minstrels, and actors carrying documents signed by persons in authority vouching for the legitimacy of travel from one place to another. These letters were testimony that a particular person was not a vagrant. But the price for the right to move somewhat freely between one point and another was surely greater conformity and less criticism of those in power than might have otherwise been the case. Patronage took its returns in the form of co-optation.

The kept artists and men-of-letters performed for relatively small audiences in controlled contexts. Adherence to religiously and aristocratically imposed prescriptions and proscriptions on art forms was required. The dramatic challenges to earlier forms, the outbursts of Beethoven and Van Gogh, reflect the weakening of the aristocracies during the hundred-year span following the French Revolution. This century also spawned bohemianism, which created social supports for those artists and writers who would not conform at work or play. Relatively impersonal support of art and artists, including wide tolerance for social and aesthetic criticism, is a rare condition.

The various writers' and artists' projects supported by the federal government of the United States was a response to mixed concerns. Organized under the Works Progress Administration (WPA), they were clearly part of a wide-scale effort to provide employment and integration for a very substantial number of Americans without jobs. Thus federal support for aesthetic and intellectual activities in the United States during the 1930s must be understood in terms of the broader historical and social context.

That the opportunity to infuse American life with a greater sense of the aesthetic influenced President Franklin D. Roosevelt in his support of these organized efforts to subsidize artists is very likely. Though his personal tastes in art were not likely to warm the hearts of the avant-garde,* he nevertheless emerged from a tradition associated with his patrician background that recognized the need to support aesthetic activities.

But this interest in art and the support of unemployed artists ran second to the more critical concern of Roosevelt and Harry Hopkins, his advisor, with a surplus population created by contractions in the economic sphere. Whether or not there was particular concern with artists and intellectuals as a special, vulnerable population or as potential leaders of a revolution against capitalist America is difficult to discern. What is clear is the fear of revolution. And this fear was based not on speculation but on perceptions of real events.

The New Deal

Federal subsidization of artists (including painters, sculptors, actors, and musicians) and writers was an offshoot of the more general reaction to unemployment following the financial crash of 1929 and the Depression that was its legacy. By the time the election campaigns of 1932 attained maturity Franklin D. Roosevelt, then governor of New York, simultaneously was advocating a cut in government spending and increased aid to the unemployed.[1] When Roosevelt delivered his acceptance speech, following a landslide victory over Herbert Hoover, he was explicitly advocating a program to employ the youth of America.[2] The reforestation program was "an obvious anticipation of the Civilian Conservation Corps" (CCC), which later became one of the most important absorbers of the nation's youth. Not only did the CCC provide employment, but it transported surplus youth who might congregate and organize in urban areas to the more remote parts of the United States, far from presumed agitators† for protest and revolution.

Real concern over revolution in the United States seems to have surfaced *after* Roosevelt took office rather than before. Although it was true that many veterans of World War I supported the mass march on

---

*His own tastes seemed to be limited to paintings and drawings of sailing ships.

†In reality, as I will show below, farmers were no less prone to revolution than others.

Washington in June 1932, seeking payment of bonuses promised for 1945, "the mood of the country during the winter 1932–33 was not revolutionary. . . . The country was less rebellious than drifting."[3] Even General Douglas MacArthur, who described the spiritless, melancholy collection of unarmed men, women, and children as "a mob . . . animated by the essence of revolution," failed in his overzealous and excessive reaction to arouse a violent response.[4] MacArthur's troops, including cavalry, tanks, and steel-helmeted infantry with fixed bayonets, attacked their foe in the government buildings downtown and in the shantytown on the Anacostia Flats outside the capital that had become the temporary homes of the veterans and their families. The army "routed the bonusers from their crude homes, hurled tear gas bombs into the colony, and set the shacks afire with their torches."[5]

The protest which followed was not what might be expected of a revolutionary mob. It came, rather, in the form of editorials in newspapers and newsreels critical of Hoover, and it was, in part at least, reflected in the rejection of the Republicans on Election Day. The only potential for violence on the part of the veterans was the physical threat against the Communist faction, who had to be protected from the other bonus marchers.[6] Thus the most dramatic protest that occurred prior to Roosevelt's election was more pacific than violent in spite of the use of force by authorities.[7]

But there surely were places in the United States where, prior to the election, portions of the populace were in a rebellious mood. From 1929 on, the Depression and its concomitant, diffusing poverty, called forth questions about government and business leaders and capitalism as a system, as well. While many went without food and clothing, farms, markets, and factories lay idle. Crops and animals, farmers and factory workers, were suddenly a surplus product in the midst of a society in need. Farmers who might have profitably sold their yields lost their land because they couldn't pay their taxes or meet bank demands. Factory owners went bankrupt. Hundreds of banks closed. Almost everybody suffered in some way.

By 1933 farmers had rebelled in many places across the country, bursting the urban stereotype of the largely conservative agrarian. "The farm strikes were only one of a series of spectacular incidents—the bonus march episode, communist-led demonstrations of the unemployed, the forty-eight-mile-long motor car "Coal Caravan" of ten thousand striking miners in southern Illinois—that led men to speculate whether the country faced imminent revolution."[8]

Talk of revolution was not uncommon, but it seemed that the widespread sense of hopelessness had yet to become translated into national collective action. In 1933, after Roosevelt took office, there was nevertheless fear on the part of the new administration that if the economic situation was not turned around and the idled integrated into organized activities, the capitalist system and its supportive institutions would soon go the way of Russia, Italy, and Germany

On March 4, 1933, Roosevelt launched a series of efforts that brought immediate, if not long-range, results. His inauguration address, including the oft-quoted statement that the only thing America had to fear was "fear itself," suddenly proved the antidote to the infection of hopelessness and insecurity that surged through the social organism. Roosevelt's rhetoric was followed immediately with action.

Five days later, following the president's edict declaring a bank holiday, Congress passed an emergency banking bill, reopening, with government assistance now pledged to private bankers, the banks. The very next day Roosevelt asked Congress to pass an emergency economy bill that cut payments to veterans and salaries of federal employees. Two days later he asked Congress to repeal the prohibition of alcohol. While the necessary amendment to the Constitution was being ratified by the states, his request honored by Congress, he turned to a quicker, more dramatic method of repeal. A bill amending the Volstead Act, the latter prohibiting beer, was passed after spirited exchange. Wine, too, was now made as accessible to the consumer as beer. And while the fate of alcohol and beer was being debated Secretary of Agriculture Henry Wallace prepared a farm bill which, after much debate, a farmer's rebellion, and a threatened strike, was passed as the compromise Agricultural Adjustment Act.

The list of bills and acts goes on and on, creating a sense of dynamic changes in all aspects of American life. Roosevelt's decisiveness, his growing charismatic leadership, and a strong feeling that someone had to do something about a deteriorating situation all contributed to his early success in saving capitalism from dissolution.[9]

> No one would ever know, General Hugh S. Johnson later said, "how close we were to collapse and revolution. We could have got a dictator a lot easier than Germany got Hitler." "I do not think it is too much to say," wrote [Rexford Guy] Tugwell, "that on March 4 we were confronted with a choice between an orderly revolution—a peaceful and rapid departure from past concepts—and a violent and disorderly overthrow of the whole capitalist structure." "At the end of February," wrote Walter Lippmann, "we were a congeries of disorderly panic-stricken mobs and factions. In the hundred days from March to June we became again an organized nation confident of our power to provide for our own security and to control our own destiny."[10]

The WPA

The first major bill directed to the integration of the unemployed into work activities was the Civilian Conservation Corps. The proposal to establish the CCC came only three weeks after Roosevelt's inauguration. But it was in total numbers and impact as an absorber of the unemployed much less significant than it appeared. Providing jobs for only 250,000 out of 15 million unemployed, its major impact, like that of some of the other bills passed during the Hundred Days, was on morale.*

It was not until a year and a half later, following a relative lull in economic upturn subsequent to the first Hundred Days, that Roosevelt turned in earnest to the matter of providing jobs. The discontent that characterized the Hoover period and early 1933 was seemingly quieted by the hope and optimism generated by the march of bills to the Congress under the guidance of Roosevelt's political field marshals. But while the new administration struggled with the realities of the situation—one-fourth of the labor force still out of work—organized dissident movements were forming. The followers of Huey Long, Francis Townsend, and Father Coughlin,—militants among the unemployed and in organized labor—were building protest movements that might very well accomplish what Johnson, Tugwell, and Lippmann had feared most, a revolution.[11] Schlesinger quotes Roosevelt as saying, in May 1938, "I am fighting Communism, Huey Longism, Coughlinism, Townsendism. . . . I want to save our system, the capitalist system; to save it is to give some heed to world thought of today. I want to equalize the distribution of wealth."[12]

In January 1935, in his message to Congress, Roosevelt put forth a set of proposals that would simultaneously attenuate the appeals of the dissidents, on the one hand, and, on the other hand, attempt to deal with a more basic problem facing the nation, the breakdown of the economy. "To restore stability, it was necessary to restore the occupational role; the long-run solution was economic recovery; the interim solution was work relief."

Roosevelt's earlier experience with the Civil Works Administration, organized by Harry Hopkins, could be described as "a quick fix."[14] Afraid that "he was creating a permanent class of reliefers whom he might never get off the payroll" and "alarmed at how much CWA was costing" (a cost buttressed, in his view, by "revelations of corruption"), he ended the CWA soon after it came into existence.[15] During its approximately one year of life, the CWA employed as many as 4,230,000 persons; built or improved roads, schools, and playgrounds; employed teachers, artists, and writers; and sponsored excavations and other diverse activities. When Roosevelt's perspective on federal employment had finally changed, the experience gained during that brief period of the CWA helped formulate the massive program which would transform the idled into employed: the WPA.

The president's changing perspective was based upon several fac-

*The Civil Works Administration provided more jobs, over 4 million, but it was short-lived.

tors. The direct relief that had been paid out, amounting to $2 billion, seemed to lead only to increasing welfare rolls. Providing work, however, would make a large surplus population—in the economic sphere—less vulnerable to appeals by dissident leaders; it could help boost morale; it could help build Roosevelt's political machine; it would be consonant with the work ethic and thus reinforce work discipline; it would continue to provide funds for pump priming; and a great many desirable projects, reminiscent of some of those accomplished under the CWA, would get done.

But above all, the WPA was a system of social control. By co-opting and integrating potentially dissident men and women into organizations that formally required disciplined behavior under the supervision of other employees of the federal government, the WPA struck a blow against the Huey Longs, the Coughlinites, the Fascists, and the Communists. The disciplines required, it is well to note, were not necessarily skills. What was required was simply showing up for work and avoiding trouble. No organization of WPA activities was more tolerant of a lack of skills than the various artists' and writers' projects.

The Federal Writers' and Artists' Projects

> The revolutionary ardor abroad in the land was a glaring fact, especially noticeable among intellectuals. Never before in American history had so many of them been drawn into the orbit of leftwing activity. The Communist party was attracting so many members that it could afford to turn away applicants who were not considered qualified. The Marxist-Leninist doctrine . . . was being embraced with a religious fervor that sometimes amounted to fanaticism.[16]

In the left-wing press, in the radical magazines, and in some of the liberal magazines, as well, proletarian themes abounded. Writing about the presumed class struggle and the Fascist threat to society was "in." Many of the best-known writers of contemporary American literature joined radical causes, and at least one of the highest-quality literary magazines owed its birth, but not its youth and maturity, to one of the Marxist-Leninist clubs. The *Partisan Review,* which in its lifetime has published most of the outstanding writers in recent American literature, began in 1934 as an "offspring of the John Reed Club in New York City"[17] but broke with the sponsors to become independent in 1937. Thus, if possible overthrow of the capitalist system was to be reckoned with, the Roosevelt administration would have to make a decisive effort to co-opt the intellectuals and their sycophants.

As I noted earlier, the CWA did, in its brief history, employ artists and writers. As the impact of the Depression grew worse and as radicalism began to claim more adherents, Roosevelt and his aide, Harry Hopkins, decided to organize as part of the overall system of the WPA a Federal Theatre Project, a Federal Writers' Project, and a Federal Art Project.

The organizations would do several things simultaneously as they exercised their social-control functions. They would employ an especially sensitive population—sensitive to political issues—and a particularly vulnerable one. The projects would also employ those who aspired to being artists and writers of all types. No less significant, many white-collar persons could be employed because they possessed sufficient education and background to come under the umbrella of "artist" or "writer." And, by no means less significant, some effort, sometimes explicit and sometimes subtle, could be made to redirect and even censor the products of the now federally employed intellectuals.

It would be an error to assume that a substantial portion of the left and the intellectuals, more generally, were unaware that they were being "bought off." From the very beginning of the New Deal the leaders of the Communist party viewed Roosevelt's efforts to employ intellectuals as counterrevolutionary. But there was too much unemployment and hunger in the land to convince the target populations that noncooperation was the best response to these modest opportunities.

Thus, while some railed out against the political implications, at least in principle, of joining with the New Dealers in federally sponsored employment, there was even more agitation from the intellectuals and artists themselves for programs that would include them. Under the CWA and another program, the Public Works of Art Project (PWAP), the New Dealers had joined some state and federal government agencies together to provide jobs for intellectuals, and this experience provided a model for those radical and nonradical artists' and writers' groups who pushed for a federal sponsored program.[18]

With the situation of the jobless growing worse and with approximately 3.5 million persons who might be considered paupers, Roosevelt and Hopkins turned to a broad program that would both stimulate the economy and deal with unemployment. The Emergency Relief Act of 1935, which established the Works Progress Administration, designed to accomplish that goal, included a seemingly "inconspicuous but significant clause authorizing . . . a nationwide program for useful employment of artists, musicians, actors, entertainers, writers . . . and others in these cultural fields."[19] The means for co-opting the intellectuals was now at hand.

But both the reader and I would be in error if we were to assume that the connection between fear of revolution, the potential role of the intellectuals in such an outcome, and the establishment of the WPA in general and the various arts projects, more particularly, was direct. Roosevelt was indeed concerned with the risks that mass unemployment posed for the system, and Harry Hopkins was clearly concerned with the debilitating effects on morale of direct aid in the form of relief. Participation in constructive work, physical or mental, was the appropriate means for quick engagement of the unemployed and equally quick consumer expenditures. Furthermore, it is well to keep in mind, Hopkins felt that the lowest economic strata should receive the most immediate attention since they would spend their income as soon as they received it.[20] The intellectuals were anything but a major concern when Roosevelt, Hopkins, Harold Ickes, and Henry Morgenthau Jr., waded through the multitiude of issues which, when clarity finally emerged, resulted in the Works Progress Administration.

Thus it was the intellectuals themselves who, through a number of organizations, agitated, persuaded, and picketed for programs to provide employment for themselves and other aesthetes.[21] The breadth and scope of the arts projects seems to have resulted from a serendipitous windfall that transformed a relatively modest proposal into a far-ranging program.

Although inclusion of those in "cultural fields," as noted above, was indeed a part of the Emergency Relief Act of 1935, the means for organizing aid to the artists and intellectuals was subject to administrative interpretation. And the interpretation leading to the administrative organization of the arts projects that finally emerged seems to have been at odds with what had initially been intended in the Hopkins and Roosevelt proposals. Instead of grants to the states for support of programs that would fall under the umbrella of the federal guidelines, a bureaucratic organization was born, with the diverse programs and projects under direct control of Washington. And, according to William F. McDonald, who authored the definitive work on the administration of the arts projects, it was a very conservative agency of the federal government, the General Accounting Office, whose interpretation of the 1935 act led to the proliferation of this administratively innovative and potentially radical government activity.[22] Although the statute and its interpretation, as reflected in the resulting directives and memoranda, tell the story with great precision, what actually occurred is less clear. But those of us who have had dealings with bureaucratic organizations will have no difficulty recognizing a familiar pattern, and thus the plausibility of McDonald's hypothesis.

In short, the appropriation of funds for the diverse categories of the WPA program was such that the problem became how to spend $300 million to support programs for "educational, professional, and clerical persons."[23] It was the press to spend funds which, probably more than any other factor, determined that the arts programs would be a federal rather than state activity and that this activity would involve as many people as it did.[24] Within the organization, concern with policies reflecting the larger goals of Roosevelt and Hopkins fell, as is often the case, by the wayside. The federal arts programs received their direct impetus less from efforts to manipulate the mass of the unemployed out of concern with protest and revolution than from the relatively mundane efforts of bureaucrats to perform their simple duties.

HOW THE PROJECTS FUNCTIONED.   With the funds at hand, the broad blueprint worked out, and the president's approval granted, four programs, headed by Jacob Baker and Edward Bruce, were begun: they covered art, music, drama, and writers.[25] But the programs were soon subject to the strains associated with the difference between their manifest and latent functions.

From the outset, the efforts to assure artistic quality or competence, at least, came into conflict with the need to absorb the unemployed, the primary mandate for the WPA as a whole. The problem as viewed from the top was how to *include* as many white-collar and educated unemployed in WPA activities as possible. But Bruce and others, with recognition of their values by those at the top including Harry Hopkins, had a genuine and profound interest in the arts and their role as missionaries to the public at large. The societal need was for *inclusiveness* rather than programs that would accept only the proven artist. Nevertheless, the combination of bureaucratic procedures and the desire to recognize those who had already demonstrated their creative capacities led to the hierarchical organization of workers into professional, skilled, and intermediate categories, corresponding to different wage scales.

Independent of the difficulties surrounding the determination of who was an artist and what was a creative contribution, with which I dealt in the chapter on bohemianism, the problem of national standards, which was implicit in the formation of the WPA, soon became manifest. And the difficulties in this sphere contributed, inadvertently, to the absorptive function of the arts projects. Because standards were difficult to establish and because there was pressure to provide jobs for as many middle-class persons as possible in the shortest time, the efforts to make the projects exclusive, for the proven alone, were undercut. And the outcome was consistent with the original intentions of the policymakers.

At the local level, however, the greatest influence on what was done was exercised by those who were the most prominent in their artistic medium. Though the bureaucrats played an important role in the overall operations of the projects (including, on occasion, censorship), the selection, assignment, and classification of recruits was in the hands of the professionals themselves. Those whose skills were perceived to be limited might be banished to an artistic Siberia.[27] And the problems were not new. Earlier, when WPA's predecessors had attempted to absorb large numbers of artistic claimants in a relatively short period of time, the same problems arose. As Lillian Brandt observed,

> Hasty assignments had meant a large proportion of misfits, necessitating an immense amount of shifting about. Musicians and actors could show their abilities in an audition. Artists, teachers, and writers had to be taken usually on their own statement of what they had done or aspired to do. A man who thought he would like to be on the Publicity Project, for example, might say that he "used to work on" *The World*, and it might be discovered later that he had at one time been a copyboy.[28]

It is well to note that the determination of level of skill was not only a problem in the sphere of the arts. The determination of who was a skilled mechanic was equally difficult.

Given the relative amorphousness of a project member's level of skill, it is difficult to raise one's expectations regarding quality of output. In any case, from my perspective on abeyance, the result of the labors of those who were earlier idled might be perceived as extra bounty, the unanticipated result of efforts to co-opt and control temporally marginal persons.

In the day-to-day workings of the arts projects, efforts and outcomes were often out of joint. On the writers' projects, for example, all manner of skills and non-skills were brought together.

> Most striking of the new departures was the WPA's Federal Writers' Project. . . . At its peak, it supported over six thousand journalists, freelance writers, novelists, poets, Ph.D.'s and other jobless persons experienced in putting words on paper. Hacks, bohemians, and local eccentrics jostled elbows with highly trained specialists and creative artists of such past or future distinction as Conrad Aiken, Maxwell Bodenheim, Vardis Fisher, and Richard Wright.[30]

But although just about every proven artist or writer participated in these projects in some way, side by side with the unproven, the aesthetic results of these activities are subject to debate among the artists themselves. The artists interviewed by Bernard Rosenberg and Norris Fliegel, for example, tended to take a dim view of the accomplishments of those artists who worked on the WPA projects.[31] A general feeling that receiving the modest income was good but that the conditions of work were poor prevailed. This view was also shared by a number of writers who worked on the writers' project.[32] The solution, from the point of view of some of the respondents who had worked on those projects, was to be allowed to work in relative solitude, deliver one's products, and pick up the checks. Of course, such a pattern, if allowed by the administrators of the WPA projects, would have jeopardized the projects' internal-control functions.[33]

The activities of these projects were, for the most part, carried out in group settings. Thus an employee was required to be on the job and was similarly obligated to perform, more or less, in conformity with the formal mandate of a particular project. One example, the recipient of a full-scale study, was the Federal Writers' Project, as described by Jerre Mangione.[34] Under the leadership of Henry Alsberg, the Washington administrators set out to do a series of handbooks, or guides, one for each state in the Union. State directors were assigned, typically with the aid of local politicians, who recommended party loyalists to administer the programs. Proven and aspiring writers applied for work and were assigned to the various aspects of writing and research that a handbook required. Although the writers did enjoy some leeway concerning the aspects of life in a given state, which would be described and interpreted as well, it is clear that censorship was widespread. Descriptions of the more sordid aspects of life in a given state or anything that resembled political narrative was subject to the scissors. The writers of the Massachusetts guide, for example, were attacked for using the guide as a medium for political agitation.[35]

In spite of the participation of amateurs and the relatively constrained circumstances under which the writing was done—groups working in offices and unoccupied factories—the outcome of this federal project was impressive, if only quantitatively. "A National Archives report indicates that up until April 1942 the [guidebook] collection consisted of 276 volumes, 701 pamphlets and 340 issuances (leaflets, articles, radio scripts)."[36]

Quality is more difficult to discern, but much that emerged found acceptance in the higher circles of intellectual and aesthetic America. Many of the books were published by the major publishing houses in the United States. Articles appeared in major journals. And a number of younger writers who later attained recognition as leading literary figures got their start on these projects. But because of the nature of creative activity and the judgments that determine what is lasting and what is trivial, it is impossible to assess the ultimate impact on the intellectual and aesthetic life of America of the various arts projects. And it is similarly impossible to determine precisely how much of a contribution the WPA effort made to the prevention of protest and revolution in a society suffering the contraction of opportunities in the economic sphere.

THE DEMISE OF THE WPA.   It is somewhat ironic that a program which was perceived by its formulators as a means for dissolving revolutionary tendencies should be attacked by others as a vehicle for fomenting revolution. The situation, approximately three years after the establishment of the federal projects in 1935, reflected this irony.

Antagonism on the part of conservatives toward Roosevelt and the

New Deal varied in intensity over the years, now stronger with the increase in programs, now weaker as the Democrats' vulnerability declined. A number of newspapers, most notably those owned by William Randolph Hearst, grasped every opportunity to discredit the Administration and particularly the WPA. Opportunists in Congress, including J. Parnell Thomas and Martin Dies, seemingly correctly assumed that an attack on the arts projects as havens for Communists would be met with a general attitude of public indifference. And any effort to locate Communists among the employees on the projects was sure to be rewarded, given the growth of Communist party membership in the early and mid-thirties. The arts projects, in sum, became the instrument that the witch-hunting doctors would use to begin dissecting the New Deal.

The Dies Congressional Committee on Un-American Activities used the public hearing as a device for presenting various and sundry accusations of heresy through carefully selected, created, and staged testimony. Plants, like Edwin Banta, who joined the Communist Party in order to inform, testified alongside those who had become disenchanted with the Party, for example, Ralph De Sola. Responsible WPA administrators, heeding the call of Congress to testify, found themselves making statements under oath that suddenly assumed new meaning once they left their tongues. And efforts to respond to, clarify, and rectify reckless charges made by the Committee were rejected outright.[37]

Although the attack of the Dies Committee and its adumbrations in the press and other mass media were not alone responsible for the demise of the WPA arts projects, there is no doubt that these provided strong rationalizations for those in Congress who wanted to withdraw support and scuttle what to them was an offensive government activity. In January 1939 the number of Writers' Project workers was cut by 25 percent without an utterance of opposition either in Congress or, apparently, among the workers or their public supporters. In April 1939, amid growing concern with a drift toward involvement in World War II, the WPA was reorganized, stripped of its independent status, and absorbed into an agency called the Federal Works Administration. In the process, the arts projects lost, for the most part, the support of the federal government.[38] The theater project was terminated immediately, but the writers', music, and art programs were allowed to continue under state sponsorship "provided that sponsors could be found to contribute at least 25 percent of the total cost of each state program."[39] Some of the projects limped along until as late as 1943, when the program succumbed. The United States was now engaged in war, and the military and its civilian support agencies now provided sufficient status vacancies to eradicate, in effect, whatever surplus populations might have otherwise existed.

The WPA and the Abeyance Process

Unlike the other organizational forms that I have used to exemplify the abeyance process, the WPA arts projects, and perhaps the WPA more generally, were perceived by a great many people as a temporary holding operation. Although somewhat fewer people were aware that social control was one of the motives for the WPA's conception, the latent level of awareness regarding this motive, as a property of some of the Establishment elites, was greater than what appears to have been the case in earlier historical periods. To be sure, there were a great many debates, as I have shown, regarding the control value of compulsory education, but the focus there was on socialization: teaching discipline and inculcating those values that would contribute to more conformity and less need for the dole. The fear of revolution was salient among the elites in the 1930s, and the use of work organizations as control systems evolved when it was found that relief alone was inadequate to curb revolutionary fervor.

The Communist elites in particular were also aware that the unemployed were being manipulated. Representing a growing vocal minority, they warned that the Roosevelt program in general was counterrevolutionary—designed to attenuate those forces in society that would finally destroy the capitalist system in the United States. But aware or not, Communists, other radicals, and a substantial portion of the intellectual and aesthetic communities in the United States struck a bargain with the federal government. The desire for physical survival far outweighed ideology. To write or paint or compose or act in conformity with the mandates of federal bureaucrats; to stay out of trouble; to attempt to maintain one's intellectual or artistic integrity in spite of the mundane and often grubby work they were required to perform—this was their lot as project workers. For many, it is clear that these activities did little harm. William de Kooning, Jackson Pollock, Nelson Algren, Saul Bellows, Ralph Ellison, Richard Wright, Alfred Kazin, Willard Motley, Harold Rosenberg, and others of their caliber went on to help establish the contemporary arts in the United States. John Cheever, Conrad Aiken, Maxwell Bodenheim, and others who were clearly established before the projects came into existence were surely not harmed by their participation in them. A great many academics were similarly engaged, including names that sociologists will recognize: Frank Manuel, Paul Radin, Kenneth Burke, St. Claire Drake, and Horace Cayton. The latter two used the data from their project activities as a basis for the classic study of social stratification among blacks in Chicago, *Black Metropolis*.[40] Few stayed out of a project for fear that co-optation was too high a price to pay for the modest livelihood WPA provided.

How the organization of the WPA, in general, and the arts projects, more specifically, performed this co-optative and abeyance function simultaneously requires a look at the pattern in terms of the variables which articulate my theoretical perspective: temporality, commitment, inclusiveness, division of labor, institutionalization, and stratification.

TEMPORALITY.   There is no question that the WPA and its suborganizations were conceived of and operationalized as relatively temporary activities. Neither Franklin D. Roosevelt nor Harry Hopkins, even in their most radical postures, wanted or expected the Emergency Relief Act of 1935 to lead to a permanent system of federally sponsored and controlled work projects.

Although support of the arts, in particular, by national government as a permanent commitment was true of Mexico and some European countries, the United States was not ready to institutionalize direct support of artists. The Mexican experience, it is well to note, which involved the support of painters like Diego Rivera and José Orozco, did impact on the United States through George Biddle, who was a personal friend of Roosevelt's. Biddle lobbied for support of the arts, beginning in 1933, and was put in touch with Edward Bruce, who, as noted above, became the primary force in the WPA for support of quality art. Although Bruce and Biddle had support in high places, including that of Mrs. Roosevelt and Mrs. Morgenthau, there was never sufficient support for the program to be more than a temporary activity.[41] Those programs that are in essence types of relief have generally operated, as Piven and Cloward have shown, for relatively short periods of history. The WPA arts projects, as federally sponsored activities, were short-lived, from 1935 until 1939. As an organization that was specifically designed to provide status vacancies to offset dissidence, the WPA is the best illustration in this study of the low-temporality dimension.

COMMITMENT.   It should be clear from everything said above that for the most part commitment to the arts projects by their employees, their administrators, and even those who were responsible for establishing them was relatively low. Although there were some at the top who felt that the programs should and would make an impact on the creation and dissemination of quality artistic and intellectual products in the United States, most others saw the projects only for what they were, a means for employing the unemployed. Edward Bruce and Eleanor Roosevelt were very much committed, although Mrs. Roosevelt was enough of a political realist to stand aside when it was time for the program to succumb.[42]

Jerry Magione, for example, in his book on the Writers' Project displays a very strong sense of commitment, a stance that was probably shared by more than a few.[43] But the sum of the observations that proliferate through the major sources I have reviewed and my conversations with numerous other observers who participated in the WPA projects suggests that commitment by those employed on the projects was generally low.

INCLUSIVENESS.   In spite of the efforts of a great many artists, who, as members of screening committees, tried to select only the proven to participate in the projects, high inclusiveness characterizes this pattern. The gatekeepers were constantly reminded by Alsberg at the top and by administrators down the line that their first responsibility was to get people off the relief rolls and into a job. Inclusiveness was enhanced by the difficulties associated with determining who was an artist or intellectual. This varied to some extent with the type of project, but those who had harbored in their souls fantasies about writing or painting a great masterpiece could now attempt to transform fantasy into reality. My example above of a claimant who described himself as formerly working on *The World*, implying that he had been a writer, no doubt reflects claims made by many who lacked proven talent but may nevertheless have gone on to great accomplishments. De Kooning, for example, was not held in very high esteem when he entered the cadres of the WPA arts project, but commitment to his own talents, an unmeasurable factor, nourished in a context that was better than mixing cement at a building site, must have made some contribution to his ultimate attainments. Awareness that promise in art is often impossible to prove aided the gatekeepers by providing rationalizations for accepting a diverse collection of artists and pretenders into their ranks. Perhaps less inclusive than public schools, the arts projects generally accepted more people than they rejected and expelled personnel only as Washington cut back payrolls.

DIVISION OF LABOR.   Because the WPA projects were manifestly understood to be holding structures, with specific artistic or intellectual accomplishments only gravy, there was limited concern with specialized skills. To be sure, a person who did not know how to handle a palette and brush would not be assigned to murals or any other kind of painting. But the pressure to absorb personnel above all else meant that many were employed who had little or no experience with a particular medium. Sometimes tasks had to be created for those with and without appropriate skills. On the Writers' Project, for example, many experienced authors were doing the work of clerks and stenographers.[44] Many a person with or without requisite skill for a given project spent his workday as a "gopher."[45] A clever cartoon in the Mangione book shows an unfinished bridge, tools, and equipment laying idle and one observer telling another "They're all transferred to the Federal Writers' Project." The thrust toward inclusiveness clearly implied that the degree of skill and specialization would be low on the arts projects. The vast majority of participants, then, did similar, often mundane, jobs.

INSTITUTIONALIZATION.   The idea of relief or government-subsidized work, except for the army and bureaucracy, runs counter to the ethos of American society. But there is no doubt that work perceived as a way to make a living or attain recognition, or as an end in itself, is very highly valued. The WPA program never enjoyed the degree or quality of acceptance that would facilitate its evolution to institutional status. It is work for pay or career advancement—primarily in a profit-making organization—that is eulogized. Thus WPA was seen as an alternative to relief but was not recognized as a desirable alternative to work in the private sector.

The fact that work is so highly valued in American society surely made the use of federally sponsored projects more palatable than relief as a means of redistributing funds. Roosevelt, realizing this, made sure to emphasize in his message to Congress proposing the establishment of the WPA the distinction between "make-work" and constructive labor. But the more rationalization required to support an activity, the more surely is that activity divergent from the accepted ways of doing things.

STRATIFICATION.   It would have been impossible to bring together so many artists and intellectuals with some degree of proven talent and skill without creating or reinforcing some patterned system of ranks. The already established—including Conrad Aiken and John Cheever, for example—were bound to enjoy higher prestige than those who had yet to prove themselves. The bureaucratic requirement which held that differential wage scales should be a concomitant of diversely evaluated talent and skill ensured that those who had already arrived would enjoy relatively greater material rewards than others, modest as these rewards were.

But more important, from the point of view of abeyance, mobility from a level of lesser skill to that of a higher level was uncommon. A job or career ceiling existed, in effect, which made it clear that upward mobility within a project organization would lead nowhere. Success, whether artistic or material, would have to be sought in realms other than the WPA. In accord with my perspective, this limited inducement for pursuing success goals within the organizations enhanced the process of expulsion when organizational contraction occurred.

The WPA, and the arts projects as a special program, came into existence for the explicit purpose of providing status vacancies in organized contexts supervised by government administrators. The program was clearly conceived as a device to help forestall protest and revolution by controlling those who might otherwise be vulnerable to the blandishments of various kinds of revolutionaries. Although it did have a desirable impact on American society, from the point of view of the arts, there was no doubt that its major mission was to temporarily hold surplus populations in abeyance until status vacancies emerged elsewhere. By the time of its demise, preparation for and engagements in World War II provided alternative positions. Following World War II, the GI Bill of Rights anticipated the creation of a surplus population and hence increased status vacancies in schools of all kinds and in industrial training programs. Government had come to realize that the abeyance process could be used for control *before* agitation and protest emerged.

CHAPTER 7

Abeyance, Surplus Population, and Social Control

"Idle Hands are the Devil's workshop"
—Samuel Smiles, *Self-Help*, 1859

The WPA projects in general and the various artists' and writers' programs in particular illustrate a direct and unambiguous effort to attenuate the potential for widespread political protest by organizing and placing under surveillance large masses of idled Americans. The source of this surplus population was not a bumper crop of births at an earlier time now impacting on society. The approximately 15 million Americans out of work were idled by a contraction of status vacancies, in abstract terms, resulting from massive strains in the economic sphere. The WPA projects provided temporary alternative positions to integrate many who were now marginal to society.

What is especially instructive in this historical case is the extent to which it is possible to discern the motives of the political elites who created the WPA organization. The historical data make it difficult, in most of the cases studied in this book, to determine whether and how elites intervene in societal processes to bring about consequences that they desire. Although there is more than a hint that the systems of compulsory apprenticeship and, later, mandatory schooling were devised as social control measures, it is also clear that other motives helped obscure the social control intentions of some of the elites engaged in establishing these systems.

The bohemians and other communal groups who might have contributed to political protest did not require manipulation by those in power. They typically placed themselves under the surveillance and control of their own chosen masters and peers. The resulting impact on the larger society was, nevertheless, the same as if they had been conscripted into the army, had joined a monastery, or had remained in school. The organizations swooning to the bohemian muse were self-co-opting.

Self-co-optation was also true in part of those medieval women who joined Beguinages. Commitment to the religious life was, for them, typically temporary but legitimate. For the individual it provided a buffer against the loneliness of urban life, and for the community it encapsulated unattached and thus presumably potentially dangerous women. Efforts to manipulate them were ambivalent, suggesting that some of the bishops did not appreciate the value of these organizations in maintaining order.

Monasticism, which emerged, in the West, out of the pressure of numbers combined with religious zeal, has since its beginning been perceived as a system that could help the Church and society stay on an even keel. As a system that encourages recruitment and incarceration of the overzealous and discipline for priests and other *religiosi* who may be going astray, monasticism exemplifies a pattern that strengthens adherence to tolerable ranges of behavior. Although intentional control of dissidence does not seem to have been one of the motives for originally organizing the monks and other less temporally bound residents, the Church hierarchy did soon learn that both abeyance and social control functions could be performed by the monasteries.

What I am suggesting is that facile statements about the manipulation of surplus populations are inadequate for understanding the manifold dimensions of the abeyance process. The assignment of personnel to positions in organizations performing this function varies from mandatory placement (as in schools, armies, and mental hospitals) to voluntary participation (as in the monasteries, Beguinages, and communes). In a formally democratic society there is seemingly more choice than in more controlled societies. The day-to-day behavior of individuals making these choices is only indirectly influenced by the efforts of elites to maintain order in society. The extent to which there is awareness of the control functions of abeyance and the intentions of elites is problematic.

Intentionality and Awareness

Tawney, on the one hand, and Piven and Cloward, on the other, suggest that intervention in the form of poor relief in sixteenth-century England or relief programs in twentieth-century America was an intentional response to the threat of social disorder. Unlike other efforts to anticipate and solve threats emerging out of surplus populations—including repression of presumed heretics during the Middle Ages in Europe, for example—economic solutions were sought in these two cases. Perhaps economic solutions are tried when the masses are perceived to be destitute, vulnerable to the most fundamental kinds of threat to physical survival. Other threats are subject to other responses. Surplus populations of the relatively well-off, for example, must be dealt with differently, particularly if those populations have an ideological base, as in religious movements. But, these matters aside, the issues associated with the conceptualization of intentionality and consciousness should be seen as problematic, requiring articulation.

When Adam Smith analyzed the functions of the market system in relation to surplus population, he focused on wages as a means of regulating demand for labor. It is clear that he understood the significance of the expansion and contraction of available personnel to fit into positions necessary to societal maintenance. That his influence among political and economic elites, at least in nineteenth-century England, was great is reflected in the widespread sale of his writings and equally widespread quotation from them. The works of Karl Marx and his colleague Friedrich Engels were similarly influential. In Book 1 of *Das Kapital* Marx held that a surplus of labor is a necessary feature of capitalist societies. Briefly, Marx's position is that in order to keep wages down and to maintain an available supply of labor to respond to the vicissitudes of the market, capitalist societies require an "industrial reserve army." By maintaining, at the lowest possible level of subsistence, a large unemployed population, competition for relatively few jobs will be great, the demands of those who work will be limited, and wages will be low. There will always be those who are so much in need that they will work for almost any wage. The "industrial reserve army" is thus warehoused, i.e., held in abeyance, in relation to expansions and contractions of status vacancies in the economic system.[1]

Although the Marxist description of surplus populations is accurate, the motives of capitalist elites remain difficult to discern. What might be termed a conspiracy against the workers is, to my mind, an outcome of the impersonal fluctuations of the market rather than conscious, intentional behavior on the part of capitalists. In fact this phenomenon is one of the best examples that social structures assume lives of their own, impacting far beyond the particular contributions of participants. The process is one that I prefer to call *synergic*; it is the cumulative and qualitative impact of independently motivated acts.[2] Ample evidence that both Marx and Engels understood this is to be found in their writings.

But from my point of view Marx's analysis of the warehousing concept refers to a special case associated with one type of system and one institution, the economic, in a particular period of history. Although the existence of diverse organizations to absorb and expel personnel facilitates the warehousing process in capitalist society, these functions of organizations are more basic to society than a purely economic explanation would indicate. They are universal functions associated with all societies at all times.[3]

Recognizing the connection between the existence of surplus populations and the threat of social disorder did not, I would hypothesize, require a great deal of sociological sophistication. How to manipulate the masses through organized efforts to co-opt and control them was a more difficult matter in emerging democratic societies. Organizations to absorb the surplus populations did emerge, but the awareness of their functions, the intentions of those who created and participated in them, and their relationship to societal need for control remains obscure. It is in the very nature of these processes that one finds difficulty in making connections between personal and group motives and intentions with societal consequences.

Robert K. Merton, in his classic paper on what he chose to call manifest and latent functions, wrestled with the problems of awareness, intentionality, and unintended consequences of group phenomena impacting on societies.[4] Although his formulation of manifest and latent functions represented a major step in articulating important dimensions in understanding the interplay between group behavior and its consequences, larger problems remain when we make efforts to understand the complexities of mass phenomena such as the emergence of surplus populations. Surplus populations have been created by elites, in the past, in order to accomplish particular goals, as, for example, in the case of the repeal of the Speenhamland Law and the enactment of the Poor Law Reform Act in England during the early nineteenth century. These legislative decisions forced peasants off the land into the urban areas and factories, where they were needed as laborers. Later, as Smelser has illustrated, a similar effort was made.[5] "In 1834 when the cotton industry was enjoying a boom accompanied by great demands for labor, the Poor Law Commissioners initiated a scheme to encourage the migration of families into the manufacturing districts."[6]

Though there are a number of instances of intended and recognized efforts on the part of the elite to impact on social structures, many cases illustrate that responses to imbalances and potential social disorder associated with surplus populations may be latent for both elites and masses.

The most recent effort to connect surplus populations and a kind of "Invisible Hand" is Richard Rubenstein's analysis of the Holocaust, *The Cunning of History*.[7] The issue of a seeming drift toward balancing out the relationship between numbers of people and the availability of status vacancies suggests that although given segments of societies act in terms of their own motives the consequences may fulfill the latent needs of a society at a given point in time. Thus the destruction of millions of Jews and others during the 1940s was at least in part a response to the problem of too many people in relation to too few *societal* resources. It is important to add, too many of the *wrong* kinds of people from the perspective of the Nazis and many other Europeans.

At a more abstract level, one that allows us to perceive the universal societal phenomena reflected in the Holocaust experience, Rubenstein holds that when there is a shortage of personnel to perform work that a dominating elite wants done those held in bondage will be treated with relatively greater care, will be kept alive and well in order to be able to better perform their assigned tasks. When there are more people than jobs the problem is, in part, how to control and/or rid the society of the surplus. I have held that organized patterns exist in societies to perform the abeyance function, an alternative to annihilation of a surplus population. Rubenstein's thesis is that whereas slavery in North America was characterized by efforts to maintain the slave as a productive unit and a valued commodity, the slaves of northern and eastern Europe were treated as expendable, to be used for a time and finally destroyed. I. G. Farben and other companies thus had a seemingly infinite supply of relatively free labor, whose only transfer potential was as victims of the death camps.

This provocative thesis helps extend the analysis of the abeyance process to a most dramatic and extreme dimension. By a gradual transformation of values, says Rubenstein, the normative checks on the propensity to commit the most extreme forms of violence between men, in a rational, systematic way, can be eroded, and what remains is a rational calculus in which people are valued or expendable according to their scarcity in the market. Although extreme in its emphasis upon the material basis for motives and behavior, Rubenstein's thesis is nevertheless important in articulating the relatively diverse impact of normative and rational processes in the organized behavior of society.

Though I have tended to set aside the analysis of the normative aspects of the abeyance process, in order to more clearly emphasize the universal, structural components, I do not feel that a complete understanding of abeyance, in an empirical sense, can be attained without understanding the institutional, normative dimension in relation to societal processes. Rubenstein's analysis does not place sufficient emphasis upon the role of nationalism and the traditions of anti-Semitism as sources of prescriptive norms in relation to the Jews and other minorities. Fritz Stern in his *The Politics of Cultural Despair*,[8] for example, describes how German philosophy and theology tended to extol the virtues of *das Volk* for more than a hundred years prior to the rise of the Nazis, simultaneously putting down the vices of the Jews and others. In the church and schools the doctrines supporting the Nazis were taught and reinforced. Joshua Trachtenberg's *The Devil and the Jews,* and Norman Cohn's *Europe's Inner Demons* similarly provide support for the thesis that the Nazi destruction of Jews and other minorities was more than rationalized by the myths associated with anti-Semitism and, more generally, the distrust of *Ausländers.*[9] The norms and values associated with relations between Germans and others did not simply facilitate the exclusion and annihilation process, but directed behavior to participate in it.

To be sure, many Germans saw the expulsion of Jews from their jobs as an opportunity to place themselves and others in valued positions. But an important component of this phenomenon was a seemingly widespread feeling, not only in Germany but elsewhere on the continent and in England as well, that the "good jobs" in society should go to "natives" rather than Jews.[10] From my perspective, in sum, the normative must be taken into account in any effort to understand what motivates and regulates people in society.

Efforts to understand the workings of society through a focus on the "Invisible Hand" metaphor reflects a concern for a critical aspect of societal processes. Louis Schneider, who devoted many years to this intellectual problem, has focused on the writings of the Scottish Moralists, and Mandeville, among others, to help clarify the issues.[11] Adam Smith, referred to above in another context, exemplified in his writing the longstanding concern with intentionality and consequences in the following discourse:

> They are led by an invisible hand to make nearly the same distribution of the necessaries of life which would have been made had the earth been divided into equal portions among all its inhabitants; and thus, *without intending, without knowing it,* advance the interest of the society and afford means to the multiplication of the species.[12]

That there has been longstanding concern with this matter of explaining the interconnections between personal motives and collective consequences does not mean that we have progressed very far in our capacity to understand this critical dimension. Indeed, the "Invisible Hand" metaphor is hardly ever seen in the literature of social science today. Given the implausibility, to say the least, of using as an alternative explanations that are based on instinct, the best we may hope to do at this time is be aware of the difficulties associated with simple explanations for complex societal processes. Explaining how self-co-optation comes about, for example, suggests one such problem.

Sociologists prefer to focus on the processes of societal interaction in organized settings, in order to help explain how the behavior of persons in groups impacts on society. In this study I focused primarily on aspects of social control at the group level. And, in attempting to assess in the context of abeyance how groups control persons, it is important to keep in mind what is meant by personal and social freedom, for this represents the other side of the coin.

Freedom and Constraint

The issues associated with freedom and constraint may appear only remotely related to my earlier discussion, but this is not the case. The concern with social order, as it is reflected in the sensitivity of elites in the past and present to the potentialities of unattached and uprooted masses, is merely an indicator of basic societal processes that remain latent for participants and observers. If we reflect, momentarily, on the interplay between persons and processes of social integration under conditions that contrast with those in the liberal democracies, it is easy to realize that surplus populations, if they should emerge, constitute no real problem. Totalitarian societies move people about, assign them to positions, and supervise them without rationalization regarding the legitimacy of the process. Deviance in society may be controlled by restricting movement of selected portions of the population, as illustrated in a recent study of the Soviet Union.[13]

Indeed, human breeding, too, may become organized, as in Nazi Germany, to develop personnel to hold designated positions in the society. Under serfdom, another example, personnel were assigned to positions, and were married and bred, according to the dictates of landowners, and, presumably, the needs of the productive system. Similarly, under slavery men, women, and children were bought, bred, and sold according to their capacity and potential for filling positions in an economic system. In none of these cases were there serious problems of population surplus, since personnel could be assigned to positions regardless of their personal needs or desires.

Liberal democratic societies depend upon more subtle processes and techniques. Formal freedom to move about; to choose occupations and spouses; to determine number of offspring—all these require societal devices that are compatible with voluntary behavior. Where there is no self-regulating mechanism at work, inducement to move, to change positions, to have more or fewer children, must be indirect. Legislation, like the Speenhamland Law cited above, may force personnel into situations that increase their vulnerability and availability to work at otherwise unattractive jobs. Organizations may be created by political elites, as in the United States during the 1930s, to attract, hold, and control the potentially dissident mass of unemployed. I refer, of course, to the New Deal programs discussed in the previous chapter. In all of those cases, consonant with a sociocultural environment that legitimizes free choice, men and women chose what seemed relatively good for them, economically, while at the same time choosing what was probably good for the survival of the political and economic system: social control over a substantial portion of their daily lives, i.e., their work lives. All of this suggests that freedom and control in liberal democratic societies may be a much more complicated process to understand than hitherto imagined.

A central problem for the sociologist, I feel, is how does a liberal democratic society maintain a degree of flexibility that simultaneously allows for a minimum of order while undergong change? Durkheim's postulate that "crime is the price that society pays for creativity" implies this question.[14] This postulate, thus interpreted, informs my approach. The paucity of interest on the part of sociologists in this subtle suggestion of Durkheim's—as well as his other, "A society of saints would be impossible"—reflects an unwillingness or inability to grapple with one of the most challenging theoretical questions to be faced in the search for a complete understanding of basic societal processes. Shelley is also sensitive to this issue. She concludes her study of Soviet criminality: "A reduction in the crime rate of major Soviet cities has been achieved only at the social cost of reducing personal freedom of movement and causing increased problems of criminality in more remote parts of the country."[16] Although it is not my intention to attempt a grandiose scheme for focusing interest and understanding on this issue, it is possible, nevertheless, to contribute to that goal, if only in a slightly oblique manner.

I am suggesting that the abeyance process, by holding people in organized activities and thus keeping them under control, is a means for formally adhering to norms of personal freedom while enhancing the flexibility that allows for creativity and change. By absorbing some portion of the potentially dissident through intentional intervention, including co-optation, and unintentional self-regulation on the part of marginal people, confrontation in the community and society at large is less likely to occur. If it does occur, protestors and deviants are likely to have a more modest impact than would otherwise be the case. In short, abeyance mitigates the impact of dissident behavior and slows down the rate of change in society. In doing so, it allows for creativity and social change with moderation. As such, it is an attentuating process in relation to a society. Where it works effectively, the potential for revolutionary change is minimal.

Abeyance and Status Vacancies

One way to conceptualize and describe the abeyance process at a more concrete level than the societal structure is to focus on movement in and out of societal positions. Abeyance may then be viewed in terms of an absorption phase and an expulsion phase. These phases, it is interesting to note, are reflected in the distinction made with respect to population movement more generally. Those leaving a society or region are referred to as "out-migrants," whereas those being received are called "in-migrants." While unattached they are referred to as "migrants," which describes them as unintegrated persons. These terms suggest implicit awareness of and concern for the absoprtion-expulsion process.

THE EXPULSION PHASE.   The expulsion phase of the abeyance process involves at least two types of conditions. In one type, persons are encouraged to move to another organizational context to fill vacant positions. In the other, personnel are expelled primarily to create positions for a presumably more select population. In this latter case, provision may or may not be made for alternative status vacancies to absorb those expelled. This is exemplified by some of my historical cases.

When the later Enclosure Acts were passed and implemented, as described by Polanyi and cited earlier, it was intended that the bulk of the now-surplus agricultural laborers would migrate to the factory towns and cities and assume jobs in the factories. This is only one example of the tranfer of personnel from one organized setting to another. Other examples include the contraction of the monastic system following the Black Death and the increase of status vacancies—i.e., the shortage of personnel—in commercial settings despite the shortage of personnel in the monastic system itself; the release of military personnel following World War II in spite of continued need for special skills within the military; and the regular expulsion of graduates of schools and colleges with the expectation that they will be absorbed into occupational positions. In all these examples there is the intention and expectation that those expelled will fill vacancies in other organizations, that they are not going to become a surplus population. The relative ease with which this transfer takes place is enhanced or inhibited by the processes reflected in my variables.

In the second type of expulsion, movement out of the organization is typically *involuntary*. The expulsion of the Jews from occupational positions in Germany and Italy during the 1930s and 1940s was in part motivated by an effort to provide loyal Nazis and Fascists with good jobs. The racial policies of Hitler and Mussolini justified the efforts of other Germans and Italians to assume positions that they coveted. Everett C. Hughes, cited above, who interviewed a sample of Germans after World War II, has noted that the occupation of important positions in German society by Jews was a not-uncommon reason given for removing the Jews from its midst. A recent study of the Jews in Italy suggests a similar pattern of displacement without efforts to justify the extermination of Jews.[17]

Another variant of the expulsion process, which for the most part does not involve either push to another organization or outright removal from a position without concern for reabsorption, is what has been called the "safety-valve" phenomenon. In this instance what is of concern is encouraging people to emigrate to another social context altogether. The frontier thesis of Frederick Jackson Turner, which held that the West of the United States was an effective safety-valve for releasing the surplus populations of the cities of the East, describes one such case. The use of the colonial empire by the British as a means for disbursing surplus populations is still another case. With respect to the social control process, the latter type of expulsion was regularly used as a means of ridding society of the politically and socially dissident. The settlement of Australia by dissidents represents a conspicuous historical case.[18]

THE ABSORPTION PHASE.   From the perspective of absorption, I would suggest at least two types of conditions. In the first, the motive is to fill positions because a shortage of personnnel has occurred or is anticipated. In the second, the social control function dominates the motives of those who manipulate the masses.

That the examples of the use of the later Enclosure Acts in England to force agricultural laborers from the land into the cities also involve motives directed to their absorption by the factory system illustrates the perspectival nature of my typology. Smelser's observation of manipulated migration in the cotton industry is similarly focused on both expulsion and absorption.

But Rubenstein's analysis of the use of Jews and other minorities as an expendable and infinite surplus population of laborers in the factories of I. G. Farben suggests a concern with absorption, i.e., filling status vacancies. To be sure, particular personnel who occupied these work positions did so for relatively short periods of time, as factory laborers ordinarily come and go, but the primary concern of the German industrialists who participated in this productive system was with keeping personnel on the job and replacing those who could no longer work. The surplus population was, of course, created by the Nazis and their German and East European allies.

Similarly, although slaves who were a marketable commodity were treated better, as Rubenstein holds, the concern of the southern planters and other white Americans who used slaves to work in their productive systems was with filling positions. Slave traders created the population from which laborers could be drawn.

The various military organizations of the United States and their current efforts to recruit personnel suggest still another example of efforts to absorb seemingly surplus youth, in this instance, into the armed forces.[19]

The second type of absorption phase is the one to which my attention has been directed in this study. Absoprtion is used to control the dissident and would-be dissident. That prisons and hospitals for those judged to be insane perform this function is clear. That the monastic system, the Beguine pattern, bohemianism, compulsory education, and the diverse programs and projects of the WPA during the 1930s performed this same function is what I have tried to demonstrate. That abeyance is an aspect of all societal organizations is what I have attempted to convey more generally. But there is a major difference between my perspective and that of Marx and Engels, on the one hand, and Richard Rubenstein, on the other. And this is reflective of diverse biases in our approaches. The cumulative intellectual impact of these two perspectives tends, however, to be complementary rather than exclusive and conflicting.

Institutional Process and Social Control

Piven and Cloward, Marx and Engels and Rubenstein emphasize the role of economic factors in the process of responding to and creating surplus population.* As I noted above, man is viewed, in their conception of capitalist society, as a commodity to be manipulated according to the ebb and flow of production and exchange. The creation of the surplus, according to Marx and Engels, is typically the result of an ironic situation: wage laborers inadvertently contribute to the process that makes them superfluous. Warehousing, unlike the organizational-integrative processes of absorbing personnel in my theory, is a *metaphor*. Neither Marx and Engels nor Rubenstein devote much attention to the aspect of socially controlling unintegrated masses through surveillance. Marx and Engels emphasize the role of wages and the way in which the poor are kept in poverty; and Rubenstein's focus is on the domination and extermination of populations who are not a social control problem because direct incarceration is the means by which domination occurs.[20]

Piven and Cloward carry the economic perspective farther by emphasizing that the way funds are distributed by the welfare system, particularly in the United States, is a social control device. When public disorder threatens, the idled masses receive welfare payments. As the threat of disorder subsides, so does the welfare system contract. Thus it is primarily the distribution of funds that is central to Piven and Cloward's analysis rather than the way in which social structural fea-

---

*It is important to note that it is only *in greater emphasis* that Marx and Engels, Rubenstein, and Piven and Cloward pay homage to economic variables. These variables are indeed important but they provide only a partial explanation for the phenomena associated with surplus populations.

tures directly exert control over the masses. In sum, their approach may be described as *payoff without integration and surveillance.* The solution to the problem of surplus population is thus conceived of as largely economic, e.g., more equitable and adequate distribution of welfare funds as necessary to the life situation of those who remain marginal to the economic system.

I cannot quarrel with Marx and Engels, Rubenstein, and Piven and Cloward. There is validity in each approach. However, it would be erroneous to assume that any one approach provides an adequate and exclusive explanation for the ways in which societal processes create and respond to marginal populations.

Marx was unambiguous in his view that the process of creating surplus populations and the need for a reserve army of unemployed had occurred "in no earlier period of human history" than the one he was writing about. What was happening under capitalism was historically and sociologically specific, he said.[21] Malthus, to whom Marx and Engels were responding in their writings on surplus population, was, to be sure, interested in the particular historical condition of society under capitalism. And it is clear that he was an apologist for those reactionary forces in England who would deprive the poor of *any* sustenance. But Malthus was also interested in the more abstract problem of balancing population and resources in society generally. His now-infamous quartet of solutions to the problem of too many people—including, disease and starvation—were conceived of as devices that unseen forces used to provide a balance between numbers and the means of subsistence.[22]

What is unacceptable in Malthus's approach is the idea that there are a limited number of status vacancies in a society and thus the significant variable is population rather than jobs. Thus, although he appreciated the fact that it is social rather than biological forces (i.e., the birthrate) that contribute to the surplus, he failed to appreciate the role that other social forces played in the persistence or decline of an unintegrated mass. Overemphasis on economic factors as creators of and impactors on surplus personnel in society obscures a wide variety of institutional patterns that also play a role in response to population imbalances. All societies in all times, I repeat, experience asymmetry between numbers of people and status vacancies. The wellspring of population and the processes by which personnel fit into and move about in a society are not simply aspects of the economy at a given point in history. Birthrates, for example, vary according to religious and other cultural prescriptions and proscriptions. Death rates, too, vary with the state of the medical arts, control of pestilence, and quality of life. The nature and quantity of positions in a society vary with religious forces, e.g., expansion-contraction of monasteries or nunneries, Crusades, and wars, to suggest only a few; political demands for soldiers and colonial administrators; and other institutional factors. The pursuit of education as an end in itself, for example, has played an important part in creating status vacancies for an intellectual core whose motives and rewards defy a simple economic explanation.

Organizations have evolved in society to provide for the absorption and expulsion of personnel as larger processes seemingly require. Though they do not always emerge in time to absorb marginal populations and though they do not necessarily work effectively, they do tend, on the whole, to help keep society on an even keel. When they fail to absorb or hold personnel under surveillance, collective protest and other forms of disorder are more likely to occur. The millennial movements described by Norman Cohn and the protests of agrarians described by Tawney (see Chapter 1), and the more recent movements of the 1930s described by Piven and Cloward (see Chapter 6), all occurred under conditions of the release of personnel from organized contexts in which they had been integrated—a release that took place without reintegration into alternative organizations. A large marginal population is perceived, realistically, as a threat to order. Thus the effective functioning of organizations that integrate marginal populations contributes to the maintenance of order. But what distinguishes these organizations from others in the society, and does their distinctive quality determine their persistence?

First of all, the functions of the organizations on which I have focused are largely, although not always, unplanned. Though it is true that the monastic system, the Beguinages, bohemian organizations, educational organizations, and the WPA projects have contributed to the control of dissidents and potential dissidents in their respective societal contexts, these outcomes are not typically the result of conscious intentions. Unlike bureaucratically organized social structures, these organizations have goals that remain relatively amorphous but within a normative-institutional framework. Since it is not clear what the activities of members might produce, in a tangible sense, it remains equally unclear what ought to be an outcome of their efforts.

Secondly, the material cost to the societies in which these patterns have emerged and within which potential dissidents are controlled is relatively small. Unlike participation in clearly recognized economic activities, which entails payment in wages, salaries, merit increases, and the like, support of those who are temporarily included in these activities is very inexpensive. By and large the nature of funding is either *eleemosynary*, i.e., charitable, or it is supported by government sponsored subsidies which reach the worker in the form of a stipend. Sometimes there is no payment at all to participants. As suggested above, these are not patterns that satisfy career aspirations. It is clear that they are materially uncompetitive with participation in main-line economic activities. Thus, from the Marxist perspective, they do function as warehousing activities in capitalist societies, since they hold personnel out of the labor force at a cost that contributes to the maintenance of low wages in the economic sphere.

Thirdly, these organizations are relatively more flexible in their activities, recruitment, and performance expectations than rationally organized social structures oriented toward specific goals. As my analysis of the six variables influencing the capacity of an organization to contribute to the abeyance function shows, these patterns tend to expand and contract as societal pressures impact on them and subside.

In general these organizations are similar to what Etzioni has called *normative*. They are organizations "in which normative power is the major source of control over most lower participants, whose orientation to the organization is characterized by high commitment."[23] All the organizations studied here fall into this type, including what Etzioni calls the "core organizations of social movements."[24]

Keeping in mind that Etzioni, and Yablonsky as well, have also made a distinction between the core and more temporary participants in organizations—a distinction that is central to my theory—it is well to articulate the differences between (1) the relatively permanent aspects of normative organizations and (2) social movements. Synthesizing the perspectives of other analysts of social movements, Etzioni holds that these movements are not organizations: "They are not oriented to specific goals; their dominant subsystems are expressive and not instrumental; there is little segregation between the various institutional spheres; and there is no systematic division of labor, power and communication. . . . Nevertheless, most movements have an organizational core which does have all these characteristics of a typical organizational structure."

The resonance between the perspective growing out of my analysis and Etzioni's lends support to the generality of applicability of my theory, even though my concern in this study is not directed to the internal processes of organizations and my own typology differs, in some ways, from his.

Abeyance and Sociological Theory

Noting the connections between organization theory in sociology and the abeyance process provides entrée into the sphere of sociological theory more generally. What are some of the other ways in which my theory links up with more general interests of sociologists?

I have already suggested how the abeyance and social control processes link up with (1) the Marxian analysis of surplus population; (2) Durkheim's proposition regarding flexibility, i.e., "crime is the price that society pays for creativity"; (3) the distinction between manifest and latent functions made by Merton and adumbrated by Schneider in his analysis of Mandeville and the Scottish Moralists, including Adam Smith; (4) Coser's perspectives on conflict and commitment; and (5) Smelser's theory of collective behavior. Still other connections are worthy of brief note.

Talcott Parsons, in attempting to describe how tendencies to conformity and deviance in society are controlled, has held that "every social system has, in addition to the obvious rewards for conformity and punishments for deviant behavior, a complex system of unplanned and largely unconscious mechanisms which serve to counteract deviant tendencies."[26] The organizational processes of simultaneous absorption and control of potential dissidents represent one such mechanism.

By siphoning off the potentially dissident in a population, the abeyance process also, I would hold, diffuses and defuses conflict. When a large unintegrated population emerges in a complex society, a number of diverse organizations provide alternative settings for the absorption of personnel, thus spreading and attentuating the impact of opposition and conflict. In the 1960s in the United States it was not only the public schools and universities which opened their doors to absorb youth. The bohemian communes, as I have shown, also absorbed a sizeable number of surplus youth.

In addition to spreading the impact of the unintegrated masses on the organized patterns that expand to absorb them, the involvement pattern defuses conflict by requiring compliance with the norms existing *within* the organization. This is analogous to the attenuation of radical tendencies that occurs when a social movement becomes transformed into an organization. The history of religious protest movements in the West provides a good number of examples of this phenomenon.

Organizations that perform the abeyance function simultaneously perform other mediating functions as well. As holding patterns these organizations are units in a network of personnel that is shifting from one activity of society to another. They may provide members with protection from destitution and with protection from the punishment communities often inflict on the unattached and marginal people in their midst. While participating in a holding pattern the member may maintain levels of skill or learn new skills, as in the WPA arts projects. The Beguinages, for example, mediated between the kinship structure and the religious structure, and the school mediates between the family and the economic system. Thus abeyance is typically only one of a number of contributions an organization may make to the maintenance or modification of societal patterns.

Other Abeyance Patterns

In addition to the role of organizations in holding personnel, other patterns typically strengthen the abeyance process. Some of these may be characterized as rites, including rites of passage, and other are associated with socialization.

TRANSITIONAL STATUS.   Within an organization there are structures that hold *individuals* in abeyance as well. Glaser and Straus, for example have suggested the concept "transitional status," which denotes

> time in terms of the social structure. It is a social system's tactic for keeping a person in passage between two statuses for a period of time. He is put in a transitional status, or sequence of them, that determines the period of time that he will be in a status passage. Thus the transitional status of the initiate will, in a particular case, carry with it the given amount of time it will take to make a non-member a member—a civilian is made a soldier by spending a given number of weeks as a basic trainee; an adolescent spends a number of years "in training" to be an adult.[27]

Using the army as an example suggests still another form of internal abeyance. The many technical training schools of the United States Army Air Corps during World War II were manpower pools that held combat soldiers in abeyance until they were needed in battle; note, for instance, the mass evacuation of many troops from these schools during the Battle of the Bulge in 1944 and 1945. This helps explain why daily physical training and continuous upgrading and reinforcement of combat skills were an integral part of the soldier's activities while attending school. Indeed, as my study of mandatory education suggests, what goes on in school generally is clearly not as important to a community or society as the fact that young people are being held in abeyance in relation to the labor market, and, simultaneously, under control. The value placed on education and the legal sanctions that reinforce attendance make education one of the most effective abeyance structures in American society.

SOCIALIZATION AND PATTERNING.   In order for abeyance processes to work, it is necessary first to socialize persons in ways that facilitate these processes and to reinforce socialization with group and organizational activities. The most general and useful descriptive concept with respect to socialization for abeyance is the Deferred Gratification Pattern, originally formulated by Schneider and Lysgaard.[28] While the DGP was most closely associated, in the sociological literature, with variations by social class, there is ample observation of ethnic patterns, which suggests that other variables are similarly associated. Not only do people in the middle classes in the United States tend to control their impulses to a greater extent than those in the working and lower classes with respect to sex, spending, and aggression, but, according to my hypotheses, they are socialized to wait in all contexts. With the help of a whole array of values and norms such as "Keep at it, success is just around the corner," Americans are taught to hold *themselves* in abeyance. When asynchronization in the system occurs, these norms play a role in the capacity of persons to cope with the holding process. Religious explanations, for example, including notions about life after death, tend to reinforce patterns of deferring gratification among some segments of the elderly population in Judeo-Christian societies. Sometimes, under extreme conditions, the holding pattern fails, or another—like the Beguinages—is too late in emerging, and a higher probability of deviance and rebellious collective action results. At still other times, as with the Calvinist experience, a rigorous system emerges that controls time and abeyance in an extremely effective manner. All these examples attest to the validity of the assumption that societies do not allow for the random expression of impulse and that the patterns which exert control enhance the abeyance process.

However, since socialization alone is incapable of controlling behavior it is necessary to explore the organizational patterns that reinforce the DGP. The quotation from Glaser and Straus suggests statuses and roles that reinforce holding patterns. It is safe to hold that all interaction involves impulse control, but engagement in organizational activities that include complementarity and reciprocity, coordination and integration, yields greater increments of reinforcement than do informal social relations. The articulation of normative and cognitive expectations, the potentially greater symbolic impact of more impersonal social interaction as size and complexity of organization or group increases, tend to enhance awareness of one's need to be patient, to await the time when one will be able to pursue desirable goals. For these patterns to be effective reinforcements, there must be supports in the larger social structure. In a relatively complex society pressures may be exerted that inhibit the process.

TIMING, SPACING, AND STATUS VACANCIES.   It is important to keep in mind that many people consciously and intentionally behave in ways that enhance the cushioning of asynchronization between status vacancies and personnel. A substantial body of literature based on demographic and survey research has been accumulating for at least twenty years on timing of pregnancy and child spacing.[30] This should come as no surprise to the social scientist, since one of the most conspicuously variable social patterns in American society has been the delay of marriage by persons in relatively higher classes. But the cause, and thus the constancy and predictability, of the pattern probably lies not only in the structuring of life-styles—including greater concern with and opportunity for extended educational and career involvement—but also in personal motives. Relative affluence allows for greater opportunity to "sow one's wild oats," to take time to decide what to do with one's life. It is sufficient to remind ourselves, in this context, that normative, cognitive, and idiosyncratic factors must be explored in order to explain the connections between personal behavior, group expectations, and societal synchronization and asychronization.

I am not suggesting, in this context, that there is a necessary correlation between apparent societal needs and the behavior of persons and groups. The structuring of behavior in a society may create strains in the system that contribute to severe imbalances between available personnel and existing status vacancies. In their classic study of Irish "countrymen," Arensberg and Kimball observed that the unwillingness of the aging father to relinquish control and ownership of his farm to his son until quite late in life led to marriages at a relatively late age, when the spouses' fertility levels were in decline. The result was a low reproduction rate, which, from some points of view, limited personnel for status vacancies in the agricultural sphere. It is well to note that from still another value perspective, that of stability, there were no strains. One more example, related to cognitive motivation, suggests how asychronization may emerge out of reproductive patterns. During the early part of the nineteenth century in England, when the factory system was expanding, it was economically feasible to have many children. The more children working, the greater the income for the family as a whole. As factory methods changed and fewer workers, i.e., children, were employable, a surplus population emerged. Without work and without school, children roamed the street panhandling and committing diverse crimes.[32] Engels, in his study of the British working class, provides a description of the scene that seems to come right out of Dickens. This particular imbalance was directly responsible, as Musgrove shows, for the rise of mandatory education and child labor laws.

Finale

I have attempted, in this study, to articulate a hitherto neglected process that is fundamental to all societies. The abeyance process is central to the relatively smooth operation of a society. This process enhances stability or change in society by integrating and placing marginal groups under the surveillance and control of functionaries in both institutionalized organizations and by control of peers in less formally organized groups.

From a theoretical perspective the process may be viewed as a buffer against diverse forms of deviance, including social protest. Abeyance attenuates the rate of social change by absorbing the potential sources of challenge to the status quo. As I have described it, it is typically a conservation process.

But awareness of this aspect of societal process can provide the planners and shapers of modern societies with an articulated method for improving the lot of ordinary citizens. Rationally organized structures of voluntary participation, recognized as simultaneously integrative and controlling, can provide alternatives for contemporary surplus populations in industrialized societies. The older members of society, particularly the very large numbers of unattached middle-aged and elderly women; unemployed, uninvolved, and unintegrated youth, particularly minority youth; and others as well could be provided with a range of alternative organized lifestyles. Like the Beguinages of the Rhineland and the Low Countries, and the communes of recent and contemporary America, urban and rural patterns could be encouraged that would provide places, on a voluntary basis, for those who are marginal to society. Although the correlation between being integrated into organized groups and living a meaningful life is less than one-to-one, the opportunity to shed loneliness and alienation is surely greater for those who are engaged with others in the intimate tasks of ordinary living.[33] And for those whose affiliation is temporary, participation in groups may help allay tendencies to despair. That these organizations may also lead to protest and demand for change is a possibility which resonates with what has gone before in the history of Western societies.

Whatever the outcome might be, I have performed my role as a sociologist. Raising the latent, inconspicuous patterns to a level of awareness that enables the professional and lay person to recognize, select, and act upon now known and better understood processes allows those who want to conserve the status quo, as well as those who want to change it, a choice. That choice, I hope, will be made on the basis of humanistic values rather than cost, economic or political.

NOTES

Prologue

1. Cf., for example, Donald Black, *The Behavior of Law* (New York: Academic Press, 1976).
2. Robert K. Merton, *Social Theory and Social Structure* (New York: Free Press, 1949).
3. Cf. Louis Schneider, ed., *The Scottish Moralists on Human Nature and Society* (Chicago: University of Chicago Press, 1967), introduction; cf. also his article, "Mandeville as Forerunner of Modern Sociology," *Journal of the History of the Behavioral Sciences* 6, no. 3 (1970); and Ephraim H. Mizruchi, *Success and Opportunity: A Study of Anomie* (New York: The Free Press, 1964), Chapter 1.
4. R. W. Southern, *Western Society and the Church in the Middle Ages* (Middlesex, England: Penguin Books, 1972), p. 219.
5. Arthur L. Stinchcombe, *Theoretical Methods in Social History* (New York: Academic Press, 1978).

1. Too Many People, Too Few Places

1. Robert K. Merton, "Manifest and Latent Functions," in *Social Theory and Social Structure* (New York: The Free Press, 1949).
2. R. H. Tawney, *The Agrarian Problem in the Sixteenth Century* (New York: Harper Torchbooks, 1967, originally 1912); N. Cohn, *The Pursuit of the Millennium* (New York: Harper Torchbooks, 1961); F. F. Piven and R. Cloward, *Regulating the Poor* (New York: Random House, 1972).
3. Cohn, *Pursuit of the Millennium*, p. 314. Italics mine. The issue of whether, and to what extent, the truly impoverished participate in revolutionary movements is an important one. I deal with it later in this chapter.
4. Tawney, *The Agrarian Problem*, p. 269.
5. Ibid.
6. *D'Ewes's Journal.* Speech of Cecil, 1597. As quoted in Ibid., p. 279.

7. Tawney, *The Agrarian Problem*, p. 280.

8. Cf. Ephraim H. Mizruchi, "Aspiration and Poverty," *Sociological Quarterly* (1967):439–446; and, for a classic, Crane Brinton, *The Anatomy of Revolution* (New York: Random House, Vintage Books, 1958).

9. In this context it is interesting to review Michael Schwartz's study of the organization of the southern agrarians into the Grange and, later, the Populist Party in the 1880s. *See* Bibliography, *under* Mizruchi.

10. Tawney, *The Agrarian Problem*, pp. 317–318.

11. See, in this context, Karl Polanyi, *The Great Transformation* (New York: Rinehart, 1944).

12. Piven and Cloward, *Regulating the Poor*, pp. 3–4. Italics mine.

13. Part 1 (Hamden, Conn.: Archon Books, 1963), and part 2 (London: Longman Green and Co., 1929, vols. 1 and 2).

14 Piven and Cloward, *Regulating the Poor*, p. 5.

15. J. R. Hale, *Renaissance Europe: 1480–1520* (London: Collins, 1971), p. 23. Italics mine.

16. Ralph Linton, *The Study of Man* (New York: Appleton-Century-Crofts, 1936). There are, of course, diverse meanings and usages associated with these concepts.

17. Pitirim Sorokin, *Social Mobility* (New York: Harper & Bros., 1927), pp. 346–377; Sorokin uses "social vacuum" in this context. S. M. Lipset and H. Zetterberg, "A Theory of Social Mobility," in R. Bendix and S. M. Lipset, eds., *Class, Status and Power*, 2nd ed. (New York: Free Press, 1966), pp. 561–573; printed from *Transactions of the Third World Congress of Sociology* 2 (1956); the quotation is from p. 565. Elbridge Sibley, "Some Demographic Clues to Stratification," *American Sociological Review* 7 (June 1942): 326. Cf., also, M. Abrahamson, E. Mizruchi, and C. Hornung, *Stratification and Mobility* (New York: Macmillan, 1976), part 4.

18. Neil J. Smelser, *Social Change in the Industrial Revolution* (Chicago: University of Chicago Press, 1959), p. 202.

19. S. N. Eisenstadt, *From Generation to Generation* (New York: Free Press, 1956).

20. Ian Kershaw, "The Great Famine and Agrarian Crisis in England, 1315–1322." *Past and Present* 59 (May 1973). Cf., also, Hans Nabholz, "Medieval Agrarian Society in Transition," pp. 493–561, and Marc Bloch, "The Rise of Dependent Cultivation and Seignorial Institutions," pp. 224–227—both in *The Cambridge Economic History*, vol. 1 (London: Cambridge University Press, 1941).

21. Friedrich Engels, *The Condition of the Working Class in England* (Stanford: Stanford University Press, 1968).

22. This aspect of change has also been noted by Engels, *Condition of the Working Class*, and by Marx and Engels in numerous contexts.

23. Max Weber, *The Methodology of the Social Sciences* (New York: Free Press, 1949).

24. Lewis A. Coser, *Greedy Institutions* (New York: Free Press, 1974).

2. Monasticism: The Total Way of Life

1. There are a great many books and papers dealing with aspects of the origins of monasticism. For my purposes some of the most useful have been A. Harnack, *Monasticism: Its Ideals and History* (New York: G. P. Putnam's Sons, n.d. [ca. 1904]); E. Gibbon, *The History of the Decline and Fall of the Roman Empire*, vol. 4, ed. with notes and intro. by J. B. Bury (London: Methuen, 1909); H. Black, *Culture and Restraint* (New York: F. H. Revell Co., 1901); H. Workman, *The Evolution of the Monastic Ideal* (London: C. H. Kelley, 1909); E. S. Duckett, *Monasticism* (Ann Arbor: University of Michigan, 1938); D. Knowles, *The Monastic Order in England* (Cambridge: Cambridge University Press, 1963); and *Christian Monasticism* (New York: McGraw-Hill, 1969); E. K. Francis, "Toward a Typology of Religious Orders," *American Journal of Sociology* 50 (March 1950): 437–449; W. E. H. Lecky, *History of European Morals* (New York: Braziller, 1955, originally published in 1869); and C. F. Montalembert, *The Monks of the West* (New York: Longmans, Green, 1896). My colleague Agehananda Bharati has written an excellent paper describing all aspects of monasticism, Oriental and Occidental. See "Monasticism," *Encyclopedia Britannica*, 1974, pp. 335–343.

2. Harnack, *Monasticism*, pp. 36–38.

3. Workman, *Evolution of the Monastic Ideal*, pp. 24–25.

4. Ibid.

5. Gibbon, *Decline and Fall*, p. 69.

6. Francis, "Toward a Typology," p. 441.

7. Lecky, *History of European Morals*, p. 101.

8. Ibid.

9. Friedrich Heer, *The Medieval World*, trans. by J. Sondheimer (New York: New American Library, Mentor Books, 1962), p. 61.

10. Ernest Barker, in F. J. C. Hearnshaw, ed., *The Social and Political Ideas of Some Great Medieval Thinkers* (London: G. G. Harrap & Co., 1923), p. 15.

11. R. W. Southern, *Western Society and the Church in the Middle Ages* (Hammondsworth, Middlesex, England: Penguin Books, 1972), pp. 225–228.

12. Ibid., p. 228.

13. Francis, "Toward a Typology," p. 437.

14. Robert MacIver, *Society* (New York: Rinehart, 1937).

15. Francis, "Toward a Typology," p. 439.

16. Montalembert, *Monks of the West*, vol. 1, p. 219. The biblical source is Acts 2: 44, 45; 4: 32, 34, 35, 37.

17. J. B. Russell, *A History of Medieval Christianity* (New York: T. Y. Crowell, 1965), p. 104.

18. Watkin Williams, *Monastic Studies* (Manchester: University of Manchester Press, 1938), p. 24.

19. J. B. Russell, *History of Medieval Christianity*, p. 105.

20. Jean Leclercq, "The Monastic Crisis of the Eleventh and Twelfth Centuries," in N. Hunt, ed., *Cluniac Monasticism in the Central Middle Ages* (Hamden, Conn.: Archon Books, 1971), p. 236.

21. Marc Bloch, *Feudal Society* (Chicago: University of Chicago Press, 1964), p. 421. J. C. Russell, "Late Ancient and Medieval Population," *Transactions of the American Philosophical Society* 48 (June 1948):98.

22. J. B. Russell, *History of Medieval Christianity*, p. 106.

23. Cf., for example, N. F. Cantor, "Obligations of the Church in English Society: Military Arrays of the Clergy, 1369–1418," in W. C. Jordan, et al., eds., *Order and Innovation in the Middle Ages* (Princeton, N.J.: Princeton University Press, 1976), pp. 293–314; and Cantor, "The Crisis of Western Monasticism, 1050–1130," *American Historical Review* 66 (1960):44–67.

24. J. B. Russell, "Late Ancient and Medieval Population," *Transactions of the American Philosophical Society* 48 (June 1948):99.

25. Ibid., p. 140.

26. For examples of this independent variation cf., for example, J. C. Russell's earlier "The Clerical Population of Medieval England," *Traditio* (1944):177–212. In this study Russell's data show that "the monastic wave reached its peak before the general population did" (p. 212). Similarly, in his 1948 paper, Russell holds that "population changes are comparatively slow" (p. 139), with which I heartily agree. If population is relatively static, in that context sex and age ratios, it cannot explain changes in religious behavior.

27. J. C. Russell, "The Clerical Population," 1944, p. 212.

28. J. R. Hale, *Renaissance Europe: 1480–1520* (London: Collins, 1971).

29. Ibid., p. 229.

30. Ibid.

31. Ibid., p. 231.

32. Workman, *Evolution of the Monastic Ideal*, p. 57.

33. Harnack, *Monasticism*, p. 45.

34. Hugh Trevor-Roper, *The Crisis of the Seventeenth Century* (New York: Harper & Row, 1966), p. 128; cf. also *The Plunder of the Arts in the Seventeenth Century* (London: Thames & Hudson, 1970), by the same author.

35. Joyce Youings, *The Dissolution of the Monasteries* (London: George Allen & Unwin, 1971), p. 23.

36. A. W. Wishart, *A Short History of Monks and Monasteries*. 2d edition. (Trenton, N.J.: A. Brandt, 1902), p. 244.

37. Lewis Coser, *Greedy Institutions* (New York: The Free Press, 1974).

38. Francis, "Toward a Typology," p. 439.

39. Hale, *Renaissance Europe*, p. 229.

40. David Knowles, Foreword to 1962 Beacon Press edition of Workman, *Evolution of the Monastic Ideal*, no pagination.

3. Beguines: Ambivalence and Heresy

1. Cf. Marc Bloch, *Federal Society* (Chicago: University of Chicago Press, 1964); J. C. Russell, *Medieval Regions and Their Cities* (Newton Abbot, England: David and Charles, 1972); Dayton Phillips, *The Beguines of Medieval Strasbourg*

(Stanford: Stanford University Press, 1941); and R. W. Southern, *Western Society and the Church in the Middle Ages* (Middlesex, England: Penguin Books, 1972).

2. My sources here are: W. L. Wakefield and A. P. Evans, eds. and trans., *Heresies of the High Middle Ages* (New York: Columbia University Press, 1969); Bernard Gui, *Manuel de l'inquisiteur*, ed. G. Mollat (Paris: Champion, 1926), trans. by M. M. McLaughlin, in J. B. Ross and M. M. McLaughlin, eds., *The Portable Medieval Reader* (New York: The Viking Press, 1949); R. I. Moore, *The Birth of Popular Heresy* (London: Edward Arnold, 1975); and J. B. Russell, ed., *Religious Dissent in the Middle Ages* (New York: Wiley, 1971). Cf. also, in this context, J. B. Russell's *Dissent and Reform in the Early Middle Ages* (Berkeley and Los Angeles: University of California Press, 1965); W. L. Wakefield, *Heresy, Crusade and Inquisition in Southern France, 1100–1250* (Berkeley and Los Angeles: University of California Press, 1974); M. Lambert, *Medieval Heresy* (New York: Holmes & Meier, 1975); G. Leff, *Heresy in the Later Middle Ages* (Manchester: Manchester University Press, 1967), vol. 1; and J. Le Goff, ed., *Hérésies et sociétés* (Paris: Mouton, 1968).

3. For an account of the changing status of women see, for example, Lina Eckenstein, *Women Under Monasticism* (New York: Russell & Russell, 1963, originally published 1896), particularly Chapter 1; and, with respect to witches, Norman Cohn, *Europe's Inner Demons* (New York: Basic Books, 1975).

4. See Eckenstein, *Women Under Monasticism*, pp. 4–5; E. E. Power, "The Position of Women," in C. G. Crump and E. F. Jacob, eds., *The Legacy of the Middle Ages* (Oxford: Oxford University Press, 1926).

5. David Herlihy, "Land, Family and Women in Continental Europe, 701–1200," *Traditio* 18 (1962):111.

6. Ibid.

7. See, for example, E. Power, "The Position of Women."

8. Ibid., p. 426.

9. Ibid., p. 427.

10. Ibid., p. 405.

11. Ibid., p. 403.

12. See, e.g., J. C. Russell, *Medieval Regions*; E. E. Power, *Medieval Women* (Cambridge: Cambridge University Press, 1975); G. Koch, *Frauenfrage und Ketzertum im Mittelalter* (Berlin: Akademie Verlag, 1962); and B. Bolton, "Mulieres Sanctae," in D. Baker, ed., *Sanctity and Secularity: The Church and the World*, Papers of the Ecclesiastical History Society of London (New York: Harper & Row, 1973), pp. 77–95; and perhaps most important in this context, Dayton Phillips, *The Beguines of Medieval Strasbourg* (Stanford: Stanford University Press, 1941).

13. J. R. Hale, *Renaissance Europe: 1480–1520* (London: Collins, 1971).

14. Bolton, in Baker, *Sanctity*, p. 86.

15. Phillips, *The Beguines*, p. 20.

16. Bolton, in Baker, *Sanctity*, p. 87.

17. R. W. Southern, *Western Society and the Church in the Middle Ages* (Middlesex, England: Penguin Books, 1972), p. 311, as paraphrased in Ibid. Bolton also reminds us of the risk of death in childbirth as a factor which might have discouraged women from marrying.
18. Bolton, in Baker, *Sanctity*, p. 87. The last sentence is paraphrased from Max Weber's *Sociology of Religion* (Boston: Beacon Press, 1963), p. 106.
19. Southern, *Western Society*, p. 309.
20. Ibid.
21. Ibid., p. 310.
22. Ibid.
23. Hugh, abbot of Cluny, as quoted by Southern, *Western Society*, p. 310.
24. Ibid.
25. For a discussion of the *Beguins* of Provence, see Leff, *Heresy*, pp. 212–230. For a discussion of the factors that played a role in the increased repression associated with dissent, see J. B. Russell, *Dissent and Reform*, pp. 251–258.
26. Southern, *Western Society*, pp. 319–331.
27. M. Erbstösser and Ernst Werner, *Ideologische Probleme des Mittelalterlichen Plebejertums* (Berlin: Akademie Verlag, 1960), pp. 27–28. With respect to the class issue, cf. also Koch, *Frauenfrage und Ketzertum*, particularly pp. 28–29; and M. Erbstösser, *Sozialreligiöse Stromungen im Späten Mittelalter* (Berlin: Akademie Verlag, 1970). Koch's assumption that those I called *Beguins* above are related to the *Beguines*, it should be kept in mind, is not consistent with my own. The class antagonisms issue that has placed these writers in opposition to Herbert Grundmann and other idealists is beyond both my concerns in this work and my capacities. I have therefore chosen to take a scholarly stance that is conservative, emphasizing those aspects of the social origins of the Beguines on which there tends to be consensus among historians of the Frauenfrage, rather than directing my energies to an issue which requires greater familiarity with the primary sources than I possess. My purposes, to repeat, are primarily limited to the role of the Beguinage as a mediating and control structure.
28. Phillips, *The Beguines*, pp. 36–37.
29. Ibid., Chapter 4.
30. Ibid., pp. 140–141.
31. Phillips, *The Beguines*, Chapter 8. With respect to overzealousness, see, for example, Robert Lerner, *The Heresy of the Free Spirit* (Berkeley and Los Angeles: University of California Press, 1972), p. 45.
32. E. W. McDonnell, *The Beguines and Beghards in Medieval Culture* (New York: Octagon Books, 1969), p. 140. Brian S. Pullan, in *Rich and Poor in Renaissance Venice* (Oxford: Basil Blackwell, 1971), has noted how Renaissance hospices "sheltered" female members of "Third Orders." "Tertiaries promised to lead an austere life and to devote themselves to good works, which included almsgiving. But the Third Orders performed another important social function, in providing a recognized status for those who joined them. They received women who did not choose or could not afford to marry or enter a

cloister: who found difficulty in solving the economic problem of the dowry" (209).

33. Herbert Grundmann, *Religiöse Bewegungen im Mittelalter* (Berlin: Verlag Dr. Emil Ebering, 1935), pp. 344–345.

34. E. W. McDonnell, *The Beguines and Beghards*, p. 438.

35. Herbert Gruudmann, *Religiöse Bewegungen*, pp. 344–345. See also his "Zur Geschichte der Beginen im 13. Jahrhundert," in *Herbert Grundmann Ausgewahlte Aufsätze* (Stuttgart: Anton Hiersemann, 1976), pp. 201–221. Cf. also the review of this paper by J. van Mierlo in *Revue d'Histoire Ecclésiastique*, vol. 28 (Louvain: Bureaux de la Revue, 1932). I thank Mrs. J. Prins for help with the German translation.

36. Lerner, *Heresy of the Free Spirit*, pp. 155–157. It is well to keep in mind that the gains which the corrupt friars might enjoy, including bribes, were also jeopardized.

37. See, in this context, Ibid.

38. See McDonnell, *Beguines and Beghards*, p. 438.

39. Lerner, *Heresy of the Free Spirit*, pp. 45–46.

40. Ibid.

41. Ibid., p. 47.

42. Ibid.

43. Lambert, *Medieval Heresy*, p. 180.

44. In this context see Edward Shils, *The Center and the Periphery* (Chicago: University of Chicago Press, 1975).

45. Southern, *Western Society*, pp. 324–325.

46. Phillips, *The Begines*, pp. 228–229.

47. For example, Southern describes property transactions carried on by Beguines other than those involving purchase of Beguinages (*Western Society*, pp. 324).

48. Bloch, in *Feudal Society*, notes that the idea of "dishonourable work" played a role in inducing women to join religious movements like those of the Beguines. For the Beguines, work was "God's work"; although menial, it was performed as a calling (p. 269).

49. See, for example, David Herlihy, "Alienation in Medieval Culture and Society," in Frank Johnson, ed., *Alienation* (New York: Seminar Press, 1973).

50. Bloch, *Feudal Society*, p. 254.

4. Bohemians: Vagabonds and Aesthetic Pretenders

1. In this context see Norman Cohn, *The Pursuit of the Millennium*, 2nd ed. (New York: Harper Torchbooks, 1961), particularly pp. 217–236.

2. Ibid., p. 221.

3. E. K. Chambers, *The Elizabethan Stage*, vol. 1 (Oxford: Clarendon Press,

1923), p. 269. The shortage of labor could be largely attributed to the Black Death.

4. R. H. Tawney, *The Agrarian Problem in the Sixteenth Century* (New York: Harper Torchbooks, 1967), Chapter 1.

5. Chambers, *Elizabethan Stage*, p. 279. The statutes in question were the Vagabonds Act and the revisions of it.

6. Ibid., Chapter 2.

7. In this context see Lewis Einstein, *The Italian Renaissance in England* (New York: Columbia University Press, 1902); and Thomas Coryat, *Coryat's Crudities*, vols. 1 and 2 (New York: Macmillan, 1905; original printing 1611).

8. See Claude Marks, *Pilgrims, Heretics and Lovers: A Medieval Journey* (New York: Macmillan, 1975).

9. Ibid., p. x.

10. See Ibid., p. 43, on attitudes toward minstrels.

11. Ibid., pp. 40–41. A classic statement on minstrels, their origins and types, is in E. K. Chambers, *The Medieval Stage*, vol. 1 (Oxford: Oxford University Press, 1903), pp. 1–86.

12. David Matza, "Subterranean Traditions of Youth," *The Annals* 338 (November 1961): 102–118. Matza's usage, it is well to keep in mind, is limited to American youth.

13. On patterned norm evasion, see especially Robert K. Merton, *Social Theory and Social Structure* (New York: The Free Press, 1949); Talcott Parsons, *The Social System* (New York: Free Press, 1951); and Robin M. Williams, Jr., *American Society*, 3rd ed. (New York: Alfred A. Knopf, 1970). Although the term "patterned norm evasion" is Williams's usage the idea is shared by several sociologists. Merton's "institutional evasions of institutional rules" was included in his Harvard lectures as early as 1938. An enlightening discussion of norm evasion is to be found in Chanoch Jacobsen, "Permissiveness and Norm Evasions," *Sociology* (May 1979): 219–233. The usage of the term "institutional evasions" does tend to conflict with my own conception of institutions in this context. Not all repetitive forms are institutionalized, in my view, since some lack normative legitimacy.

14. See Marks, *Pilgrims*.

15. Chambers, *Medieval Stage*, p. 38.

16. Ibid., p. 45.

17. Ibid., p. 54.

18. Ibid., p. 62.

19. Ibid., p. 68.

20. Chambers, *Medieval Stage*, p. 1. Erich Auerbach in his book *Mimesis* (Princeton: Princeton University Press, 1953), deals with important aspects of Western literature—differentiating between two models, the Greek classic, as reflected in Homer, and the Old Testament. That there are important sociological aspects of this distinction, and that they have a bearing on the nature of the drama and reactions to it during medieval and post-medieval periods, is worthy of investigation but beyond the scope of this work. What

I have in mind is the matter of whether the ideas to be communicated are "up front" and easily discerned, as in the Greek drama, or whether a greater amount of inference and interpretation is required, as in the Old Testament. I would hypothesize that as the drama shifted to greater obscurity and suggestiveness there was greater concern on the part of authorities.

21. Chambers, *Elizabethan Stage*, p. 269. Cf. also W. J. Chambliss, "The Law of Vagrancy." *Warner Modular Publications* Module 4 (1973):1–10.

22. Ibid., p. 270.

23. Ibid., p. 271.

24. Quoted by Chambers, Ibid., pp. 306–307.

25. T. H. Jameson, *The Hidden Shakespeare* (New York: Minerva Press, 1969).

26. In this context see A. Stinchcombe, *Theoretical Methods in Social History* (New York: Academic Press, 1978).

27. C. Grana, *Bohemian versus Bourgeois* (New York: Basic Books, 1964), p. 26.

28. Aspects of bohemianism are dealt with in a number of Balzac's works. See, for example, *Lost Illusions* and *The Human Comedy*. Both Grana's study and Malcolm Easton's *Artists and Writers in Paris* (New York: St. Martin's Press, 1964) provide excellent treatment of literary themes relevant to understanding the bohemian ideal.

29. Easton, *Artists and Writers*, p. 26. On Saint-Simon as a contributor to the emerging views of the artist, see Frank Manuel, *The Prophets of Paris* (New York: Harper Torchbooks, 1965), pp. 162–168.

30. Easton, *Artists and Writers*, p. 28.

31. Translated and quoted in Ibid.

32. Henri Murger, *Vie de Bohème*, trans. N. Cameron (London: The Novel Library, 1949).

33. Easton, *Artists and Writers*, p. 113.

34. Ibid., p. 127.

35. Ibid., p. 127.

36. T. Zeldin, *France: 1848–1945*, Oxford History of Modern Europe, vol. 2 (Oxford: Clarendon Press, 1977), p. 204.

37. Quoted and translated in Grana, *Bohemian versus Bourgeois*, p. 54. From *Oeuvres Complètes*, vol. 1 (Paris: 1845), pp. 162–163.

38. R. Miller, *Bohemia: The Protoculture Then and Now* (Chicago: Nelson-Hall, 1977).

39. In this context see Albert Parry's *Garrets and Pretenders* (New York: Dover Books, 1960, originally 1933). Parry's work is, to my mind, the most significant historical study of American bohemianism to date. Still another useful book is Emily Hahn, *Romatic Rebels* (Boston: Houghton-Mifflin Co., 1967).

40. Parry, *Garrets and Pretenders*, Chapter 16.

41. M. Cowley, *Exile's Return* (New York: Viking Press, 1968, originally 1934).

42. Ibid., p. 69.

43. Matza, "Subterranean Traditions of Youth." Although I accept Cowley's view that the bohemian doctrine had an impact on the behavior pattern of

Americans, and his perceptive articulation as well, I am less inclined to agree that this represented a "revolution in morality" (p. 63). The traditional pattern of morality may persist in a society or substructure at the same time that deviant behavior persists. Patterned norm evasion, to which I referred above, is one such category of behavior. Which "morals" have changed since World War I and to what degree is problematic. Careful research, yielding unequivocal results, has not been forthcoming at this date. The best analysis of American values, to my mind, is still Williams, *American Society*.

44. Cowley, *Exile's Return*, pp. 60–61.
45. Caroline Ware, *Greenwich Village 1920–1930* (New York: Harper & Row, 1965, originally 1935); Harvey Zorbaugh, *The Gold Coast and the Slum* (Chicago: University of Chicago Press, 1929).
46. Cf. chapters 15 and 16 in Parry, *Garrets and Pretenders*.
47. Ware, *Greenwich Village*, pp. 251–252.
48. Ibid., pp. 252–256.
49. Émile Durkheim, *Suicide*, trans. G. Simpson (New York: The Free Press, 1951, originally 1897), p. 252.
50. L. Veysey, *The Communal Experience* (New York: Harper & Row, 1973).
51. Ibid.
52. My own observations here are reinforced by those described by Harry T. Moore, "Enter Beatniks: The Bohème of 1960," in Parry *Garrets and Pretender*, pp. 376–395; Lawrence Lipton, *The Holy Barbarians* (New York: Julian Messner, 1958); Francis J. Rigney and L. Douglas Smith, *The Real Bohemia* (New York: Basic Books, 1961); and John Gruen, *The New Bohemia* (New York: Grosset & Dunlap, 1967). With respect to the hippies and the San Francisco context, see Howard Becker, ed., *Culture and Civility in San Francisco* (New Bruswick, N.J.: Transaction books, 1971), and Miller, *Bohemia: The Protoculture*. One of the best sociological works on the hippies is Lewis Yablonsky's *The Hippie Trip* (New York: Pegasus, 1968). An interesting series of portraits appears in Leonard Wolf, ed., *Voices from the Love Generation* (Boston: Little, Brown, 1968).
53. This point is one of several important themes in Harvey C. Greisman, "Social Movements and the Mass Society: Requiem for the Counter-Culture," in E. H. Mizruchi, ed., *The Substance of Sociology*, 2nd ed. (New York: Appleton-Century-Crofts, 1973).
54. Although Jack Kerouac in his best-known book, *On the Road* (New York: Viking, 1957), holds that "beat" is short for "beatific," most observers agree that the reference is to the disillusioned appearance of these youths.
55. L. Yablonsky, *The Violent Gang* (New York: Macmillan, 1962). The hippies are dealt with in his *The Hippie Trip* (New York: Pegasus, 1968).
56. *The Hippie Trip*, pp. 293–294.
57. Ibid., p. 294.
58. Tawney, *The Agrarian Problem*; see also Chambers, *The Elizabethan Stage*.
59. See Veysey, *The Communal Experience*.
60. Matza, "Subterranean Traditions," has suggested several patterns which aid in the integration of bohemians into conventional society.

61. Parry, *Garrets and Pretenders*, p. XXII.
62. Grana, *Bohemian versus Bourgeois*.

5. Compulsory Apprenticeship and Education: The Quintessence of Control

1. R. H. Tawney, *The Agrarian Problem in the Sixteenth Century* (New York: Harper Torchbooks, 1967, originally 1912), chapter 1.
2. M. Weber, *The Protestant Ethic and the Spirit of Captialism* (London: Allen Unwin, 1930).
3. E. M. Leonard, *The Early History of English Poor Relief* (London: Frank Cass & Co., 1965, originally 1900).
4. O. J. Dunlop, *English Apprenticeship and Child Labor* (New York: Macmillan, 1912) p. 29. For a number of relevant readily available and readable documents see A. E. Bland et al., eds., *English Economic History: Select Documents* (London: G. Bell and Sons, Ltd., 1930), especially chapter 5.
5. Ibid.
6. Ibid., p. 30. Note that while Dunlop and others use 1562 as the date of passage M. G. Davies in *The Enforcement of English Apprenticeship* (Cambridge, Mass.: Harvard University Press, 1965), uses 1563.
7. This is a central theme in E. M. Leonard, *The Early History of English Poor Relief.*
8. Davies, *The Enforcement*, p. 11.
9. Dunlop, *English Apprenticeship*, p. 61.
10. Ibid.
11. Ibid., p. 63. It is important to keep in mind that the apprentice *was not* required to serve his term in his own community nor to later practice his craft in the place where he served his apprenticeship.
12. Ibid.
13. As quoted by Dunlop, *English Apprenticeship*, p. 69. In this instance we note that the guilds were reluctant to perform more than a limited role in absorbing surplus youth.
14. Ibid., p. 70.
15. See Davies, *The Enforcement*, in this context.
16. Ibid., pp. 20–21.
17. Dunlop, *English Apprenticeship*, p. 124.
18. Leonard, *The Early History*, p. 14.
19. Ibid., pp. 14–15.
20. Ibid.
21. Ibid.
22. Ibid., p. 303.
23. Ibid., p. 39. For a number of documents supporting this position see the Appendices in Leonard.

24. Frank Musgrove, *Youth and the Social Order* (Bloomington: Indiana University Press, 1965) has an excellent discussion of these issues. It is important to keep in mind that the decline in infant mortality was also a factor in the rapid growth of surplus populations.

25. K. Marx, *Kapital* (Chicago: C. H. Kerr & Co., 1908), p. 693.

26. In this context see F. Engels, *The Condition of the Working Class in England* (Stanford, Calif.: Stanford University Press, 1968), especially pages 92–103.

27. Rousseau's position is developed in *Emile,* Book 4, and Locke's are dealt with in his *Thoughts Concerning Education.* See Musgrove, *Youth,* chapter 3 for a discussion of these issues.

28. See Polanyi, K. *The Great Transformation* (New York: Rinehart & Co., 1944).

29. "Education," in F. J. C. Hearnshaw, ed., *Medieval Contributions to Modern Civilization* (London: G. G. Harrap and Co., 1921), P. 211.

30. In this context see E. P. Thompson, *The Making of the English Working Class* (New York: Vintage Books, 1963) especially chapter XI.

31. Musgrove, *Youth,* p. 74

32. Ibid., p. 74.

33. Ibid., p. 76.

34. I will deal with the larger issues in chapter 7.

35. In this context see Carl F. Kaestle, "Between the Scylla of Brutal Ignorance and the Charybdis of the Literary Education: Elite Attitudes toward Mass Schooling in Early Industrial England and America." In Lawrence Stone, ed., *Schooling and Society* (Baltimore: Johns Hopkins University Press, 1976), pp. 177–191.

36. Ibid., pp. 178–9.

37. Ibid.

38. Ibid.

39. Ibid.

40. Andres Irvine, *Reflections on the Education of the Poor* (London: 1815), pp. 32–33, as paraphrased by Kaestle, "Between the Scylla", pp. 180–181. Italics mine.

41. C. Kaestle, "Between the Scylla", p. 182.

42. Ibid.

43. The discrepancy between the laws is noted by M. B. Katz, *The Irony of Early School Reform* (Boston: Beacon Press, 1968)p. 167.

44. Public Document, State of Massachusetts 23, 1858, pp. 8–10, as quoted by Katz, *The Irony,* p. 194.

45. M. B. Katz Class, Bureaucracy and Schools (New York: Praeger, 1975).

46. J. Spring, *Education and the Rise of the Corporate State* (Boston: Beacon Press, 1972) p. 76.

47. Ibid.

48. Ibid.

49. E. A. Ross, *Social Control* (New York: Macmillan, 1919).

50. Ibid., p. 170.

51. Ibid. p. 171.
52. From Pelet, "Napoleon in Council", p. 206, as quoted by Ross, *Social Control*, p. 174.
53. Ibid.
54. Ibid., p. 175.
55. L. Coser, *Greedy Institutions* (New York: Free Press, 1974).
56. E. G. West, *Education and the State* (London: The Institute of Economic Affairs, 1965).
57. J. Coleman et al., *The Adolescent Community* (New York: Free Press, 1961).
58. H. and J. Schwendinger, "Marginal Youth and Social Policy," *Social Problems* 24 (December 1976): 186.

6. Co-opted Aesthetes and Aspirants: The WPA Writers' and Artists' Projects

1. This is, perhaps ironically, what the Republicans under Ronald Reagan advocated in the 1980 presidential campaign. There are, I would like to note, a great many ironies, paradoxes and plain "twists of history" reflected in the comparison between the Reagan campaign and the 1932 Roosevelt campaign. In this context see William E. Leuchtenburg, *Franklin D. Roosevelt and the New Deal* (New York: Harper and Row, 1963) especially Chapter I, "The Politics of Hard Times."   2. Leuchtenburg, *Franklin D. Roosevelt*, p. 11.
3. Ibid., p. 26.
4. Ibid., p. 15.
5. Ibid.
6. Ibid.
7. I imply, of course, that violence often occurs when force is used to attempt to contain protest. In this context see, William Gamson, *The Strategy of Social Protest* (Homewood, Ill.: Dorsey Press, 1975) and Charles Tilly et al., *The Rebellious Century, 1830–1930* (Cambridge, Mass.: Harvard University Press, 1975).
8. Leuchtenburg, *Franklin D. Roosevelt*, pp. 24–25. Cf. also, Arthur Schlesinger, *The Age of Roosevelt: The Coming of the New Deal*, vol. 2 (Boston: Houghton Miffin, 1958) pp. 43–44, and Maxine Davis, *They Shall Not Want*, (New York: Macmillan, 1937) pp. 19–21.
9. Roosevelt's general attitude is reflected in a comment made at Oglethorpe University. "It is common sense to take a method and try it. If it fails, admit it frankly and try another. But above all, try something." In Sidney Lens, *Poverty: America's Enduring Paradox* (New York: Crowell, 1971) p. 261.
10. Schlesinger, *Coming of the New Deal*, vol. 2, p. 22.
11. A typical example of the violent atmosphere was the longshoremen strike in San Francisco on May 9, 1934, described by Schlesinger, *Coming of the New Deal*, vol. 2, pp. 390–393.

12. Arthur Schlesinger, *The Age of Roosevelt, Vol. III, The Politics of Upheaval* (Boston: Houghton Mifflin, 1960) p. 525. As quoted by F. F. Piven and R. Cloward, *Regulating the Poor* (New York: Random House, 1972), fn. p. 89.

13. Ibid., p. 89.

14. Leuchtenburg, *Franklin D. Roosevelt*, p. 122.

15. Ibid. Cf., also, Robert E. Sherwood, *Roosevelt and Hopkins* (New York: Harper, 1948) pp. 53–55.

16. Jerre Mangione, *The Dream and the Deal* (Boston: Little, Brown, 1972) p. 30.

17. Ibid., p. 32.

18. Ibid., p. 38.

19. Ibid., p. 39.

20. Schlesinger, *Politics of Upheaval*, vol. 3, p. 267.

21. Perhaps the best and most complete treatment of the origins, organization and consequences of the federal arts projects, although too little focused on the political aspects, is William F. McDonald, *Federal Relief Administration and the Arts* (Columbus: Ohio State University Press, 1969). Treatment of the internal political occurences in this context, from the inside and outside, is masterfully displayed by Schlesinger, *Politics of Upheaval*, vol. 3.

22. McDonald, *Federal Relief Administration*, p. 128.

23. Ibid., pp. 126–132 for a detailed analysis of the interpretation of the statute and its consequences.

24. Even though, it is well to keep in mind, as compared with the WPA in general, the numbers employed were modest.

25. While the McDonald book is the most comprehensive on the public aspects of the projects a number of more specific and more personal accounts provide interesting insights into the day-to-day activities of the Directors and their subordinates. J. Mangione, *The Dream and the Deal* (Boston: Little, Brown, 1972) is one such source; J. D. Mathews, *The Federal Theatre, 1935–1939* (Princeton: Princeton University Press, 1967) is another. Cf. The bibliographies and references in Mangione, Mathews and McDonald.

26. Cf., for example Mangione, *Dream and the Deal*, p. 42.

27. One example of worthy note was the tendency, on the arts project, to assign the seemingly unpromising to doing murals. de Kooning, now recognized as a major contemporary artist, was so assigned presumably because he was judged to have limited talent. Personal communication from Bernard Rosenberg. Cf., in this context B. Rosenberg and N. Fliegel, *The Vanguard Artist* (Chicago: Quadrangle Books, 1965).

28. "Relief of the Unemployed in New York City, 1929–1937" Welfare Council of New York City, as quoted by McDonald, *Federal Relief Administration* p. 89. Professor McDonald received permission for the quotation from the Community Council of Greater New York.

29. McDonald, *Federal Relief Administration*, p. 197.

30. Dixon Wecter, *The Age of the Great Depression*, 1948, as quoted by Mangione, *Dream and the Deal*, p. 51.

31. Rosenberg and Fliegel, *Vanguard Artist*, pp. 322–325.

32. Mangione, *Dream and the Deal*, Chapter 4.

33. Another problem, as perceived by some of the artists, was the internal squabbles surrounding efforts of diverse political groups to control the projects and the activities of the FBI to counter these efforts. ". . . artists felt harassed at both ends." Rosenberg and Fliegel, *Vanguard Artist*, p. 323.

34. Mangione, *Dream and the Deal*.

35. Ibid., p. 291. It was not long after that incident that the federal phase of the projects was terminated.

36. Ibid., p. 352.

37. For a vivid description of these occurrences, see Mangione, *Dream and the Deal*, chapter 8 "Congress Sees Red." There was also a Woodrun Committee whose activities Mangione describes.

38. Mathews, *Federal Theatre*, p. 307.

39. Mangione, *Dream and the Deal*, p. 330.

40. St. Claire Drake and Horace Cayton, *Black Metropolis* (New York: Harcourt Brace & World, 1945).

41. On Biddle and Bruce see McDonald, *Federal Relief Administration*, pp. 357–261.

42. See Mangione, *The Dream and the Deal*, pp. 8–13, for a description of his personal experience with Mrs. Roosevelt regarding this matter.

43. Ibid.

44. Ibid., p. 100.

45. This term has come into use in recent years to describe an errand runner. "Go for this" and "Go for that" is, of course, the basis for this usage. Mangione, *The Dream and the Deal*, p. 107.

7. Abeyance, Surplus Population, and Social, Control

1. See, in this context, Ronald Meek, ed., *Marx and Engels on the Population Bomb* (Berkeley, Cal.: Ramparts Press, Inc. 1971); and F. Engels, *The Condition of the Working Class in England* (Stanford, Calif.: Stanford University Press, 1968).

2. The idea of synergy originates in sociological theory in the works of the late Lester Frank Ward. See his *Pure Sociology* (New York: Macmillan, 1903). My interpretation of Ward's concept is admittedly narrow and applicable primarily to this context.

3. I am not suggesting that Marx was a simple economic determinist. The discussion of surplus labor in Book 1 of *Das Kapital* does emphasize, however, the economic sources and functions of surplus populations.

4. R. Merton, *Social Theory and Social Structure* (New York: Free Press, 1957, Revised and Enlarged Edition) p. 51.

5. K. Polanyi, *The Great Transformation* (New York: Rinehart & Co., 1944).

6. N. Smelser, *Social Change in the Industrial Revolution* (Chicago: University of Chicago Press, 1959) p. 202.

7. R. Rubenstein, *The Cunning of History* (New York: Harper, Colophon Books, 1978).

8. Fritz Stern, *The Politics of Cultural Despair* (Berkeley: University of California Press, 1974).

9. J. Trachtenberg, *The Devil and the Jews* (New Haven: Yale University Press, 1943); and N. Cohn, *Europe's Inner Demons* (New York: Basic Books, 1975).

10. Everett C. Hughes, "Good People, Dirty Work," *Social Problems*, 10 (Summer, 1962): 3–11. Cf. also I. Bick, "Honorable Conduct: The Jews of Pisa Under the Nazis and Facists," Ph. D. Dissertation, Dept. of Sociology, Syracuse University, 1980.

11. Louis Schneider, ed. *The Scottish Moralists on Human Nature and Society*, (Chicago: University of Chicago Press, 1967) Introduction; cf. also, his article, "Mandeville as Forerunner of Modern Sociology," *Journal of the History of the Behavioral Sciences*, 6, no. 3, (1970); and *The Sociological Way of Looking at the World*, New York: McGraw-Hill, 1975.

12. In Schneider, Ibid., p. 106. Italics mine.

13. Louise Shelley, "The Geography of Soviet Criminality," *American Sociological Review*, 45 (February 1980): 111–122. I thank Albert K. Cohen for bringing this paper to my attention.

14. E. Durkheim, *The Rules of Sociological Method* (New York: Free Press, 1964). In this context see also Talcott Parsons's discussion of flexibility based on E. C. Devereaux, Jr.'s Harvard dissertation in *The Social System* (New York: Free Press, 1951), pp. 307–308.

15. Ibid.

16. Shelley, "Geography of Soviet Criminality", p. 121

17. Bick, "Honorable Conduct".

18. In this context see, Harriet Martineau, *The History of England during the Thirty Years Peace: 1816–1846* (London: Charles Knight, 1849) chapter 4.

19. Sometimes the need for personnel is sufficiently great to induce changes in the division of labor in an organization. Cf., for example Richard D. Schwartz, "Functional Alternatives to Inequality", *American Sociological Review* 20 (August, 1955): 424–430. For a description and analysis of the control aspects of two types of Israeli settlements, the same ones used for the above analysis, see the same author's, "Social Factors in the Development of Legal Control", *Yale Law Journal* 63 (February 1954): 471–491.

20. These are, in Amitai Etzioni's terms, coercive organizations. Their task is to keep inmates in. Thus they are beyond the typology which I have proposed in this study. They nevertheless help us gain perspective and understanding. Cf. Etzioni's, *Complex Organizations*, Revised Ed. (New York: Free Press, 1975), pp. 23–39.

21, In Meek, *The Population Bomb*, p. 96. From *Kapital*, vol. 1.

22. Malthus, nevertheless recognized that modern industry required a surplus

population. See Marx's quotation from Malthus's, *Principles of Political Economy,* in Meek, Ibid., p. 98.

23. Etzioni, *Complex Organizations,* p. 40. High commitment is not always associated with this type of organization. See my table, p. 25.

24. *Ibid.,* p. 41. Cf. also, Lewis Yablonsky's analysis of hippies, above.

25. Ibid., p. 52.

26. *The Social System* (New York: Free Press, 1951) p. 321. Parsons's perspective here is adumbrated in Smelser's typology of factors influencing collective behavior. My analysis, thus, articulates aspects of Smelser's study. N. Smelser, *A Theory of Collective Behavior* (New York: Free Press, 1962).

27. B. Glaser and A. Straus, *Discovery of Grounded Theory* (Chicago: Aldine, 1967), p. 85. Cf. also L. San Giovanni, *Ex-Nuns* (Norwood, N.J.: Ablex Publishing Corporation, 1978).

28. L. Schneider and S. Lysgaard, "The Deferred Gratification Pattern," *American Sociological Review* 18 (1953): 142–149.

29. Cf., for example, Barry Schwartz, *Queuing and Waiting: Studies in the Social Organization of Access and Delay* (Chicago: University of Chicago Press, 1975). Cf, for example, John Braithwaite, "The Myth of Social Class and Criminality Reconsidered." *American Sociological Review,* 46 (February 1981): 36–57.

30. Recent examples of this type of research is, R. M. Stolzenberg and L. Waite, "Age Fertility Expectations and Plans for Employment," *American Sociological Review,* 42 (1977): 769–781; H. B. Presser, "The Timing of the First Birth, Female Roles and Black Fertility," *Milbank Memorial Fund Quarterly* 69 (1971): 329–361; H. B. Presser, "Perfect Fertility Control: Consequences for Women and the Family," in C. F. Westoff et al., eds., *Toward the End of Growth: Population in America* (Englewood Cliffs, N.J.: Prentice-Hall, 1973), pp. 133–144. A very important, well articulated, theory which meshes with the theory proposed here is Harrison White's. See his *Chains of Opportunity* (Cambridge, Mass.: Harvard University Press, 1970).

31. C. Arensberg and S. T. Kimball, *The Irish Countryman* (New York: Harcourt, Brace, Jovanovich, 1937). For a study of age cohorts which is relevant to my theory see J. Waring, "Social Replenishment and Social Change," in A. Foner, ed., *Age in Society* (Beverly Hills, Calif.: Sage, 1976).

32. Ibid.

33. Cf. Mizruchi, *Success and Opportunity,* (New York: The Free Press, 1964). and my earlier papers on anomie and alienation.

BIBLIOGRAPHY

ABBOTT, GRACE. *The Child and the State: Legal Status in the Family Apprenticeship and Child Labor Law, Selected Documents with Introductory Notes.* Chicago: University of Chicago Press, 1938.

ADAMS, HENRY H. *Harry Hopkins, A Biography.* New York: Putnam, 1977.

ADAMSON, J. W. "Education." In F. J. C. Hearnshaw, ed., *Medieval Contributions to Modern Civilization.* London: G. G. Harrop, 1921.

ALLAN, GRAHAM. "A Theory of Millenialism: The Irvington Movement as an Illustration." *British Journal of Sociology* 25 (September 1974).

ALLEN, FRANCIS R. *Sociocultural Dynamics.* New York: Macmillan, 1971.

ALLMAND, C. T., ED. *War, Literature and Politics in the Late Middle Ages.* Liverpool: Liverpool University Press, 1976.

ALTBACH, PHILIP G., AND LAUFER, ROBERT, EDS. *The New Pilgrims: Youth Protest in Transition.* New York: McKay, 1972.

_____, EDS. *Students Protest, The Annals,* vol. 395. Philadelphia: American Academy of Political and Social Science, 1971.

ARENSBERG, CONRAD, AND KIMBALL, SOLON T. *The Irish Countryman.* New York: Harcourt Brace Jovanovich, 1937.

ARIÈS, PHILIPPE. *Centuries of Childhood.* Trans. by R. Baldick. New York: Random House (Vintage Books), 1962.

ASH, ROBERTA. *Social Movements in America.* Chicago: Markham, 1972.

ASTON, TREVOR, ED. *Crisis in Europe, 1560–1660.* New York: Doubleday (Anchor Books), 1967.

AUERBACH, ERICH. *Mimesis.* Princeton, N.J.: Princeton University Press, 1953.

AYDELOTTE, FRANK. *Elizabethan Rogues and Vagabonds.* Oxford: Clarendon Press, 1913.

AYLMER, G. E., ED. *The Levellers in the English Revolution.* Ithaca, N.Y.: Cornell University Press, 1975.

BAINTON, ROLAND. *Concerning Heretics.* New York: Octagon, 1965.

BALFE, JUDITH H. "Shame, Guilt and the Development of Mariolatry," in M. C. Nelson and J. Ikenberry, eds., *Psychosexual Imperatives.* New York: Human Sciences Press, 1979.

_____. "Women and Puritanism." Unpublished paper, 1975.

BARKUN, MICHAEL. *Disaster and the Millennium.* New Haven: Yale University Press, 1974.

_____. "Millenarian Transformations: Processes of Change in Chiliastic Movements." Paper presented to the Annual Meeting of the International Society for the Comparative Study of Civilizations (U.S.), Philadelphia, 1976.

BAY, CHRISTIAN. *The Structure of Freedom.* Stanford, Calif.: Stanford University Press, 1958.

BECKER, HOWARD S. *Outsiders: Studies in the Sociology of Deviance.* New York: Free Press, 1963.

————, ED. *Culture and Civility in San Francisco.* New Brunswick, N.J.: Transaction Books, 1971.

BERK, RICHARD A. *Collective Behavior.* Dubuque, Iowa: Brown, 1974.

BERTALANFFY, LUDWIG VON. *General System Theory.* New York: Braziller, 1968.

BICK, ISABELLA, "Honorable Conduct: The Jews of Pisa under the Nazis and Facists," Ph.D. Dissertation, Dept. of Sociology, Syracuse University, 1980.

BINDER, FREDERICK M. *The Age of the Common School, 1830–1865.* New York: Wiley, 1974.

BIRNBAUM, NORMAN, AND LENZER, GERTRUDE, EDS. *Sociology and Religion.* Englewood Cliffs, N.J.: Prentice-Hall, 1969.

BLACK, H. *Culture and Restraint.* New York: F. H. Revell, 1901.

BLAND, A. E., ET AL., EDS. *English Economic History: Selected Documents.* London: G. Bell and Sons, 1930.

BLAU, HERBERT. *The Impossible Theatre.* New York: Macmillan, 1964.

BLOCH, MARC, *Feudal Society.* 2 vol. Trans. by L. A. Manyon. Chicago: Phoenix Books, University of Chicago Press, 1964.

————. *Melanges Historiques.* 2 vol. Paris: S.E.V.P.E.N., 1963.

————. "The Rise of Dependent Cultivation and Seigniorial Institutions," *The Cambridge Economic History,* I. London: Cambridge University Press, 1941. Pp. 224–277.

BOGUE, ALLAN G., ED. *Emerging Theoretical Models in Social and Political History.* Beverly Hills, Calif.: Sage, 1973.

BOISSONNADE, PROSPER. *Life and Work in Medieval Europe.* Trans. with intro. by Eileen Power. New York: Knopf, 1927.

BOLTON, BRENDA. "Mulieres Sanctae." In D. Baker, ed., *Sanctity and Secularity: The Church and the World.* Papers of the Ecclesiastical History Society of London. New York: Harper & Row, 1973.

————. "Vitae Matrum: A Further Aspect of the Frauenfrage." In B. Bolton, *Medieval Women.* London: Blackwell, 1978.

BOOTH, SALLY SMITH. *Seeds of Anger: Revolts in America, 1607–1771.* New York: Hastings House, 1977.

BENSMAN, JOSEPH, AND VIDICH, ARTHUR. *The New American Society.* Chicago: Quadrangle, 1971.

BOULDING, ELISE. *The Underside of History: A View of Women Through Time.* Boulder, Colo.: Westview Press, 1976.

BOYD, CATHERINE E. *A Cisterian Nunnery in Medieval Italy.* Cambridge: Harvard University Press, 1943.

————. *Tithes and Parishes in Medieval Italy.* Ithaca, N.Y.: Cornell University Press, 1952.

BRAEMAN, JOHN, BREMNER, ROBERT H., AND BRODY, DAVID, EDS. *The New Deal.* Vol. 1. Columbus, Ohio: Ohio State University Press, 1975.

BRAUDEL, FERNAND. *Afterthoughts on Material Civilization and Capitalism.* Trans. by P. M. Ranum. Baltimore: Johns Hopkins University Press, 1977.

————. *Capitalism and Material Life: 1400–1800.* Trans. by M. Kochan. New York: Harper & Row, 1973.

————. *Ecrits Sur L'Histoire.* Paris: Flammarion, 1969.

————. "History and the Social Sciences." In P. Burke, ed., *Economy and Society in Early Modern Europe.* London: Routledge and Kegan Paul, 1972.

————. *The Mediterranean and the Mediterranean World in the Age of Philip II.* Trans. by S. Reynolds. New York: Harper & Row, 1972.

BRAUNGART, RICHARD. "The Historical and Generational Pattern of Youth Movements: A Global Perspective." Paper presented at the Fourth Annual Meeting of the International Society of Political Psychology, Mannheim, West Germany, June 1981.

BRENNER, M. HARVEY. *Mental Illness and the Economy.* Cambridge: Harvard University Press, 1973.

BRINTON, CRANE. *The Anatomy of Revolution.* New York: Random House (Vintage Books), 1958.

BROWN, ROBERT. *Explanation in Social Science.* Chicago: Aldine, 1963.

BUCKLEY, WALTER F., ED. *Modern Systems Research for the Behavioral Scientist.* Chicago: Aldine, 1968.

————. *Sociology and Modern Systems Theory.* Englewood Cliffs, N.J.: Prentice-Hall, 1967.

BULLOUGH, WILLIAM A. *Cities and Schools in the Gilded Age.* Port Washington, N.Y.: Kennikat Press, 1974.

BURKE, PETER. *Popular Culture in Early Modern Europe.* New York: New York University Press, 1978.

————. ED. *Economy and Society in Early Modern Europe.* London: Routledge and Kegan Paul, 1972.

BUTTNER, THEODORA, AND WERNER, ERNST. *Circumcellionen Und Adamiten.* Berlin: Akademie-Verlag, 1959.

CAHNMAN, WERNER, AND BOSKOFF, ALVIN, EDS. *Sociology and History.* New York: Free Press, 1964.

The Cambridge Medieval History. Cambridge: University Press, 1964.

CAMPBELL, ANNA. *The Black Death and Men of Learning.* New York: Columbia University Press, 1931.

CANTOR, NORMAN F. "Obligations of the Church in English Society: Military Arrays of the Clergy, 1369–1418." In W. C. Jordan et al., eds., *Order and Innovation in the Middle Ages.* Princeton, N.J.: Princeton University Press, 1976, pp. 293–314.

————. "The Crisis of Western Monasticism, 1050–1130." *American Historical Review* 66 (1960):44–67.

CANTOR, NORMAN F., AND WERTHMAN, MICHAEL S., EDS. *Medieval Society, 400–1450,* 2d ed. New York: Crowell, 1972.

————. *Renaissance, Reformation and Absolution,* 2d ed. New York: Crowell, 1972.

CHAMBERS, EDMUND K. *The Medieval Stage.* Vol. 1. Oxford, Oxford University Press, 1903.

————. *The Elizabethan Stage.* Vol. 1. Oxford: Clarendon Press, 1923.

CHAMBLISS, WILLIAM J. "The Law of Vagrancy." *Warner Modular Publications,* Module 4 (1973):1–10.

_____. "The State, the Law and the Definition of Behavior as Criminal or Delinquent." In Daniel Glaser, ed., *Handbook of Criminology.* Chicago: Rand McNally, 1974.

_____. "Markets, Profits, Labor and Smack." Unpublished paper.

CHENU, MARIE D. *Nature, Man and Society in the Twelfth Century.* Selected, Ed., and Transl. by J. Taylor and L. K. Little. Chicago: University of Chicago Press, 1968 (1957).

CIPOLLA, CARLO M., ED. *The Economic Decline of Empires.* London: Methuen, 1970.

CLAWSON, DAN. Pre-Capitalist Work Patterns and the Rise of the Factory." *Discourse* (SUNY, Stony Brook), Spring, 1977.

CLARK, JAMES M. *The Great German Mystics, Eckhart, Tauler and Suso.* Oxford: Basil Blackwell, 1949.

COBB, RICHARD C. *The Police and the People: French Popular Protest 1789–1820.* Oxford: Clarendon Press, 1970.

_____. *Reactions to the French Revolution.* London: Oxford University Press, 1972.

COBBAN, ALFRED. *Aspects of the French Revolution.* New York: George Braziller, 1968.

COHEN, ALBERT K., "Introduction" to Musgrove, Frank, *Youth and the Social Order.* Bloomington, Ind.: Indiana University Press, 1965.

COHN, NORMAN. *The Pursuit of the Millennium,* 2d ed. New York: Harper Torchbooks, 1961.

_____. *Europe's Inner Demons.* New York: Basic Books, 1975.

COLEMAN, JAMES, ET AL. *The Adolescent Society.* New York: Free Press, 1961.

CONKIN, PAUL K. *FDR and the Origins of the Welfare State.* New York: Crowell, 1967.

CONNOR, WALTER D. "The Manufacture of Deviance: The Case of the Soviet Purge, 1936–1938." *American Sociological Review* 37 (August 1972).

_____. *Deviance in Soviet Society.* New York: Columbia University Press, 1972.

CONSTABLE, GILES. "Cluniac Administration and Administrators in the Twelfth Century." In W. C. Jordan et al., eds., *Order and Innovation in the Middle Ages.* Princeton, N.J.: Princeton University Press, 1976, pp. 17–30.

COOK, BRUCE. *The Beat Generation.* New York: Scribner, 1971.

CORNWALL, JULIAN. *Revolt of the Peasantry 1549.* London: Routledge & Kegan Paul, 1977.

CORYAT, THOMAS. *Coryat's Crudities.* Vol. 1 and 2. New York: Macmillan, 1905 (originally 1611).

COSER, LEWIS A. *The Social Functions of Conflict.* New York: Free Press, 1956.

_____. *Men of Ideas.* New York: Free Press, 1965.

_____. *Continuities in the Study of Social Conflict.* New York: Free Press, 1967.

_____. *Greedy Institutions.* New York: Free Press, 1974.

_____. "The Alien as a Servant of Power: Court Jews and Christian Renegades." *American Sociological Review* 37 (October 1972).

COULTON, GEORGE G. *Life in the Middle Ages.* 4 vols. Cambridge: University Press, 1967.

COWLEY, MALCOLM. *Exile's Return.* New York: Viking Press, 1968 (originally 1934).

CRUMP, C. G., AND JACOB, E. F., EDS. *The Legacy of the Middle Ages.* Oxford: Oxford University Press, 1926.

CUROE, P. *Educational Attitudes of Organized Labor in the U.S.* New York: Teachers College, Columbia, No. 201, 1926.

DAVIES, MARGARET G. *The Enforcement of English Apprenticeship.* Cambridge, Mass.: Harvard University Press, 1965.

DAVIS, GLENN. *Childhood and History in America.* New York: Psychohistory Press, 1976.

DAVIS, MAXINE. *They Shall Not Want.* New York: Macmillan, 1937.

DAVIS, NATALIE Z. *Society and Culture in Early Modern France.* Stanford, Calif.: Stanford University Press, 1975.

_____. "The Rites of Violence: Religious Riot in Sixteenth-Century France." *Past and Present* 59 (May 1973).

_____. "The Reasons of Misrule: Youth Groups and Charivaris in Sixteenth-Century France." *Past and Present* 50 (February 1971).

DEACON, ALAN, AND HILL, MICHAEL. "The Problem of 'Surplus Women' in the Nineteenth Century: Secular and Religious Alternatives." In M. Hill, ed., *A Sociological Yearbook of Religions in Britain.* London: SCM Press, 1972.

DELANEY, SHEILA, ED. *Counter-Tradition: The Literature of Dissent and Alternatives.* New York: Basic Books, 1971.

DENISOFF, R. SERGE, AND PETERSON, RICHARD A., EDS. *The Sounds of Social Change.* Chicago: Rand McNally, 1972.

DEWEY, ROBERT E., AND GOULD, JAMES A. *Freedom: Its History, Nature and Varieties.* New York: Macmillan, 1970.

DRAKE, ST. CLAIR, AND CAYTON, HORACE. *Black Metropolis.* New York: Harcourt Brace Jovanovich, 1945.

DROZE, WILMON H., WOLFSKILL, GEORGE, AND LEUCHTENBURG, WILLIAM E. *Essays On the New Deal.* Austin: University of Texas Press, 1969.

DUCKETT, ELEANOR S. *Monasticism.* Ann Arbor, Mich.: University of Michigan Press, 1938.

_____. *Saint Dunstan of Canterbury.* London: Collins, 1955.

_____. *Death and Life in the Tenth Century.* Ann Arbor, Mich.: University of Michigan Press, 1967.

DUFFIELD, MARCUS. *King Legion.* New York: Jonathan Cape and Harrison Smith, 1931.

DUNCAN, HUGH D. *The Rise of Chicago as a Literary Center from 1885–1920.* Totowa, N.J.: Bedminster Press, 1964.

DUNCAN-JONES, RICHARD. *The Economy of the Roman Empire: Quantitative Studies.* Cambridge: Cambridge University Press, 1974.

DUNLOP, O. J. *English Apprenticeship and Child Labor.* New York: Macmillan, 1912.

DURKHEIM, ÉMILE. *The Division of Labor in Society.* Trans. by G. Simpson. New York: Free Press, 1947 (originally 1893).

_____. *Suicide.* Trans. by G. Simpson. New York: Free Press, 1951 (originally 1897).

_____. *The Rules of Sociological Method.* Trans. by Sarah Solovay and John Mueller. Ed. by George Catlin. New York: Free Press, 1964 (originally 1895).

EASTON, MALCOLM. *Artists and Writers in Paris.* New York: St. Martin's Press, 1964.

EBAUGH, HELEN R. F. *Out of the Cloister.* Austin: University of Texas Press, 1977.

ECKENSTEIN, LINA. *Women Under Monasticism.* New York: Russell & Russell, 1963 (originally 1896).

EHRENREICH, BARBARA, AND ENGLISH, DEIRDRA. "Witches, Midwives and Nurses." *Monthly Review,* October 1973.

EINSTEIN, LEWIS. *The Italian Renaissance in England.* New York: Columbia University Press, 1902.

EISENSTADT, S. N. *From Generation to Generation.* New York: Free Press, 1956.

———. *Modernization: Protest and Change.* Englewood Cliffs, N.J.: Prentice-Hall, 1966.

———. ED. *Political Sociology.* New York: Basic Books, 1971.

EKIRCH, ARTHUR A., JR. *Ideologies and Utopias: The Impact of the New Deal on American Thought.* Chicago: Quadrangle, 1969.

ELLACOTT, S. E. *Conscripts on the March.* New York: Abelard-Schuman, 1966.

ELTON, GEOFFREY R. *Star Chamber Stories.* London: Methuen, 1974.

———. *Policy and Police.* Cambridge: Cambridge University Press, 1972.

ENGELS, FRIEDRICH. *The Condition of the Working Class in England.* Trans. by W. O. Henderson and W. H. Chaloner. Stanford, Calif.: Stanford University Press. 1968 (originally 1845).

ENSIGN, F. *Compulsory School Attendance and Child Labor.* Iowa City: Athens Press, 1921.

ERASMUS, CHARLES J. *In Search of the Common Good.* New York: Free Press, 1977.

ERBSTÖSSER, MARTIN, AND WERNER, ERNST. *Ideologische Probleme des Mittelalterlichen Plebejertums.* Berlin: Akademie Verlag, 1960.

———. *Sozialreligiöse Stromungen im Späten Mittelalter.* Berlin: Akademie Verlag, 1970.

ERIKSON, KAI. *Wayward Puritans.* New York: Wiley, 1966.

ETZIONI, AMITAI. *A Comparative Analysis of Complex Organizations,* rev. and enl. New York: Free Press, 1975.

GODWIN, GEORGE. *The Great Revivalists.* Boston: Beacon Press, 1950.

GOODRIDGE, R. MARTIN. "The Ages of Faith—Romance or Reality." *Sociological Review* 23 (May 1975).

GOUBERT, PIERRE. *The Ancien Regime: French Society 1600–1705.* Trans. by S. Cox. New York: Harper Torchbooks, 1974.

GOULDNER, ALVIN W. "The Metaphoricality of Marxism and the Context-Freeing Grammar of Socialism." Unpublished Paper. *University of Amsterdam,* 1974.

GRAHAM, HUGH D., AND GURR, TED R. *Violence in America: Historical and Comparative Perspectives.* 2 vols. A Staff Report to the National Commission on the Causes and Prevention of Violence. Washington: U.S. Government Printing Office, 1969.

GRANA, CESAR. *Bohemian versus Bourgeois.* New York: Basic Books, 1964.

GREENE, THOMAS H. *Comparative Revolutionary Movements.* Englewood Cliffs, N.J.: Prentice-Hall, 1974.

GREER, COLIN. *The Great School Legend.* New York: Basic Books, 1972.

GREISMAN, HARVEY C. "Social Movements and Mass Society: Requiem for the Counter-Culture." In E. H. Mizruchi, ed., *The Substance of Sociology,* 2nd ed. New York: Appleton-Century-Crofts, 1973.

GROB, GERALD N. *Mental Institutions in America: Social Policy to 1875*. New York: Free Press, 1973.

GRUEN, JOHN. *The New Bohemia*. New York: Grosset & Dunlap, 1967.

GRUNDMANN, HERBERT. *Religiöse Bewegungen im Mittelalter*. Berlin: Verlag Dr. Emil Ebering, 1935.

_____. "Zur Geschichte der Beginen im 13. Jahrhundert." In *Herbert Grundmann Ausgewahlte Aufsätze* Stuttgart: Anton Hiersemann, 1976.

GUIBERT OF NOGENT. *Self and Society in Medieval France*. Memoirs, edited with an Introduction by John F. Benton. New York: Harper Torchbooks, 1970.

GURR, TED ROBERT. *Why Men Rebel*. Princeton, N.J.: Princeton University Press, 1971.

GUSFIELD, JOSEPH R. *Symbolic Crusade*. Urbana: University of Illinois Press, 1963.

HAHN, EMILY. *Romantic Rebels*. Boston: Houghton Mifflin, 1967.

HALE, J. R. *Renaissance Europe: 1480–1520*. London: Collins, 1971.

HALL, JEROME. *Theft, Law and Society*, 2nd ed. Indianapolis: Bobbs-Merrill, 1952 (originally 1935).

HALLMANN, DR. E. *Die Geschichte des Ursprungs der belgishen Beghinen*. Berlin: 1843.

FARIS, ROBERT E. L., ED. *Handbook of Modern Sociology*. Chicago: Rand McNally, 1964.

FEIGELSON, NAOMI. *The Underground Revolution: Hippies, Yippies and Others*. New York: Funk & Wagnalls, 1970.

FIELD, DANIEL. *Rebels in the Name of the Tsar*. Boston: Houghton Mifflin, 1975.

FINLEY, M. I. "Manpower and the Fall of Rome." In Carlo M. Cipolla, ed., *The Economic Decline of Empires*. London: Methuen, 1970.

FLACKS, RICHARD. *Youth and Social Change*. Chicago: Markham Publishing Company, 1971.

FRANCIS, E. K. "Toward a Typology of Religious Orders." *American Journal of Sociology* 50 (March 1950).

FRAZIER, THOMAS R., ED. *The Underside of American History*. Vol. 2. New York: Harcourt Brace Jovanovich, 1971.

GAMSON, WILLIAM H. *Power and Discontent*. Homewood, Ill.: Dorsey Press, 1968.

_____. *The Strategy of Social Protest*. Homewood, Ill.: Dorsey Press, 1975.

GASQUET, F. A. Introduction to C. F. Montalembert, *The Monks of the West*. New York: Longmans, Green, 1896.

GERTH, H. H., AND MILLS, C. WRIGHT, EDS. *From Max Weber: Essays in Sociology*. Trans. by the editors. London: Routledge & Kegan Paul, 1948.

GIBBON, EDWARD. *The History of the Decline and Fall of the Roman Empire*. Vol. 4. London: Methuen, 1909.

GIELE, JANET Z. "Age Cohorts and Changes in Women's Roles." Paper presented at the Annual Meeting of the American Sociological Association, New York, 1973.

GILLIS, JOHN R. *Youth and History*. New York: Academic Press, 1974.

GINGER, RAY. *Age of Excess: The United States from 1877–1914*. New York: Macmillan, 1965.

GLASER, BARNEY, AND STRAUS, ANSELM. *Discovery of Grounded Theory*. Chicago: Aldine, 1967.

GLASS, DAVID V. *Population: Policies and Movements in Europe.* London: Frank Coss and Co., 1967.

GLEASON, SARELL, E. *An Ecclesiastical Barony of the Middle Ages.* Cambridge, Mass.: Harvard University Press, 1936.

HANNA, PAUL R., ET AL. *Youth Serves the Community.* New York: Appleton-Century-Crofts, 1936.

HARNACK, ADOLPH. *Monasticism: Its Ideals and History.* New York: Putman, n.d. (ca. 1904).

──────. *The Mission and Expansion of Christianity in the First Three Centuries.* 2 vols. Trans. and ed. by J. Moffatt. New York: Putnam, 1908.

HARRIS, S., ED. *Education and Public Policy.* Berkeley, Calif.: McCuthen, 1965.

HASKINS, C. H. *The Rennaissance of the Twelfth Century.* Cambridge: Cambridge University Press, 1928.

HASSETT, WILLIAM D. *Off the Record with F.D.R.* New Brunswick, N.J.: Rutgers University Press, 1958.

VON HAYEK, F. A. *Law, Legislation and Liberty.* 3 vol. Chicago: University of Chicago Press, 1973.

HEARNSHAW, F. J. C. ED. *Medieval Contributions to Modern Civilization.* London: G. G. Harrap and Co., 1921.

──────. ED. *The Social and Political Ideas of Some Great Medieval Thinkers.* London: G. G. Harrap and Co., 1923.

HEER, DAVID M. *Society and Population,* Englewood Cliffs, N.J.: Prentice-Hall, 1968.

HEER, FRIEDRICH. *The Medieval World, Europe 1100–1350.* Trans by J. Sondheimer. New York: New American Library (Mentor Books), 1962.

HERLIHY, DAVID. "Alienation in Medieval Culture and Society." In Frank Johnson, ed., *Alienation.* New York: Seminar Press, 1973.

──────. "Families in Fifteenth-century Tuscany: Ideals and Reality." Mimeographed.

──────. "Land, Family and Women in Continental Europe, 701–1200." *Traditio* 18 (1962):89–120.

──────. ED. *The History of Feudalism.* New York: Walker & Co., 1971.

──────. ED. *Medieval Culture and Society.* New York: Harper Torchbooks, 1968.

HILL, CHRISTOPHER. *The World Turned Upside Down.* New York: Viking Press, 1972.

HILLERBRAND, HANS J. "Religious Dissent and Toleration: Introductory Reflections." In B. K. Kiraly, ed., *Tolerance and Movements of Religious Dissent in Eastern Europe,* East European Quarterly. Boulder, Distributed by Columbia University Press, 1975.

HILLERY, GEORGE A., JR. "The Convent: Community, Prison or Task Force?" *Journal for the Scientific Study of Religion* 8 (Spring 1969).

──────. "Social Structure and Resistance to Change." *Sociologia Ruralis* 12 (1972).

HILTON, RODNEY. *Bond Men Made Free: Medieval Peasant Movements and the English Rising of 1381.* New York: Viking Press, 1973.

HINDLEY, GEOFFREY. *Medieval Warfare.* London: Wayland Publishers, 1971.

"Historical Population Studies." *Daedalus* 97 (Spring 1968).

"Historical Studies Today." *Daedalus* 100 (Winter 1971).

HOBSBAWM, E. J. *The Age of Revolution: Europe 1789–1848*. London: Weidenfeld and Nicholson, 1962.

———. *Industry and Empire: The Making of Modern English Society*. Vol. 2. New York: Pantheon Books, 1968.

———. *Primitive Rebels*. New York: Norton, 1965.

———. AND RUDE, GEORGE. *Captain Swing*. London: Lawrence and Wishart, 1969.

HOERDER, DIRK. *Crowd Action in Revolutionary Massachusetts 1765–1780*. New York: Academic Press, 1977.

HOFSTADTER, RICHARD, AND LIPSET, SEYMOUR MARTIN, EDS. *Turner and the Sociology of the Frontier*. New York: Basic Books, 1968.

HOLLISTER, C. WARREN, ED. *The Twelfth Century Renaissance*. New York: Wiley, 1969.

HOLMES, MICHAEL S. *The New Deal in Georgia*. Westport, Conn.: Greenwood Press, 1975.

HOMANS, GEORGE. *English Villagers of the Thirteenth Century*. Cambridge, Mass.: Harvard University Press, 1941.

HORNE, THOMAS A. *The Social Thought of Bernard Mandeville*. New York: Columbia University Press, 1978.

HOWARD, DONALD S. *The WPA and Federal Relief Policy*. New York: Russel Sage Foundation, 1943.

HUGHES, EVERETT C. "Good People, Dirty Work." *Social Problems* 10 (Summer 1962).

HUIZINGA, JOHAN. *The Waning of the Middle Ages*. Garden City, N.Y.: Doubleday (Anchor Books), 1956 (originally 1924).

HUMPHREYS, CLAIRE B. *The Sociology of Religious Orders*. Ph.D. dissertation, SUNY Buffalo, 1972.

HUNT, NOREEN, ED. *Cluniac Monasticism in the Central Middle Ages*. Hamden, Conn.: Anchor, 1971.

ICKES, JANE. *The Secret Diary of Harold Ickes—The First 1000 Days*. New York: Simon & Schuster, 1953.

———. *The Secret Diary of Harold Ickes—The Inside Struggle, 1936–1941*. New York: Simon & Schuster, 1954.

"Intellectuals and Change." *Daedalus* 101 (Summer 1972).

JAFFE, JULIAN F. *Crusade Against Radicalism*. Port Washington, N.Y.: Kennikat Press, 1972.

JAMES, MARQUIS. *A History of the American Legion*. New York: William Green, 1923.

JAMESON, THOMAS H. *The Hidden Shakespeare*. New York: Minerva Press, A Division of Funk and Wagnalls, 1969.

JARAUSCH, KONRAD H. "The Sources of German Student Unrest, 1815–1848." In Lawrence Stone, ed., *The University in Society*. Vol. 2. Princeton, N.J.: Princeton University Press, 1974.

JARRETT, BEDE. *Social Theories of the Middle Ages, 1200–1500*. London: Earnest Benn, 1926.

JOHNSON, FRANK, ED. *Alienation: Concept, Term, and Meanings*. New York: Seminar Press, 1973.

JOHNSON, MARY ANNE, AND OLSEN, JAMES. *Exiles from the American Dream.* New York: Walker and Co., 1975.

JONES, ALFRED H. *Roosevelt's Image Brokers.* Port Washington, N.Y.: Kennikat Press, 1974.

JONES, A. H. M. *The Roman Economy.* Oxford: Basil Blackwell, 1974.

JORDAN, W. C., ET AL., EDS. *Order and Innovation in the Middle Ages.* Princeton, N.J.: Princeton University Press, 1976.

JOSEPHSON, MATTHEW. *Infidel in the Temple: A Memoir of the 1930's.* New York: Knopf, 1967.

KAESTLE, CARL F. "Between the Scylla of Brutal Ignorance and the Charybdis of a Literary Education: Elite Attitudes Toward Mass Schooling in Early Industrial England and America." In Lawrence Stone, ed., *Schooling and Society.* Baltimore: Johns Hopkins University Press, 1976, pp. 177–191.

KANTER, ROSABETH M. *Commitment and Community.* Cambridge, Mass.: Harvard University Press, 1972.

KATZ, MICHAEL B. *Class, Bureaucracy and Schools,* exp. ed. New York: Praeger, 1975.

————. *The Irony of Early School Reform: Educational Innovation in Mid-Nineteenth Century Massachusetts.* Boston: Beacon Press, 1970.

KEEN, MAURICE. *A History of Medieval Europe.* New York: Praeger, 1967.

KELSEN, HANS. *Society and Nature.* Chicago: University of Chicago Press, 1943.

KENISTON, KENNETH. *The Uncommitted: Alienated Youth in American Society.* New York: Harcourt Brace Jovanovich, 1965.

————. *Young Radicals.* New York: Harcourt Brace Jovanovich, 1968.

KEROUAC, JACK. *On the Road.* New York: Viking, 1957.

KERSHAW, IAN. "The Great Famine and Agrarian Crisis in England, 1315–1322." *Past and Present* 59 (May 1973).

KIRBY, JOHN B. *Black Americans in the Roosevelt Era.* Knoxville: University of Tennessee Press, 1980.

KNOWLES, DAVID. *The Monastic Order in England.* Cambridge: Cambridge University Press, 1963.

————. *Christian Monasticism.* New York: McGraw-Hill, 1969.

————. Introduction to 1962 edition of H. Workman, *The Evolution of the Monastic Ideal.* Boston: Beacon Press, 1962.

————. *The Religious Orders in England.* Cambridge: Cambridge University Press, 1948.

KNOWLES, DAVID, AND HADCOCK, R. NEVILLE. *Medieval Religious Houses.* London: Longmans, Green, 1953.

KOCH, G. *Frauenfrage und Ketzertum im Mittelalter.* Berlin: Akademie Verlag, 1962.

KORNBLUH, JOYCE L., ED. *Rebel Voices: An I.W.W. Anthology.* Ann Arbor, Mich.: Ann Arbor Paperbacks, 1968.

KRIEGEL, ANNIE. *The French Communists.* Trans. by E. P. Halperin. Chicago: University of Chicago Press, 1972.

LABARRE, WESTON. "Materials for a History of Studies of Crisis Cults: A Bibliographic Essay." *Current Anthropology* 12 (February 1971).

LACROIX, PAUL. *Military and Religious Life in the Middle Ages and at the Period of the Rennaissance.* London: Bickers and Son, n.d.

LADURIE, EMMANUEL LE ROY. *Montaillou*. New York: Random House (Vintage Books), 1979.

LAMBERT, M. *Medieval Heresey*. New York: Holmes & Meier, 1976.

LANGER, WILLIAM. "The Black Death." In K. Davis, ed., *Cities: Their Origin, Growth and Human Impact*. San Francisco: Freeman, 1973.

_____. "The Next Assignment." *American Historical Review* 63 (January 1958).

LAPIERE, RICHARD T. *A Theory of Social Control*. New York: McGraw-Hill, 1954.

LAQUEUR, WALTER. "Reflections on Youth Movements." *Commentary* 47 (June 1969).

_____, and Mosse, George L. eds. *Education and Social Structure in the Twentieth Century*. New York: Harper Torchbooks, 1967.

LASLETT, PETER. *The World We Have Lost*, 2d ed. New York: Scribner, 1971.

_____. *Family Life and Illicit Love in Earlier Generations*. Cambridge: Cambridge University Press, 1977.

_____, AND RICHARD WALL, EDS. *Household and Family in Past Time*. Cambridge: Cambridge University Press, 1972.

LAUFER, ROBERT. "Sources of Generational Consciousness and Conflict." In P. Altbach and R. Laufer, eds., *The New Pilgrims*. New York: McKay, 1972.

LECKY, W. E. H. *History of European Morals*. New York: Braziller, 1955 (originally 1869).

LECLERCQ, JEAN. "The Monastic Crisis of the Eleventh and Twelfth Centuries." In N. Hunt, ed., *Cluniac Monasticism in the Central Middle Ages*. Hamden, Conn.: Archon Books, 1971.

_____. *Monks and Love in Twelfth-Century France*. Oxford: Clarendon Press, 1979.

LEFF, GORDON. *Heresy in the Later Middle Ages*. Vol. 1 and 2. Manchester: Manchester University Press, 1967.

LE GOFF, J., ED. *Hérésies et sociétés*. Paris: Mouton, 1968.

LEMERT, EDWIN M. *Social Pathology*. New York: McGraw-Hill, 1951.

LENS, SIDNEY. *Poverty: America's Enduring Paradox*. New York: Crowell, 1971.

LEONARD, E. M. *The Early History of English Poor Relief*. Cambridge: Cambridge University Press, 1900.

LERNER, ROBERT. *The Heresy of the Free Spirit*. Berkeley and Los Angeles: University of California Press, 1972.

_____. *The Age of Adversity*. Ithaca, N.Y.: Cornell University Press, 1968.

The Letters of St. Bernard of Clairvaux. Trans. by B. S. James. London: Burns Oates, 1953.

LEUCHTENBURG, WILLIAM E. *Franklin D. Roosevelt and the New Deal*. New York: Harper & Row, 1963.

_____. *The Perils of Prosperity, 1914–32*. Chicago: University of Chicago Press, 1958.

_____. ED. *The New Deal: A Documentary History*. Columbia: University of South Carolina Press, 1968.

LEVY, JEAN-PHILIPPE. *The Economic Life of the Ancient World*. Trans. by J. G. Biram. Chicago: University of Chicago Press, 1967.

LIPSET, SEYMOUR MARTIN. *Revolution and Counter-Revolution: Change and Persistence in Social Structures*, rev. ed. Garden City, N.Y.: Doubleday (Anchor Books), 1970.

————. *Rebellion in the University.* Boston: Little, Brown, 1972.

LIPSET, S. M., AND ZETTERBERG, H. "A Theory of Social Mobility." In R. Bendix and S. M. Lipset, eds., *Class, Status and Power,* 2d ed. New York: Free Press, 1966.

LIPTON, LAWRENCE. *The Holy Barbarians.* New York: Julian Messner, 1958.

LOPEZ, R. S. "Still Another Rennaissance?" *American Historical Review* 57 (1951–52).

LORD, RUSSEL, ED. *Democracy Reborn.* New York: Reynal and Hitchcock, 1944.

LOURDAUX, W., AND VERHELST, D., EDS. *The Concept of Heresy in the Middle Ages.* Louvain: University of Louvain Press, 1976.

LOWI, THEODORE J. *The End of Liberalism,* 2d ed. New York: Norton, 1979.

————. *The Politics of Disorder.* New York: Basic Books, 1971.

MacIVER, ROBERT. *Society.* New York: Rinehart, 1937.

MacMULLEN, RAMSAY. *Enemies of the Roman Order: Treason, Unrest and Alienation in the Empire.* Cambridge, Mass.: Harvard University Press, 1966.

MALAMENT, BARBARA C., ED. *After the Reformation: Essays in Honor of J. H. Hexter.* Philadelphia: University of Pennsylvania Press, 1980.

MANGIONE, JERRE. *The Dream and the Deal: The Federal Writers' Project, 1935–1943.* Boston: Little, Brown, 1972.

MANNING, PETER K. *Youth: Divergent Perspectives.* New York: Wiley, 1973.

MARCH, JAMES G., ED. *Handbook of Organizations.* Chicago: Rand McNally, 1965.

MARKS, CLAUDE. *Pilgrims, Heretics and Lovers: A Medieval Journey.* New York: Macmillan, 1975.

MARTIN, MALACHI. *Three Popes and the Cardinal.* New York: Farrar, Straus & Giroux, 1972.

MARTINEAU, HARRIET. *The History of England During the Thirty Year's Peace: 1816–1846.* 2 vols. London: Charles Knight, 1849.

MARTINES, LAURA, ED. *Violence and Civil Disorders in Italian Cities, 1200–1500.* Berkeley and Los Angeles: University of California Press, 1972.

MARX, KARL. *Kapital.* Chicago: C. H. Kerr & Co., 1908.

MASUR, GERHARD, *Prophets of Yesterday.* New York: Macmillan, 1961.

MATHEWS, JANE DeHART. *The Federal Theatre, 1935–1939: Plays, Relief, and Politics.* Princeton, N.J.: Princeton University Press, 1967.

MATZA, DAVID. "Subterranean Traditions of Youth." *The Annals* 338 (November 1961).

MAYHEW, HENRY. *London Labour and the London Poor.* 4 vols. London: Frank Cass and Co., 1967 (originally 1851–1862).

————, AND BINNY, JOHN. *The Criminal Prisons of London.* London: Frank Cass and Co., 1968 (originally 1862).

McCONNELL, THOMAS R., ET AL. *From Elite to Mass to Unviersal Higher Education.* Berkeley, Calif.: Center for Research and Development in Higher Education, University of California, 1973.

McDONALD, WILLIAM F. *Federal Relief Administration and the Arts.* Columbus: Ohio University Press, 1969.

McDONNELL, E. W. *The Beguines and Beghards in Medieval Culture.* New York: Octagon Books, 1969.

McFARLANE, K. B. *Wycliffe and English Non-Conformity.* Middlesex, England: Pelican Books, 1972.

McKee, Samuel, Jr. *Labor in Colonial New York: 1664–1776*. New York: Columbia University Press, 1935.

Meadows, Paul. "Movements of Social Withdrawal." *Sociology and Social Research* 29 (September–October 1944).

Meek, Ronald L. *The Rise and Fall of the Concept of the Economic Machine*. Leicester, England: Leicester University Press, 1965.

———, ed. *Marx and Engels on the Population Bomb*. Berkeley, Calif.: Ramparts Press, 1971.

Merton, Robert K. *Social Theory and Social Structure*. New York: Free Press, 1949.

van Mierlo, J. "Review of Grundmann's 'Zur Geschichte der Beginen im 13. Jahrhundert." In *Revue d'Histoire Ecclesiastique*, vol. 28. Louvain: Bureaux de la Revue, 1932.

Miller, Richard C. *Bohemia: The Protoculture Then and Now*. Chicago: Nelson-Hall, 1977.

Miskimin, Harry A. *The Economy of Early Rennaissance Europe, 1300–1460*. Cambridge: Cambridge University Press, 1975.

Mitchell, David. *1919: Red Mirage*. New York: Macmillan, 1970.

Mizruchi, Ephraim H. *Success and Opportunity: A Study of Anomie*. New York: Free Press, 1964.

———. "Aspiration and Poverty." *Sociological Quarterly* 8 (Autumn 1967).

———. "Bohemianism and the Urban Community." *Journal of Human Relations* 8 (Autumn 1959).

———. "Bohemianism, Social Structure and Deviant Behavior." Paper presented at the annual meeting of the Society for the Study of Social Problems, San Francisco, 1969.

———. "On the Uses of History in the Development of Social Problems Theory." Paper presented at the annual meeting of the Society for the Study of Social Problems, New York, 1976.

———. Review of M. Schwartz *Radical Protest and Social Structure*. *Contemporary Sociology* 10, no. 3 (May 1981).

———. "Social Structure and Anomia in a Small City." *American Sociological Review* 25 (October 1960).

———. "Social Structure, Social Integration and Abeyance." Paper presented at the annual meeting of the American Sociological Association, Montreal, 1974.

———. "Alienation, Mediating Processes and Social Control." Paper Presented at the 8th World Congress of Sociology, Toronto, 1974.

———, Glassner, B., and Pastorello, T., eds. *Time and Aging*. Bayside, N.Y.: General Hall, 1982.

Mollat, G., ed. *Manuel de l'inquisiteur*. Paris: Champion, 1926. Trans. by M. M. McLaughlin, in J. B. Ross and M. M. McLaughlin, eds., *The Portable Medieval Reader*. New York: Viking Press, 1949.

Mols, Roger. *Introduction a la Demographie Historique Des Villes D'Europe du XIV au XVIII siecle*. 2 vols. Louvain: University of Louvain, 1955.

Montalembert, Charles F. *The Monks of the West*. New York; Longmans, Green, 1896.

Moore, Barrington, Jr. *Social Origins of Dictatorship and Democracy*. Boston: Beacon Press, 1967.

_____. *Political Power and Social Theory.* New York: Harper Torchbooks, 1965.

MOORE, ROBERT I. *The Birth of Popular Heresy.* London: Edward Arnold, 1975.

MOORE, WILBERT E. *The Impact of Industry.* Englewood Cliffs, N.J.: Prentice-Hall, 1965.

MOREAU, E. *Histoire de l'Eglise en Belgique.* Brussels: L'Edition Universelle, 1945.

MORALL, JOHN B. *The Medieval Imprint: Hammondsport.* Middlesex, England: Penguin Books, 1970.

MOUSNIER, ROLAND. *Peasant Uprisings in Seventeenth-Century France Russia, and China.* Trans. by Brian Pearce. New York: Harper & Row, 1970.

MURGER, HENRI. *Vie de Bohéme.* Trans. by N. Cameron. London: Novel Library, 1949.

MURRAY, ALEXANDER. *Reason and Society in the Middle Ages.* Oxford: Clarendon Press, 1978.

MURRAY, GILBERT. *Five Stages of Greek Religion.* New York: Doubleday (Anchor Books), 1951 (originally 1912 and 1925).

MURVAR, VATRO. "Messianism in Russia: Religious and Revolutionary." *Journal for the Scientific Study of Religion* 10 (Winter 1971).

MUSGROVE, FRANK. *Youth and the Social Order.* Bloomington: Indiana University Press, 1964.

_____. *Patterns of Power and Authority in English Education.* London: Methuen, 1971.

_____. *Ecstasy and Holiness.* Bloomington: Indiana University Press, 1974.

NABHOLZ, HANS. "Medieval Agrarian Society in Transition." In *The Cambridge Economic History.* Vol. 1. London: Cambridge University Press, 1941, pp. 493–561.

NANDAN, YASH, ED. *Emile Durkheim: Contributions to L'Anée Sociologique.* New York: Free Press, 1980.

NASH, G. B., ED. *The Private Side of American History.* New York: Harcourt Brace Jovanovich, 1975.

NELSON, BENJAMIN. "Eros, Logos, Nomos, Polis: Their Changing Balances and the Vicissitudes of Communities and Civilization." In A. W. Eister, ed., *Changing Perspectives in the Scientific Study of Religion.* New York: Wiley, 1974.

NIGG, WALTER. *The Heretics.* Ed. and trans. by R. and C. Winston. New York: Knopf, 1962.

NISBET, ROBERT. *Tradition and Revolt.* New York: Random House, 1968.

_____. *Social Change and History.* New York: Oxford University Press, 1969.

NOGGLE, BURL. *Into the Twenties: The United States from Armistice to Normalcy.* Urbana: University of Illinois Press, 1974.

NORTH, DOUGLASS C., AND THOMAS, ROBERT P. *The Rise of the Western World.* Cambridge: Cambridge University Press, 1973.

OBERSCHALL, ANTHONY. *Social Conflict and Social Movements.* Englewood Cliffs, N.J.: Prentice-Hall, 1973.

OGG, FREDERIC A. *A Source Book of Medieval History.* New York: American Book Company, 1908.

OZMENT, STEVEN E., ED. *The Reformation in Medieval Perspective.* Chicago: Quadrangle Books, 1971.

PAINTER, SIDNEY. *Feudalism and Liberty.* Ed. by F. A. Cazel, Jr. Baltimore: Johns Hopkins University Press, 1961.

_____. *A History of the Middle Ages.* New York: Knopf, 1953.

PARRY, ALBERT. Garrets and Pretenders: A History of Bohemianism in America. New York: Dover, 1960 (originally 1933).

PARSONS, TALCOTT. *The Social System.* New York: Free Press, 1951.

_____. *The Structure of Social Action.* New York: Free Press, 1949.

_____, AND SMELSER, NEIL. *Economy and Society.* New York: Free Press, 1956.

PELLS, RICHARD H. *Radical Visions and American Dreams.* New York: Harper & Row, 1973.

PERKINS, FRANCES. *The Roosevelt I Knew.* New York: Viking Press, 1946.

PERRUCCI, ROBERT. *Circle of Madness.* Englewood Cliffs, N.J.: Prentice-Hall, 1974.

_____. "The Significance of Intra-Occupational Mobility." *American Sociological Review* 27 (December 1961).

PHILLIPS, DAYTON. *The Beguines of Medieval Strasbourg.* Stanford: Stanford University Press, 1941.

PIVEN, FRANCES FOX, AND CLOWARD, RICHARD. *Regulating the Poor.* New York: Random House (Vintage Books), 1972.

_____. *Poor People's Movements.* New York: Random House (Vintage Books), 1979.

PLUMB, J. H. *The Growth of Political Stability in England, 1675–1725.* Middlesex, England: Penguin Books, 1973.

_____. *The Italian Renaissance.* New York: Harper Torchbooks, 1965.

POLANYI, KARL. *The Great Transformation.* New York: Rinehart & Co., 1944.

POLENBERG, RICHARD. *War and Society: The United States, 1941–1945.* Philadelphia: Lippincott, 1972.

POSTAN, MICHAEL M. *Essays on Medieval Agriculture and General Problems of the Medieval Economy.* Cambridge: Cambridge University Press, 1973.

POWELL, ELWIN H. *The Design of Discord: Studies of Anomie.* New York: Oxford University Press, 1970.

POWELL, JAMES M. Introduction to *The Liber Augustalis.* Trans. by J. M. Powell. Syracuse, N.Y.: Syracuse University Press, 1971.

_____. "The Papacy and the Early Franciscans." *Franciscan Studies* 36 (1976).

_____, ED. *Medieval Studies.* Syracuse, N.Y.: Syracuse University Press, 1976.

POWER, EILEEN E. "The Position of Women." In E. G. Crump and E. F. Jacob, eds., *The Legacy of the Middle Ages.* Oxford: Oxford University Press, 1926.

_____. *Medieval People.* London: Methuen, 1963.

_____. *Medieval Women.* Ed. by M. M. Postan. Cambridge: Cambridge University Press, 1975.

_____. AND TAWNEY, R. H., EDS. *Tudor Economic Documents.* London: Longmans, Green, 1935–37.

PULLAN, BRIAN S. *Rich and Poor in Renaissance Venice.* Oxford: Basil Blackwell, 1971.

RAFTIS, J. AMBROSE. *Tenure and Mobility.* Toronto: Pontifical Institute of Medieval Studies, 1964.

_____. *The Estates of Ramsey Abby.* Toronto: Pontifical Institute of Medieval Studies, 1957.

REEDER, D. A., ED. *Urban Education in the Nineteenth Century.* New York: St. Martin's Press, 1978.

RENARD, G., AND WEULERSSE W. *Life and Work in Modern Europe, Fifteenth to*

Eighteenth Centuries. Trans. by M. Richards, Foreward by E. Power. New York: Knopf, 1926.

The Rennaissance: Six Essays. New York: Harper Torchbooks, 1962.

"Revolution on the Campus." *American Scholar,* Autumn 1969.

RICHARD, I. A. *Speculative Instruments.* Chicago: University of Chicago Press, 1955.

RIGNEY, FRANCIS J., AND SMITH, L. DOUGLAS. *The Real Bohemia.* New York: Basic Books, 1961.

ROBBINS, HELEN. "A Comparison of the Effects of the Black Death on the Economic Organization of France and England." *Journal of Political Economy* 36 (1928).

ROBY, PAMELA, ED. *The Poverty Establishment.* Englewood Cliffs, N.J.: Prentice-Hall, 1974.

Roehl, Richard. *Patterns and Structure of Demand, 1000–1500.* The Fontana Economic History of Europe, vol. I, sec. 3. London: 1970.

ROOSEVELT, ELEANOR. *This I Remember.* New York: Harper & Row, 1949.

ROSENBERG, BERNARD, AND FLIEGEL, NORBERT. *The Vanguard Artist.* Chicago: Quadrangle Books, 1964.

ROSS, E. A. *Social Control.* New York: Macmillan, 1919.

ROSS, J. B., AND McLAUGHLIN, M. M., EDS. *The Portable Medieval Reader.* New York: Viking Press, 1949.

ROTHMAN, DAVID J. *The Discovery of the Asylum.* Boston: Little, Brown, 1971.
————. *Conscience and Convenience.* Boston: Little, Brown, 1980.

RUBENSTEIN, RICHARD. *The Cunning of History.* New York: Harper Colophon Books, 1978.

RUDE, GEORGE. *The Crowd in History, 1730–1848.* New York: Wiley, 1964.
————. *Revolutionary Europe 1783–1815.* New York: Harper Torchbooks, 1964.
————. *Europe in the Eighteenth Century.* London: Weidenfeld and Nicholson, 1972.

RUSSELL, D. E. H. *Rebellion, Revolution and Armed Force.* New York: Academic Press, 1974.

RUSSELL, JEFFREY B. *A History of Medieval Christianity.* New York: Crowell, 1965.
————. *Dissent and Reform in the Early Middle Ages.* Berkeley and Los Angeles: University of California Press, 1965.
————. "Interpretations of the Origins of Medieval Heresy." *Medieval Studies* 25. (1963).
————, ED. *Religious Dissent in the Middle Ages.* New York: Wiley, 1971.

RUSSELL, JOSIAH C. "Late Ancient and Medieval Population." *Transactions of the American Philosophical Society* 48 (June 1948).
————. "The Clerical Population of Medieval England." *Traditio,* 2 (1944).
————. *Medieval Regions and Their Cities.* Newton Abbot, England: David and Charles, 1972.

SALTMARSH, JOHN. "The Plague and Economic Decline in the Later Middle Ages." *Cambridge Historical Journal* 7 (1941).

SAMAHA, JOEL. *Law and Order in Historical Perspective.* New York: Academic Press, 1974.

SAN GIOVANNI, LUCINDA. *Ex-Nuns: A Study of Emergent Role Passage.* Norwood, N.J.: Ablex Publishing Corporation, 1978.

SCHAPIRO, J. SALWYN. *Liberalism and the Challenge of Facism.* New York: McGraw-Hill, 1949.

SCHILLING, BERNARD N. *Conservative England and the Case Against Voltaire.* New York: Columbia University Press, 1950.

SCHLESINGER, ARTHUR M., JR. *The Age of Roosevelt.* 3 vols. Boston: Houghton Mifflin, 1960.

SCHNEIDER, LOUIS, ED. *The Scottish Moralists.* Chicago: University of Chicago Press, 1967.

_____. *The Sociological Way of Looking at the World.* New York: McGraw-Hill, 1975.

_____. *Classical Theories of Social Change.* Morristown, N.J.: General Learning Press, 1976.

_____. "Mandeville as Forerunner of Modern Sociology." *Journal of the History of Behavioral Sciences* 6, no. 3, (1970).

_____. "The Sociology of Religion: Some Areas of Theoretical Potential." *Sociological Analysis* 31 (Fall 1970).

SCHNORE, LEO F. *The Urban Scene.* New York: Free Press, 1965.

SCHWARTZ, BARRY. *Queuing and Waiting: Studies in the Social Organization of Access and Delay.* Chicago: University of Chicago Press, 1975.

SCHWARTZ, MICHAEL. *Radical Protest and Social Structure.* New York: Academic Press, 1976.

SCHWARTZ, RICHARD D. "Functional Alternatives to Inequality," *American Sociological Review* 20 (August 1955).

_____. "Social Factors in the Development of Legal Control: A Case Study of Two Israeli Settlements." *Yale Law Journal* 63 (February 1954).

SCHWENDINGER, HERMAN, AND SCHWENDINGER, JULIA. "Marginal Youth and Social Policy." *Social Problems* 24 (December 1976).

SCOTT, JONATHAN F. *Historical Essays on Apprenticeship and Vocational Education.* Ann Arbor, Mich.: Ann Arbor Press, 1914.

SELZNICK, PHILIP. *TVA and the Grass Roots.* New York: Harper Torchbooks, 1966.

SHELLEY, LOUISE. "The Geography of Soviet Criminality." *American Sociological Review* 45 (February 1980).

SHERWOOD, ROBERT E. *The White House Papers of Harry L. Hopkins.* 2 vols. London: Eyre and Spottiswoode, 1948.

_____. *Roosevelt and Hopkins, An Intimate History.* New York: Harper & Row, 1948.

SHILS, EDWARD. *The Center and the Periphery: Essays in Macrosociology.* Chicago: University of Chicago Press, 1975.

SIBLEY, ELBRIDGE. "SOME DEMOGRAPHIC CLUES TO STRATIFICATION." *American Sociological Review* 7 (June 1942).

SILVER, HAROLD. *The Concept of Popular Education.* London: Macgibbon and Kee, 1965.

SIMON, RITA JAMES, ED. *As We Saw the Thirties.* Urbana: University of Illinois Press, 1967.

SKOCPOL, THEDA. *States and Social Revolutions.* New York: Cambridge University Press, 1979.

SKOLNICK, JEROME H. *The Politics of Protest.* New York: Ballantine Books, 1969.

SMELSER, NEIL J. *Social Change in the Industrial Revolution.* Chicago: University of Chicago Press, 1959.

———. *Theory of Collective Behavior.* New York: Free Press, 1962.

———, AND LIPSET, S. M., EDS. *Social Structure and Mobilization in Economic Development.* Chicago: Aldine, 1966.

SMITH, ADAM. *The Theory of Moral Sentiments.* New Rochelle, N.Y.: Arlington House, 1969 (originally 1759).

———. *The Wealth of Nations.* Ed. by Andrew Skinner. Books 1 and 2. Middlesex, England: Penguin Books, 1970 (originally 1776).

SMITH, GEOFFREY S. *To Save A Nation: American Countersubversives, the New Deal, and the Coming of World War II.* New York: Basic Books, 1973.

SNYDER, DAVID, AND TILLY, CHARLES. "Hardship and Collective Violence in France, 1830 to 1960." *American Sociological Review* 37 (October 1972).

SOKOLSKY, GEORGE. "America Drifts Toward Fascism." *American Mercury* 32 (July 1934).

SOLOMON, MAYNARD. *Marxism and Art.* New York: Knopf, 1973.

SOROKIN, PITIRIM. *The Sociology of Revolution.* Philadelphia: Lippincott, 1925.

———. *Social and Cultural Mobility.* New York: Free Press, 1959 (originally 1927).

———. *Man and Society in Calamity.* New York: Dutton, 1943.

———. *Social and Cultural Dynamics,* Vol. 3, *Fluctuation of Social Relationships, War and Revolution,* Vol. 4, *Basic Problems, Principles and Methods.* New York: American Book Co., 1941.

SOUTHERN, R. W. *Western Society and the Church in the Middle Ages.* Middlesex, England: Penguin Books, 1972.

SPATES, JAMES L. "Counterculture and Dominant Culture Values." *American Sociological Review* 41 (October 1976).

SPRING, JOEL. *Education and the Rise of the Corporate State.* Boston: Beacon Press, 1972.

———. *A Primer of Libertarian Education.* New York: Free Life Editions, 1975.

STEAD, WILLIAM H. *Democracy Against Unemployment.* New York: Harper & Row, 1942.

STEARNS, PETER N., ED. *The Impact of the Industrial Revolution.* Englewood Cliffs, N.J.: Prentice-Hall, 1972.

———. *European Society in Upheaval.* New York: Macmillan, 1967.

STERN, FRITZ. *The Politics of Cultural Despair.* Berkeley: University of California Press, 1974.

STINCHCOMBE, ARTHUR L. *Constructing Social Theories.* New York: Harcourt Brace Jovanovich, 1968.

———. *Theoretical Methods in Social History.* New York: Academic Press, 1978.

STONE, LAWRENCE, *The Causes of the English Revolution, 1529–1642.* New York: Harper Torchbooks, 1972.

———. *The Crisis of the Aristocracy 1558–1641.* Abridged. London: Oxford University Press, 1967.

———, ED. *Schooling and Society.* Baltimore: Johns Hopkins University Press, 1976.

———, ED. *The University in Society.* 2 vols. Princeton, N.J.: Princeton University Press, 1974.

STRAYER, JOSEPH R. *The Albigensian Crusades.* New York: Dial Press, 1971.

SWENSEN, RUSSEL B. *Social Processes in the Rise of Early Christian Heresies.* Chicago: University of Chicago Libraries, 1937.

SWIFT, D. *Ideology and Change in the Public Schools.* New York: Charles B. Merrill, 1971.

SYKES, GERALD. *The Cool Millennium.* Englewood Cliffs, N.J.: Prentice-Hall, 1967.

TALMON, J. L. *The Origins of Totalitarian Democracy.* New York: Praeger, 1960.

TALMON, YONINA. "Pursuit of the Millennium: The Relation Between Religous and Social Change." In N. Birnbaum and G. Lenzer, eds., *Sociology and Religion.* Englewood Cliffs, N.J.: Prentice-Hall, 1969. Abridged from *European Journal of Sociology* 3 (1962).

TAWNEY, R. H. *The Agrarian Problem in the Sixteenth Century.* New York: Harper Torchbooks, 1967 (originally 1912).

———. *The Radical Tradition.* New York: Pantheon Books, 1964.

THOMAS, DOROTHY SWAIN. *Social Aspects of the Business Cycle.* New York: Gordon and Breach, 1967 (originally 1927).

THOMIS, MALCOLM I. *Responses to Industrialization: The British Experience 1780–1850.* Hamden, Conn.: (Archon Books), 1976.

THOMPSON, E. P. *The Making of the English Working Class.* New York: Vintage Books, 1963.

THRUPP, SYLVIA, ED. *Change in Medieval Society: Europe North of the Alps, 1050–1500.* New York: Appleton-Century-Crofts, 1964.

———, ED. *Millenial Dreams in Action.* New York: Schocken Books, 1970.

TILLY, CHARLES. *From Mobilization to Revolution.* Reading, Mass.: Addison-Wesley, 1978.

———, TILLY, LOUISE, AND TILLY, RICHARD, *The Rebellious Century, 1830–1930.* Cambridge, Mass.: Harvard University Press, 1975.

TIRYAKIAN, EDWARD A. "Toward the Sociology of Esoteric Culture." *American Journal of Sociology* 78 (November 1972).

———, ED. *Sociological Theory, Values and Sociological Change: Essays in Honor of P. A. Sorokin.* New York: Harper Torchbooks, 1967.

Touraine, Alain. *The May Movement.* New York: Irvington Publishers, 1979.

TRANTER, N. L., ED. *Population and Industrialization.* London: A. and C. Block, 1973.

TRACHTENBERG, JOSHUA. *The Devil and the Jews.* New Haven: Yale University Press, 1943.

TRATTNER, WALTER I. *From Poor Law to Welfare State.* New York: Free Press, 1974.

TRAUGOTT, MARK. "Reconceiving Social Movements." *Social Problems* 26 (October 1978).

TREVOR-ROPER, HUGH. *The Crisis of the Seventeenth Century.* New York: Harper & Row, 1966.

———. *The Plunder of the Arts in the Seventeenth Century.* London: Thames & Hudson, 1970.

———. *The European Witch-Craze of the Sixteenth and Seventeenth Centuries and Other Essays.* New York: Harper Torchbooks, 1969.

TUGWELL, REXFORD G. *F.D.R.: Architect of an Era.* New York: Macmillan, 1967.

TYACK, DAVID B., *George Ticknor and the Boston Brahmins.* Cambridge, Mass.: Harvard University Press, 1967.

SMELSER, NEIL J. *Social Change in the Industrial Revolution.* Chicago: University of Chicago Press, 1959.

⸻. *Theory of Collective Behavior.* New York: Free Press, 1962.

⸻, AND LIPSETT, S. M., EDS. *Social Structure and Mobilization in Economic Development.* Chicago: Aldine, 1966.

SMITH, ADAM. *The Theory of Moral Sentiments.* New Rochelle, N.Y.: Arlington House, 1969 (originally 1759).

⸻. *The Wealth of Nations.* Ed. by Andrew Skinner. Books 1 and 2. Middlesex, England: Penguin Books, 1970 (originally 1776).

SMITH, GEOFFREY S. *To Save A Nation: American Countersubversives, the New Deal, and the Coming of World War II.* New York: Basic Books, 1973.

SNYDER, DAVID, AND TILLY, CHARLES. "Hardship and Collective Violence in France, 1830 to 1960." *American Sociological Review* 37 (October 1972).

SOKOLSKY, GEORGE. "America Drifts Toward Fascism." *American Mercury* 32 (July 1934).

SOLOMON, MAYNARD. *Marxism and Art.* New York: Knopf, 1973.

SOROKIN, PITIRIM. *The Sociology of Revolution.* Philadelphia: Lippincott, 1925.

⸻. *Social and Cultural Mobility.* New York: Free Press, 1959 (originally 1927).

⸻. *Man and Society in Calamity.* New York: Dutton, 1943.

⸻. *Social and Cultural Dynamics,* Vol. 3, *Fluctuation of Social Relationships, War and Revolution,* Vol. 4, *Basic Problems, Principles and Methods.* New York: American Book Co., 1941.

SOUTHERN, R. W. *Western Society and the Church in the Middle Ages.* Middlesex, England: Penguin Books, 1972.

SPATES, JAMES L. "Counterculture and Dominant Culture Values." *American Sociological Review* 41 (October 1976).

SPRING, JOEL. *Education and the Rise of the Corporate State.* Boston: Beacon Press, 1972.

⸻. *A Primer of Libertarian Education.* New York: Free Life Editions, 1975.

STEAD, WILLIAM H. *Democracy Against Unemployment.* New York: Harper & Row, 1942.

STEARNS, PETER N., ED. *The Impact of the Industrial Revolution.* Englewood Cliffs, N.J.: Prentice-Hall, 1972.

⸻. *European Society in Upheaval.* New York: Macmillan, 1967.

STERN, FRITZ. *The Politics of Cultural Despair.* Berkeley: University of California Press, 1974.

⸻. *Constructing Social Theories.* New York: Harcourt Brace Jovanovich, 1968.

STINCHCOMBE, ARTHUR L. *Constructing Social Theories.* New York: Harcourt Brace Jovanovich, 1968.

⸻. *Theoretical Methods in Social History.* New York: Academic Press, 1978.

STONE, LAWRENCE, *The Causes of the English Revolution, 1529–1642.* New York: Harper Torchbooks, 1972.

⸻. *The Crisis of the Aristocracy 1558–1641.* Abridged. London: Oxford University Press, 1967.

⸻, ED. *Schooling and Society.* Baltimore: Johns Hopkins University Press, 1976.

⸻, ED. *The University in Society.* 2 vols. Princeton, N.J.: Princeton University Press, 1974.

STRAYER, JOSEPH R. *The Albigensian Crusades.* New York: Dial Press, 1971.

SWENSEN, RUSSEL B. *Social Processes in the Rise of Early Christian Heresies.* Chicago: University of Chicago Libraries, 1937.

SWIFT, D. *Ideology and Change in the Public Schools.* New York: Charles B. Merrill, 1971.

SYKES, GERALD. *The Cool Millennium.* Englewood Cliffs, N.J.: Prentice-Hall, 1967.

TALMON, J. L. *The Origins of Totalitarian Democracy.* New York: Praeger, 1960.

TALMON, YONINA. "Pursuit of the Millennium: The Relation Between Religious and Social Change." in N. Birnbaum and G. Lenzer, eds., *Sociology and Religion.* Englewood Cliffs, N.J.: Prentice-Hall, 1969. Abridged from 9 *European Journal of Sociology* 3 (1962).

TAWNEY, R. H. *The Agrarian Problem in the Sixteenth Century.* New York: Harper Torchbooks, 1967 (originally 1912).

————. *The Radical Tradition.* New York: Pantheon Books, 1964.

THOMAS, DOROTHY SWAIN. *Social Aspects of the Business Cycle.* New York: Gordon and Breach, 1967 (originally 1927).

THOMIS, MALCOLM I. *Responses to Industrialization: The British Experience 1780–1850.* Hamden, Conn.: (Archon Books), 1976.

THOMPSON, E. P. *The Making of the English Working Class.* New York: Vintage Books, 1963.

THRUPP, SYLVIA, ED. *Change in Medieval Society: Europe North of the Alps, 1050–1500.* New York: Appleton-Century-Crofts, 1964.

————, ED. *Millenial Dreams in Action.* New York: Schocken Books, 1970.

TILLY, CHARLES. *From Mobilization to Revolution.* Reading, Mass.: Addison-Wesley, 1978.

————, TILLY, LOUISE, AND TILLY, RICHARD. *The Rebellious Century, 1830-1930.* Cambridge, Mass.: Harvard University Press, 1975.

TIRYAKIAN, EDWARD A. "Toward the Sociology of Esoteric Culture." *American Journal of Sociology* 78 (November 1972).

————, ED. *Sociological Theory, Values and Sociological Change: Essays in Honor of P. A. Sorokin.* New York: Harper Torchbooks, 1967.

TOURAINE, ALAIN. *The May Movement.* New York: Irvington Publishers, 1979.

TRANTER, N. L., ED. *Population and Industrialization.* London: A. and C. Block, 1973.

TRACHTENBERG, JOSHUA. *The Devil and the Jews.* New Haven: Yale University Press, 1943.

TRATTNER, WALTER I. *From Poor Law to Welfare State.* New York: Free Press, 1974.

TRAUGOTT, MARK. "Reconceiving Social Movements." *Social Problems* 26 (October 1978).

TREVOR-ROPER, HUGH. *The Crisis of the Seventeenth Century.* New York: Harper & Row, 1966.

————. *The Plunder of the Arts in the Seventeenth Century.* London: Thames & Hudson, 1970.

————. *The European Witch-Craze of the Sixteenth and Seventeenth Centuries and Other Essays.* New York: Harper Torchbooks, 1969.

TUGWELL, REXFORD, G. *F.D.R.: Architect of an Era.* New York: Macmillan, 1967.

TYACK, DAVID B. *George Ticknor and the Boston Brahmins.* Cambridge, Mass.: Harvard University Press, 1967.

Author Index

Subject Index